Heresy and Inquisition in the Middle Ages

Volume 3

Heresy, Inquisition and Life Cycle in Medieval Languedoc

YORK MEDIEVAL PRESS

York Medieval Press is published by the University of York's Centre for Medieval Studies in association with Boydell & Brewer Limited. Our objective is the promotion of innovative scholarship and fresh criticism on medieval culture. We have a special commitment to interdisciplinary study, in line with the Centre's belief that the future of Medieval Studies lies in those areas in which its major constituent disciplines at once inform and challenge each other.

All enquiries of an editorial kind, including suggestions for monographs and essay collections, should be addressed to: The Academic Editor, York Medieval Press, University of York, Centre for Medieval Studies, The King's Manor, York, YO1 7EP (E-mail: gmg501@york.ac.uk).

Publications of York Medieval Press are listed at the back of this volume.

Heresy and Inquisition in the Middle Ages
ISSN 2046–8938

Series editors
John H. Arnold, Department of History, Classics and Archaeology, Birkbeck, University of London
Peter Biller, Department of History, University of York

Heresy had social, cultural and political implications in the middle ages, and countering heresy was often a central component in the development of orthodoxy. This series publishes work on heresy, and the repression of heresy, from late antiquity to the Reformation, including monographs, collections of essays, and editions of texts.

Heresy, Inquisition and Life Cycle in Medieval Languedoc

Chris Sparks

THE UNIVERSITY of York

YORK MEDIEVAL PRESS

First published 2014

A York Medieval Press publication
in association with The Boydell Press
an imprint of Boydell & Brewer Ltd
PO Box 9, Woodbridge, Suffolk IP12 3DF, UK
and of Boydell & Brewer Inc.
668 Mt Hope Avenue, Rochester, NY 14620, USA
website: www.boydellandbrewer.com
and with the
Centre for Medieval Studies, University of York
www.york.ac.uk/medieval-studies

ISBN 978–1–903153–52–9

A CIP catalogue record for this book is available from the British Library

This book is about the importance of human relationships

It is dedicated to my friends

Contents

List of Tables viii

Acknowledgements ix

List of Abbreviations x

A Note on Names xi

Introduction 1

1. Childhood 27
2. Youth 71
3. Marriage 94
4. Death 123

Conclusion 151

Glossary 157

Bibliography 159

Index 169

Tables

1.1 Child initiates from Le Mas-Saintes-Puelles 54
1.2 Other child initiates: girls. 57
1.3 Other child initiates: boys. 59
2.1 Young deponents before Bernard Gui 86

Acknowledgements

The research on which this book was based would not have been possible without the funding provided by an AHRC doctoral award. I am also grateful to the Department of History at York, who supported my MA studies with a Fee Waiver Scholarship, and whose faculty and staff have always been both friendly and encouraging. Thanks are also due to Caroline Palmer at Boydell & Brewer, and to Pete Biller and John Arnold who have been generous and wonderfully efficient editors. A great many people have supported me during the years that this book has been in development. Thanks are due to the School of History at Queen Mary, University of London, and in particular to Emma Yates, who is the most supportive boss, and friend, one could wish for. I am also indebted to Miri Rubin, for her advice and guidance, and for her careful and generous proof-reading. My parents have been, as ever, a source of unwavering and unconditional support, for which I am more grateful than I can say. The single largest debt I owe as an author is to Pete Biller. I have often had cause to draw on Pete's seemingly inexhaustible supplies of advice, scholarship, encouragement, friendship, coffee, and all-round generosity of spirit, without which this book would never have been written at all.

Abbreviations

D21	Paris, Bibliothèque nationale de France, Collection Doat vol. 21.
D22	Paris, Bibliothèque nationale de France, Collection Doat vol. 22.
D23	Paris, Bibliothèque nationale de France, Collection Doat vol. 23.
D24	Paris, Bibliothèque nationale de France, Collection Doat vol. 24.
D25	Paris, Bibliothèque nationale de France, Collection Doat vol. 25.
D26	Paris, Bibliothèque nationale de France, Collection Doat vol. 26.
GA	*L'inquisiteur Geoffroy d'Ablis et les cathares du comté de Foix (1308–1309)*, ed. and trans., A. Pales-Gobilliard (Paris, 1984)
Gui, *Sentences*	Bernard Gui, *Le livre des sentences de Bernard Gui: 1308–1323*, ed. A. Pales-Gobilliard, 2 vols. (Paris, 2002).
JF	*Le registre d'inquisition de Jacques Fournier, 1318–1325*, ed. J. Duvernoy, 3 vols. (Toulouse, 1965)[1]
JFD	*Le registre d'inquisition de Jacques Fournier (évêque de Pamiers) 1318–1325*, ed. and trans. J. Duvernoy, 3 vols. (Paris, The Hague and New York, 1978).
Mansi	G. D. Mansi, ed., *Sacrorum conciliorum nova et amplissima collection*, 53 vols. (1757–98)
Montaillou (En)	E. Le Roy Ladurie, *Montaillou: The Promised Land of Error*, trans. B. Bray (London, 1978).
Montaillou (Fr)	E. Le Roy Ladurie, *Montaillou, village occitan de 1294 à 1324* (Paris, 1975).
MS 609	Toulouse, Bibliothèque municipale, MS 609.[2]
SS	*Les statuts synodaux français du XIIIe siècle, précédés de l'historique du synode diocésain depuis ses origines*, ed. O. Pontal, 2 vols. (Paris, 1971).[3]

1 References to this work are given in the format 'x.yyy–yy', where 'x' represents the volume number and 'y' the page number.

2 The abbreviation '(DT)' indicates that the preceding citation or quote relies solely upon Jean Duvernoy's transcription, and that the photostat was illegible.

3 Canon numbers are given in square braces: [ ]. References are to vol. 2 unless otherwise stated.

A Note on Names

I have Anglicized the first names of deponents where possible, falling back to modern French or Occitan where a translation was not evident. Place-names (which appear mostly in Latin) have been converted to modern French, but translated as ablatives even when they appear to form part of a surname (hence, 'John of X of Y').[1]

I have avoided the term 'Perfect' and its Latin equivalents, and have described the Cathar ministers as 'good men' and 'good women'.[2] In order to preserve the ambiguity that exists in the term's verbal use, I have avoided capitalisation. I have, however, included reference to the Cathar Church and the Cathar community. That organisation's reality – the arguments for which I find largely convincing – is discussed below.[3] The term 'Cathar' is itself problematic: the good men and good women never referred to themselves by that name. There is as yet, however, no comfortable shorthand which can be used to describe either the collectivity of good men and good women in Languedoc or the faith they preached. The alternatives are to use 'Cathar', or to coin a new term. I have opted for the former; the latter would add confusion without removing baggage.

Finally, a note on 'inquisition', a term whose precise meaning has often caused confusion. From its development, or formalisation, during the pontificate of Innocent III, inquisition was a widely used judicial procedure in ecclesiastical courts. Its distinguishing feature was that, under it, judges proceeded against suspects *ex officio* without the need for a formal accuser. Thus, whilst the procedure is perhaps most famous for its use in the prosecution of heresy, that was in fact only one of the areas in which it was employed.[4] The formal

1 Here, the 'Index Nominum' of *Saisimentum Comitatus Tholosani*, ed. Y. Dossat (Paris, 1966), at pp. 339–486 is invaluable.

2 M. G. Pegg, 'On Cathars, Albigenses, and Good Men of Languedoc', *Journal of Medieval History* 27 (2001), 181–95; M. G. Pegg, *The Corruption of Angels: The Great Inquisition of 1245–1246* (Princeton, 2001), pp. 15–19, 141–51; M. G. Pegg, 'Heresy, Good Men, and Nomenclature', in *Heresy and the Persecuting Society in the Middle Ages: Essays on the Work of R. I. Moore*, ed. M. Frassetto, Studies in the History of Christian Traditions (Leiden, 2006), pp. 227–39; M. G. Pegg, 'Albigenses in the Antipodes: An Australian and the Cathars', *Journal of Religious History* 35, no. 4 (2011), 577–600.

3 See pp. 3–5 and p. 137, n. 82, below.

4 There is often some confusion on this point, on which – and for clarification – see H. A. Kelly, 'Inquisition and the Prosecution of Heresy: Misconceptions and Abuses', *Church History* 58 (1989), 439–51.

title 'inquisitor of heretical depravity' has here for brevity's sake been reduced to 'inquisitor', as it was in many of those official's own documents.

Writers on medieval heresy have also to decide whether they will talk about 'Inquisition', or 'inquisition', where the capitalised form denotes a more-or-less formalised and continuous institution and the lower-case a more ad hoc process whose form and success at any given moment depended largely upon the particular individual to whom it had been entrusted.[5] Richard Kieckhefer believes that the evolution from inquisition to Inquisition has often been seen 'as proceeding at a more rapid pace than the sources in fact suggest'.[6] Alan Friedlander, on the other hand, is of the opinion that 'there existed already in the early fourteenth century something more than a "personal" inquisition inseparable from the inquisitors who performed it'.[7] Other opinions vary.[8] It is certainly true that evidence from Languedoc does not seem to support so high a degree of institutionalisation as has sometimes been assumed. I have largely avoided using either 'Inquisition' or 'inquisition' in an abstract sense, preferring instead to talk of 'inquisitors'. Indeed, it was probably a matter of little concern to those facing pursuit, interrogation or imprisonment by Languedocian inquisitors whether their persecutors were agents of a formal bureaucracy or merely zealous and well-funded individuals.

5 The fundamental article here is: R. Kieckhefer, 'The Office of the Inquisition and Medieval Heresy: The Transition from Personal to Institutional Jurisdiction', *Journal of Ecclesiastical History* 46 (1995), 47–53.

6 Ibid., p. 59.

7 Friedlander bases this upon the argument that the question of whether Bernard Délicieux had impeded the 'agent' or the 'function' of inquisition was of importance to both the friar and the papally appointed judges during his trial in 1318–19. Alan Friedlander, *The Hammer of the Inquisitors: Brother Bernard Délicieux and the Struggle against the Inquisition in Fourteenth-Century France* (Leiden, 2000), pp. 270–2.

8 Mark Pegg agrees wholeheartedly with Kieckhefer: 'At no time, however, and this must never be forgotten, were Bernart de Caux and Jean de Saint-Pierre ever representatives of a fully functioning self-perpetuating institutional "Inquisition"'; Pegg, *The Corruption of Angels*, p. 32. James Given notes Kieckhefer's arguments, but tends to present the inquisitional exercise of power as institutional. For instance, he says that 'Despite the admiration one may feel for the assiduous way in which the Languedocian inquisitors went about their task of regulating belief and practice, one can never forget that their institution was above all dedicated to repression, and that its agenda was essentially negative.' See J. Given, *Inquisition and Medieval Society: Power, Discipline, and Resistance in Languedoc* (Ithaca, 1997), pp. 32, 216. John Arnold argues that heresy inquisitors in Languedoc were becoming in the thirteenth century 'a kind of professional group'. He also suggests that we might talk of 'Inquisition' (capital I) 'as a mechanism for producing "truth", using a particular kind of authority and language that lays claim to continuity in its textual repetition.' Thus, for Arnold, 'The process extend[s] beyond the individual inquisitor.' See J. Arnold, *Inquisition and Power: Catharism and the Confessing Subject in Medieval Languedoc* (Philadelphia, 2001), pp. 77–8, 90.

Introduction

This book examines the beliefs and lived religion of men and women attached to the dualist Christian sect known as Catharism in the Languedoc region of southern France between the late twelfth and early thirteenth centuries. Its main sources are the interview records of mendicant inquisitors charged with the identification and elimination of heterodoxy. The ordained ministers of the Cathar sect – called 'good men' and 'good women' by sympathisers, 'heretics' by the inquisitors – are not its principal concern, however. Instead its primary focus is on the large number of non-ordained men and women who made up the majority of its membership.

A great deal of material has been written about the Languedocian Cathars.[1] Many of these studies focus on the theology of the sect, on its rituals, or on the careers of its leaders.[2] Others have mapped the history of the movement in Languedoc from its emergence there in the mid-eleventh century to its gradual dwindling at the hands of orthodox persecutors.[3] Catharism also plays a large part in the tourist industry in the modern *région* of Languedoc-Roussillon, whose *Pays Cathare* road signs will be familiar to any modern tourist.[4] There are at least two series of *bandes dessinées* – comic books – devoted to the Cathars, and they have recently appeared in UK households in Kate Mosse's *Labyrinth* series of novels, and its television adaptation.

Yet whilst Catharism has always been seen as a 'popular' heresy, its populace – the ordinary men and women who made up the bulk of its support and whose interest so concerned the Catholic Church – have generally been ignored. The orthodox enemies of Catharism in the eleventh and twelfth centuries saw the people the sect attracted as an inert mass, incapable of the imaginative leap to heresy until they were corrupted by the 'leaven' of

1 A comprehensive and relatively recent survey of some of this work can be found in B. Hamilton, 'The Legacy of Charles Schmidt to the Study of Christian Dualism', *Journal of Medieval History* 24 (1998), 191–214. See also the articles in *Cahiers de Fanjeaux*, vol. 14 (Toulouse, 1979), which is entitled 'Historiographie du Catharisme'.

2 On ritual, see J. Duvernoy, *Le Catharisme: la religion des Cathares* (Toulouse, 1976). On both ritual and careers, J. M. Vidal, 'Les derniers ministres de l'albigéisme en Languedoc: leurs doctrines', *Revue des questions historiques* 79 (1906), 57–107, and J. M. Vidal, 'Doctrines et morale des derniers ministres albigeois', *Revue des questions historiques* 86 (1909), 5–48.

3 For example, M. Lambert, *The Cathars* (Oxford, 1998).

4 A good English-language introduction to this world is E. McCaffrey, 'Imagining the Cathars in Late-Twentieth-Century Languedoc', *Contemporary European History* 11 (2002), 409–27. See also C.-O. Carbonell, 'Vulgarisation et récupération: le Catharisme a travers les mass-médias', *Cahiers de Fanjeaux* 14 (1979), pp. 361–80.

heretical ministers.[5] This way of seeing religious groupings remains current in the historiography of heresy: with some notable exceptions, historians of Catharism seem to have been relatively untouched by the 'rise of the laity' in the wider field of religious history.[6]

Studies of unordained people within Languedoc have focussed on political, economic or social factors rather than on popular religion. These have thus been highly successful in mapping the context for Catharism, but have often failed to integrate the experience of Catharism into that context.[7] Even Emmanuel Le Roy Ladurie's *Montaillou*, acclaimed for its powerful evocation of everyday life, does not engage with popular religion meaningfully.[8] Le Roy Ladurie's work, which generated both praise and controversy, is a

5 'The Lump and the Leaven' is the title of the first chapter of J. H. Arnold, *Inquisition and Power: Catharism and the Confessing Subject in Medieval Languedoc* (Philadelphia, 2001), pp. 19–47.

6 The 'rise of the laity' is described in P. Biller, 'Popular Religion in the Central and Later Middle Ages', in *Companion to Historiography*, ed. M. Bentley (London, 1997), pp. 221–46. Its lack of impact on heresy studies (with the exception of Waldensianism) is discussed at pp. 237–9.

7 John Mundy has published works on the social and political context of Catharism in the region's principal city (Toulouse). See J. H. Mundy, *Liberty and Political Power in Toulouse, 1050–1230* (New York, 1954); J. H. Mundy, *Men and Women at Toulouse in the Age of the Cathars* (Toronto, 1990); J. H. Mundy, *Society and Government at Toulouse in the Age of the Cathars* (Toronto, 1997). In part because of the wealth of detail and breadth of the themes which he covers, and in part because it was not his intent so to do, Mundy's studies of men and women in Languedoc do not provide a picture of Catharism as a lived religion. Other historians have produced detailed articles on Catharism within specific regions or localities, though, again, lived religion is not their primary concern. See, for example: W. L. Wakefield, 'Heretics and Inquisitors: The Case of Le Mas-Saint-Puelles', *Catholic Historical Review* 69 (1983), 209–26, and W. L. Wakefield, 'Heretics and Inquisitors: The Case of Auriac and Cambiac', *Journal of Medieval History* 12 (1986), 225–37. One particular group of lay supporters – women – has received more serious attention as part of Catharism. The fundamental article here is R. Abels and E. Harrison, 'The Participation of Women in Languedocian Catharism', *Mediaeval Studies* 41 (1979), 215–51, which carefully compiled statistics from the inquisitors' registers disproving the previously popular idea that Catharism had had special appeal to women because it offered them a more elevated role than either secular society or Roman Catholicism. See also P. Biller, 'The Common Woman in the Western church in the Thirteenth and Early Fourteenth Centuries', *Studies in Church History* 27 (1990), 127–57, especially pp. 156–57, which suggests a third possibility – that Catharism was actively *unattractive* to women, perhaps because its anti-materialist doctrine often manifested itself as a particular revulsion for their sex.

8 E. Le Roy Ladurie, *Montaillou, village occitan de 1294 à 1324* (Paris, 1975). Translated (and significantly abridged) as E. Le Roy Ladurie, *Montaillou: The Promised Land of Error*, trans. B. Bray (London, 1978), I have mostly referred to the English translation, but on occasion have made use of material only available in the more detailed French text. To avoid confusion, I have used the abbreviations *Montaillou* (En) and *Montaillou* (Fr) to indicate whether I am referring to the original or the translation. Where appropriate, I have given references to both.

'microhistory' reconstructed from fourteenth-century testimonies before the bishop-inquisitor Jacques Fournier of men and women from the eponymous village in the foothills of the Pyrenees.[9] Its narrative is set firmly within a rich local context that includes Catharism, but *Montaillou* is not primarily devoted to lived religion. Instead, its main focus was the establishment of a broader image of peasant life, mentality and 'outlook'; although always a background presence, Catharism was not a major area of interest for Le Roy Ladurie, who 'does not take [it] seriously, and does not discuss it systematically', according to one of his reviewers.[10] The religious beliefs and experiences of non-elite followers of Catharism, then, have thus far received little attention. Even those works which treat the interior world of these people seek to explain a moment of conversion – 'the attraction of Catharism' – rather than the realities of life within the sect. The model is still a top-down one in which believers examine the claims of Catharism and either subscribe or do not, but themselves bring nothing to it.[11] This is a very limited picture of the significance of religion in people's lives.

One recent historian of heresy in Languedoc, Mark Pegg, has placed lived religion firmly in the foreground. Like *Montaillou* before it, Pegg's 2001 monograph *The Corruption of Angels* was a tightly focussed study of one set of deposition records which covered a geographically limited area (the Lauragais region to the south-east of Toulouse). Pegg shares with Le Roy Ladurie both literary flair and an eye for the picturesque, but his work has concentrated more intently on the lived reality of Catharism.[12] Pegg's text is deceptively brief, but its few words are chosen with exquisite care.[13] His argument is provocative and iconoclastic: historians studying 'Catharism' – a term he rejects as anachronistic – have been seduced by medieval polemicists' views of heresy. They have constructed a fictional 'Cathar church' which did not exist in the minds of its supposed ministers, and most certainly not in those

9 A thorough – if brutal – re-evaluation of Le Roy Ladurie's text is given in L. E. Boyle, 'Montaillou Revisited: Mentalité and Methodology', in *Pathways to Medieval Peasants*, ed. J. A. Raftis (Toronto, 1981), pp. 120–40.

10 J. B. Russell, 'Review: Montaillou: The Promised Land of Error', *Catholic Historical Review* 66 (1980), 678–80. Chapter 19 of Le Roy Ladurie, *Montaillou* (En), (pp. 306–7) is devoted to 'Religion in Practice'. Here, though, Le Roy Ladurie is primarily concerned with orthodox Christianity; only three pages (pp. 324–6) deal with Catharism. This focus may have reflected the demographic make-up of a village which retained an orthodox majority, but in light of the fact that the vast bulk of evidence in Fournier's register concerns those sympathetic to Catharism it is a little unexpected. See also the comments in Boyle, 'Montaillou Revisited', p. 134.

11 An example of this approach can be found in Wakefield, 'Heretics and Inquisitors: The Case of Le Mas-Saint-Puelles'.

12 M. G. Pegg, *The Corruption of Angels: The Great Inquisition of 1245–1246* (Princeton, 2001).

13 Deceptively in that the text rests securely on a large and meticulously constructed set of footnotes which are sometimes lengthier than the chapters they support.

of ordinary believers.[14] No trace of this Cathar church exists in his source, he argues: this mid-thirteenth-century inquisition register instead tells the story of an 'intimate, intensely local, and deliberately unadorned way of living with the holy', which was retrospectively reshaped by inquisitors (and historians) into the conventional heresy they had expected to find all along.[15] This challenge to the 'conventional picture of Catharism' has reinvigorated the study of high-medieval heresy, and brought it once again before a wider audience.[16] Its resolution, Pegg has argued, could have profound consequences for our understanding of heterodoxy and, by extension, for our understanding of the Middle Ages themselves: 'if heresy is fundamentally misunderstood, then Latin Christianity is fundamentally misunderstood, and so what it means to study the medieval world is fundamentally misunderstood'.[17] The faith of ordinary people is a key facet of this understanding.

Pegg's bombast is compelling, and his refreshingly inclusive approach to the study of lived religion – encompassing elite and non-elite members, and foregrounding the non-elite majority – is something I hope to emulate here. *The Corruption of Angels* is firmly grounded in the local environment, deeply evocative and eloquently written. Its arguments are powerful, but not entirely convincing. In particular, the following points should be noted: first, that there is significant counter evidence to his claims; second, that much of this evidence can be found in the testimonies of ordinary men and women collected by Languedocian inquisitors (some within the register he used); and, finally, that Pegg does not seriously engage with the problems this material presents to his attempts to demolish the idea of 'Catharism'.[18]

14 This argument can be found primarily in chapter 3 of Pegg, *The Corruption of Angels*, pp. 15–19.

15 Pegg, *The Corruption of Angels*, p. 130. Cf references to testamentary bequests to the 'church of the heretics' in MS 609 discussed below, p. 00 n. 82.

16 For a summary of the debate, see C. Taylor, 'Evidence for Dualism in Inquisitorial Registers of the 1240s: A Contribution to a Debate', *History* 98 (2013), 319–45. Amongst recently published works, the most well known amongst non-specialists is R. I. Moore, *The War on Heresy* (Cambridge MA, 2012), which incorporates many of Pegg's arguments. See also M. G. Pegg, 'Albigenses in the Antipodes: An Australian and the Cathars', *Journal of Religious History* 35, no. 4 (2011), 577–600, and M. G. Pegg, *A Most Holy War: The Albigensian Crusade and the Battle for Christendom* (Oxford, 2008), which contains elements of this argument (for example, pp. 169–71 on the Charter of Niquita), but suggests that the Crusade changed Catharism and that what inquisitors began to investigate in 1245 was 'only two decades old', 'no more than atrophied nostalgia for the vivid and distinctive world of the good men before war' (p. 187).

17 Pegg, 'Albigenses in the Antipodes: An Australian and the Cathars', p. 580.

18 Claire Taylor has recently explored evidence of dualist belief in the inquisitors' records. Focusing on the earliest registers, she argues that deposition records represent a range of 'emergent' variations on dualist belief amongst Cathar followers, rather than a clearly formulated 'ideal type'. They are thus accurate records of a complex reality, she argues, rather than neat inquisitorial fabrications. Taylor, 'Evidence for Dualism'. See also B. Hamilton, review of *The Corruption of Angels*, by M. Pegg, *American Historical Review*

It is perhaps understandable that 'conventional' Cathar historiography has yet rarely followed Pegg in concentrating on lay involvement. Catharism – both as a belief system and as a body of people – privileged the elite, to a much greater extent than the Catholic Church. The dichotomy between the purified and saved elect and their worldly followers could not have been clearer: they existed on opposite sides of the dualist divide. The tiny religious elite entirely controlled access to salvation. These good men were purified living saints, intermediaries between man and God; the un-consoled, by contrast, were not even able to pray without their ministers' intervention. Salvation could not be attained through individual effort, but was bestowed in one fell swoop through the ritual of *consolamentum*.

Theologically speaking, Catharism was an exclusive club with a long waiting list but few fully active members. Yet the practical reality of Catharism can never really have matched this rigid theological and ecclesial hierarchy. The bulk of the Cathar movement was made up of men and women outside its official structures. They were not faceless crowds, but individuals who interacted with ministers in small groups, increasingly in domestic settings.[19] They funded the Cathar church;[20] they provided the good men and good women with buildings in which to live and food to eat; they attended services and paid ritual respect to the preachers; in later years they protected their fugitive ministers from discovery by orthodox forces. Ultimately, of course, they were the pool from which new members of the elite were drawn. Whilst they had no active theological role within Catharism itself, then, these men and women were nevertheless a fundamentally important part of the institution, without which it could not have existed.[21]

What is more, there are good reasons to suspect both that the needs and demands of the non-elite majority within Catharism differed from those of the hierarchy, and that their influence was not negligible. Carol Lansing has argued that ordinary followers in northern Italy exercised some discretion in matters of belief, and that doctrine mattered little to them. Instead, they made pragmatic assessments of Cathar ministers, and followed particularly attractive tenets 'without necessarily adopting or caring about dualism'.[22] In thirteenth-century Quercy, Claire Taylor suggests, 'many people engaged

107 (2002), 925–6, and Biller, review of *The Corruption of Angels*, by M. Pegg, *Speculum* 78 (2003), 1366–70.

19 Arnold, *Inquisition and Power*, pp. 157–8; J. H. Arnold, 'The Preaching of the Cathars', in *Medieval Monastic Preaching*, ed. C. Muessig (Leiden, 1998), pp. 191–4.

20 On which, see A. Roach, 'The Cathar Economy', *Reading Medieval Studies* 12 (1986), 51–71.

21 Cf. C. Bruschi, *The Wandering Heretics of Languedoc* (Cambridge, 2009), p. 193, which states that 'messengers' had a 'crucial role' logistically (and thus for the inquisitors), but 'within the community they carried little religious weight and authority'.

22 C. Lansing, *Power and Purity: Cathar Heresy in Medieval Italy* (New York, 1997), p. 95. See in general chapter 5, pp. 81–105.

with ideas about the nature of creation and made decisions for themselves about which ones they found convincing'.[23] Non-elite members of the Cathar movement in Languedoc were not entirely passive, as Pegg has amply demonstrated. Peter Biller has suggested that Cathar followers in the region sometimes set the agenda in their interactions with good men by encouraging them to fill roles usually played by orthodox clergy. The settlement of disputes and the burial of the dead were two areas in which Cathar ministers did not keep rigidly to their theology, but adapted to meet the demands of un-consoled followers; this book will identify further examples.[24] Followers' demands were informed not just by Cathar teaching but also by personal and social concerns and the enduring influence of long-established ecclesiastical norms.

A better testing-ground than the Languedoc for the examination of interactions between the non-elite members of a religious movement and its hierarchy could not be wished for. Over the course of the thirteenth and fourteenth centuries the Cathar Church was subject to extreme outside pressures in the form of orthodox persecution. These pressures acted to make good men ever more reliant on their followers for the essentials of their life: shelter, sustenance, and secrecy. If its ordinary membership really did have an influence on the direction of Catharism as a movement, this must surely have become stronger as the practical support they provided became ever more necessary during this period.

Although generations of historians of Catharism have contributed towards a sophisticated knowledge of its theological and hierarchical structures, our picture of Catharism as a movement will always be lacking until it encompasses the experiences of the wider membership. This has partly to do with building up an understanding of lay belief, but its significance is wider too.[25] If we wish to gain a more complete understanding of the way Catharism worked on the ground and to reconstruct a picture of the faith as it was actually experienced, these men and women must be included, and included not simply in the context in an assessment of the movement's 'reception', but as independent actors within it. This book aims to fill that gap. At its core is an attempt to answer two basic questions: what did non-elite members do within the Cathar movement, and what did they think about it?

Like all studies of Languedocian Catharism, this study relies primarily on the records of interviews conducted by hostile judicial courts. The officials of these courts – inquisitors (primarily Dominicans) and their lieutenants – were more interested in eliciting confessions to specific crimes and in uncovering

23 C. Taylor, *Heresy, Crusade and Inquisition in Medieval Quercy*, Heresy and Inquisition in the Middle Ages 2 (York, 2011) p. 191.

24 P. Biller, 'Cathar Peacemaking', in *Christianity and Community in the West: Essays for John Bossy*, ed. S. Ditchfield (Aldershot, 2001), pp. 1–23.

25 Arnold, *Inquisition and Power*, pp. 157–8.

networks of heretics and their supporters than in recording for posterity the complex lives of Cathar followers. Yet the depositions they collected overflow with snatches of conversation between ordinary followers, and with snapshots of their lives. Far from being arid territory for the historian, in fact, the rich detail which can be collated from the inquisitors' registers can instead be overwhelmingly fruitful.

Depositions are not complete narratives composed by a single, predictable author, but collections of often disjointed episodes ranging across time and space: a deponent might testify about events that took place within the week that they were interviewed, or those from which they are separated by half a century or more. Indeed, whilst the formal structure that inquisitors and their scribes imposed lends the finished documents a semblance of predictable uniformity, the inquisitorial registers are just as much the product of the deponents themselves, a diverse group of people ranging in age from early teens to late sixties, interviewed at different times and in widely varying circumstances. If we are to work with these rich sources, we need an interpretive framework which assists with the creation of a coherent narrative whilst giving room for the representation of diversity.

The life-cycle model

One interpretive scheme which has been of some recent interest to medieval historians is that of the life cycle.[26] The life-cycle model is well suited to the analysis of medieval faith, because religious affiliation was governed by age-specific rules and expectations. Questions about life stage crop up regularly when reading about religion in the Middle Ages. Three gender-specific examples: Was Humbert of Romans right when he complained that adolescent girls were too distracted by fashion and socialising to have any time for religion?[27] What effect did marriage have on the faith and adherence of young women?[28] How can deathbed entry into religious orders be viewed within the context of lifelong patterns of belief?[29] These questions and others like them are useful and important, but changing patterns of religious adher-

26 A few examples: S. Shahar, *Childhood in the Middle Ages* (New York, 1990); P. J. P. Goldberg and F. Riddy, eds., *Youth in the Middle Ages* (York, 2004); P. J. P. Goldberg, *Women, Work and Life Cycle in a Medieval Economy* (Oxford, 1992); S. Shahar, *Growing Old in the Middle Ages: 'Winter Clothes Us in Shadow and Pain'* (London, 1996).

27 P. Biller, 'Abundance and Scarcity of Food in the Inquisition Records of Languedoc', in *Cross, Crescent and Conversion: Studies on Medieval Spain and Christendom in Memory of Richard Fletcher*, ed. S. Barton and P. Linehan (Leiden, 2008), p. 276.

28 This question was posed in Biller, 'The Common Woman', p. 132.

29 According to Shahar 'throughout the High and Late Middle Ages there seem to have been more mature or elderly women who entered convents … than there were men who became monks in maturity': Shahar, *Growing Old in the Middle Ages*, pp. 99–100.

ence have not until now been analysed within the frame of a life cycle. This book attempts to do so.

The life-cycle model is particularly well suited to the meaningful analysis of the disparate bits of information contained in the deposition records. Drawing together testimony from across a broad range of inquisitors' registers, it is possible to collect a significant body of material about specific groups. Although deponents' ages are often difficult to ascertain, many of the experiences recounted within the deposition records can be located within one of the life-cycle stages. By imposing order on the varied deposition material, I hope that the life-cycle model will facilitate a coherent representation of the rich complexity of people's interactions with the Cathar faith, and allow for diversity and change to be represented.

Religious orthodoxy has a part to play in this story, too. Contrary to the impression one might receive from the attention devoted to it, Catharism in Languedoc only ever claimed a minority of the population as adherents. The demands made by the Catholic Church on its followers were not always particularly heavy, and orthodox practice was by no means entirely abandoned by those who followed the good men.[30] 'What is still underrated', wrote Andrew Roach in 1986, 'is the way in which the orthodox and the heretical interacted to fulfil people's spiritual needs.'[31] Taking heed of this comment, I investigate the role played by diverse external factors in shaping people's life-cycle adherence, and take particular care to set its subjects' Catharism against a wider backdrop of secular and orthodox practice.

While the life cycle is the model, then, which life cycle? Human life can be divided into many differing cycles. The Middle Ages recognised several: three-, five-, six- or seven-part divisions, and more, each with their own precisely defined boundaries.[32] As one might expect, these schemes were implicitly gendered, describing not the ages of mankind but of *man* specifically.[33] Even if this were not the case, though, they are unsuitable for use here. Medieval discussion about the Ages of Man was either a scholarly exploration of symbolism, or – if more 'scientific' – was based on ideas about the natural world foreign to us today. It was not intended to reflect the realities

30 On low expectations for lay Catholics, see N. Tanner and S. Watson, 'Least of the Laity: The Minimum Requirements for a Medieval Christian', *Journal of Medieval History* 32 (2006), 395–423.

31 Roach, 'The Cathar Economy', p. 67.

32 On 'ages of man' in medieval thought, see: E. Sears, *The Ages of Man: Medieval Interpretations of the Life Cycle* (Princeton, 1986). Also helpful as a general introduction is J. A. Burrow, *The Ages of Man: A Study in Medieval Writing and Thought* (Oxford, 1986). M. Dove, *The Perfect Age of Man's Life* (Cambridge, 1986), is somewhat narrower in focus.

33 Dove, *Perfect Age*, discusses the 'ages of woman's life' on pp. 20–5, noting that woman's experience was considered as deviation from a male norm, and that women were generally not considered to experience the 'perfect age' which is her subject. Dove, *Perfect Age*. See also material on the 'ages of woman' in Sears, *Ages of Man*.

of most people's lives, and would have meant little to most people.[34] In any case, we cannot work with precisely defined life stages, for the depositions only very rarely provide information about deponents' ages.

Rather than attempt to follow a medieval model, therefore, this book's chapters follow themes which have been important in the historiography of life stages. It is divided into four chapters which deal consecutively with childhood, youth, married life, and old age and death. The broad changes which took place during the life stage will emerge over the course of these chapters. Each chapter also reflects on work on the life cycle by other historians. The earlier stages of the life cycle in particular have not been without controversy. In fact, their validity as categories of analysis for medievalists has been challenged outright: the existence of medieval childhood has been questioned and vigorously defended, and its historical specificity has been reasserted; similar debates are now taking place over the status of youth. Both sides in these debates would agree, though, that 'childhood' and 'youth' are at least partly subject to cultural construction and in that sense historical products. This study attempts to engage with these debates from the perspective of a history of popular religion; its own contribution is made in an attempt to ascertain the status of children and young people within Catharism and to describe their place within and responses to it.[35]

One related area which is *not* discussed is parenthood. On the earliest stage of this process there is some evidence in the early registers: two pregnant women were told that they had demons in their bellies, and another that she could not be saved if she died whilst in that state;[36] two more did not perform the *melioramentum*.[37] Later, some women reacted against the application to

34 On 'scientific' ideas about the ages of man, see Burrow, *The Ages of Man*, chapter 1: 'Nature', (pp. 5–54). Burrow argues (at pp. 92–3) that 'Many medieval people, we may suppose, knew little more about the formal doctrines of the *aetates hominum* than they might have learned from a sermon on Septuagesima Sunday or a wall-painting in a chamber.' Sears comments in her introduction that 'it should be frankly stated at the outset that the theme of the ages of man was a bookish one … [medieval] descriptions of the ages of man do not mirror medieval life so much as they reflect medieval meditations … on the nature and meaning of human existence': Sears, *Ages of Man*, p. 6.

35 See below, pp. 27–93.

36 Ermessende Viguier (told she had a demon in her belly by good women), MS 609, fols. 239v–40r; Guillemette of Saint-Flour (told by her neighbour 'that she should pray to God to release her from the demon in her belly'), D25, fol. 40r. In *circa* 1232 Peirone Claustra was informed by two good men whom she and her husband put up for the night that 'si decederet praegnans non posset saluari'; D22, fol. 57r.

37 Guillemette *de Bono Loco*, D21, fol. 296r–v, and Domina Ermengaud of Mazerolles, MS 609, fol. 124r. Note that it is not clear that there was a prohibition against pregnant women performing the *melioramentum*, and it may merely have been impractical, especially if they were nearing full-term. In the latter case, this is almost certain. Ermengaud met the good men when riding, and to perform the rite would have involved dismounting from her horse, kneeling on the ground, and remounting: 'quia ipsa testis erat tunc pregnans

sick infants of ascetic prohibitions following the *consolamentum*.[38] Yet, tantalising though they are, there is disappointingly little evidence concerning the topic beyond these few cases.[39] The same is true of evidence relating to the care of older children: whilst some depositions bear upon parents' relationships to children, they are almost all related from the child's point-of-view.[40]

'What about *Montaillou*', readers may be asking themselves, 'has not the life cycle been covered there already?' It is a pertinent question. Yet whilst Le Roy Ladurie used elements of a life-cycle model in his work, it was not employed systematically.[41] The short chapter on childhood ('and other ages in life') deals for the most part not with children but with parents, and primarily with those nursing infants.[42] Montaillou itself, according to Le Roy Ladurie, did not possess anything that could be called a 'youth culture', and so young people too receive short shrift.[43] These omissions are hardly surprising, for Le Roy Ladurie was interested above all in the kinship ties of the *domus* (household), a sphere within which the primary actors were adult males. I do not aim to reconstruct the totality of society, economy and outlook from the registers, only that portion of it that touches upon lived religion. This book devotes far greater attention to the life cycle, but my interest in it is instrumentalist. The chapter-headings of *Montaillou* reflect the range of themes which Le Roy Ladurie wanted to investigate; mine reflect the desire to divide my single large theme – the nature of lived religion amongst Cathar followers – into meaningful as well as manageable portions.

The sources consulted

There is another important difference between this book and the studies by both Le Roy Ladurie and Pegg: its source base is wider. It is true that the register on which *Montaillou* is based is remarkable for the length of its depositions (in 314 folios the depositions of just ninety-five people are recorded),

non descendit nec dimiserunt eam dicti heretici descendere de eqitatura et ideo non adoravit'.

38 Biller, 'The Common Woman', pp. 154–7.

39 A possible addition is the case of a pregnant woman expelled from her husband's death-bed reception because of pregnancy and grief. It is not clear, though, whether pregnancy was the reason for her expulsion. See p. 139 n. 91 below.

40 See below, pp. 27–70.

41 Le Roy Ladurie, *Montaillou* (En). Chapter headings in this work include 'Marriage and the condition of women', 'Childhood and other ages in life', 'Death in Montaillou'. Chapter 16 deals in part with youth.

42 See ibid., chapter 12 (pp. 204–17); of that chapter, only pp. 214–16 deal directly with non-infant children, and these are concerned not with children per se, but with their acculturation.

43 Ibid., p. 216.

but it is still just one enquiry covering a very narrow time period.[44] In terms of its breadth, Pegg's source is at the other end of the scale: its 260 folios record the testimony of around 5,500 men and women. Yet it too captures only a particular moment in the history of inquisition and heresy.[45] These are detailed snapshots, but they are snapshots nevertheless. During the century and a half between the start of Pegg's coverage and the end of Le Roy Ladurie's, the movement led by the good men underwent fundamental changes. These developments are best viewed as being in constant flow. Whether or not its brand of Catharism had local peculiarities, Montaillou in the early fourteenth century was no more 'an island in time' than had been the Lauragais a century earlier.[46] Micro-histories are extraordinarily valuable, but their intense specificity can sometimes emphasise local colour and individual eccentricity at the expense of situating these within wider developments.[47] Hoping to avoid such a charge, this book casts its nets widely, examining ten inquisitorial records of varying sizes which range in date from the 1240s to the 1320s. These sources comprise almost all the extant material of their type from the period.[48] The following pages discuss the character, content and context of each in turn, ordered chronologically by period covered.

I. Toulouse MS 609: records of an inquest of 1245–46

Between May 1245 and August 1246, the Dominicans Bernard of Caux and Jean of Saint-Pierre undertook a large-scale investigation of the Lauragais region to the south-east of Toulouse. The depositions were all taken in the city, in the basilica dedicated to its martyred first bishop, Saint-Sernin. Little is known about the two friars, and they may have been foreigners in

44 On the register, see below pp. 22–4.

45 Indeed, the raw figures are somewhat misleading. Many of those who testified before the 1245–46 inquest denied all knowledge of heresy and thus left short depositions, often no more than a single line in the register.

46 Montaillou as an 'island in time' is discussed in Le Roy Ladurie, *Montaillou* (En), p. 282. See David Herlihy, 'Review: Montaillou: Cathars and Catholics in a French Village, 1294–1324', *Social History* 4 (1979), 519, for a critique.

47 See: Hamilton, review of *The Corruption of Angels*, by M. Pegg; Biller, review of *The Corruption of Angels*, by M. Pegg; Boyle, 'Montaillou Revisited', pp. 131–3.

48 Notable amongst those works not consulted are the records of an investigation in 1299 at Albi, published in *The Inqusition at Albi 1299–1300*, ed. G.W. Davis (New York, 1948). These are particularly dry and have an unusually limited range: all deponents were male, wealthy and locally powerful, and all were arrested together. Also not consulted is Paris, Bibliothèque nationale de France MS 12856, the record of an inquiry by Bernard de Castanet and Jean Galand in 1286–90, which has been surveyed in A. de la Presle-Evesque, 'Le manuscrit BNF latin 12856. Analyse, texte, traduction' (unpublished Ph.D. thesis, École Pratique des Hautes Études, Section des Sciences Religieuses, 1995).

Languedoc.[49] The inquisitor-historian Bernard Gui described Bernard of Caux (the senior of the pair) in glowing terms as 'inquisitor and persecutor and hammer of heretics, a blessed man filled with God'.[50] Of Jean of Saint-Pierre we know 'absolutely nothing'.[51] Other material from enquiries by these two inquisitors survives, most notably a register of sentences dating from 1244–48 published by Célestin Douais; sixty-three other pieces can be found scattered throughout the Doat collection, some of which have been consulted here.[52]

The results of the 1245–46 investigation – along with some later work undertaken by those inquisitors – were copied about fifteen years later for the inquisitors William Bernard of Dax and Reginald of Chartres.[53] Two of an original ten or more volumes survive today as MS 609 of the Bibliothèque municipale de Toulouse.[54] This register, composed of 260 folios, is one of the oldest known paper documents in France.[55] It records the depositions of around 5,500 men and women who gave evidence during the enquiry, grouped in the register by village. This is an astounding number which makes the register the most comprehensive surviving text of its kind from the Middle Ages.[56]

Villagers were summoned *en masse* to Toulouse during 1245–46, not through any detailed selection process. The enquiry was thus something of a fishing expedition, and many deponents did not bite. Compared to the other collections consulted for this study, the Toulouse manuscript appears to be a

49 Y. Dossat, *Les crises de l'inquisition Toulousaine au XIIIe siécle (1233–1273)* (Bordeaux, 1959), p. 155.

50 Bernard Gui, *De fundatione et prioribus conventuum provinciarum Tolosanae et Provinciae Ordinis Praedicatorum*, ed. P. A. Amargier, *Monumenta ordinis fratrum praedicatorum historica* 24 (Rome, 1961), p. 109. Yves Dossat considered Bernard of Caux to be a better inquisitorial exemplar than the more extraordinary Gui; see Y. Dossat, 'Une figure d'inquisiteur: Bernard de Caux', *Cahiers de Fanjeux* 6 (1971), 253–72 (p. 253).

51 Dossat, *Crises*, p. 155.

52 The register is Bibliothèque nationale de France MS Lat 9992. It is published in C. Douais, ed., *Documents pour servir à l'histoire de l'inquisition dans le Languedoc*, 2 vols. (Paris, 1900), II, 1–89. For a detailed summary of the register, see ibid, I, cxlix–cliii.

53 On the date of copying, see Dossat, *Crises*, p. 57.

54 The lost volumes are attested to in the register itself by (contemporary) marginal notes which cross-reference them. See MS 609, fols. 43v, 99r.

55 Various studies have been made of the manuscript itself; amongst the most important and accessible are: Douais, ed., *Documents*, I, cliii–clxi; Dossat, *Crises*, pp. 56–70; Pegg, *The Corruption of Angels*, pp. 20–7 and especially its notes on pp. 151–60. On its status as one of France's oldest paper documents, see Dossat, *Crises*, p. 56.

56 Various estimates have been made, but these are almost all in the region of 5,500. For a summary, see Pegg, *The Corruption of Angels*, p. 169 n. 52. The exception, Molinier, gave a figure of between 8,000 and 10,000. He was, however – as he admitted – extrapolating based on a limited sample. See C. Molinier, *L'Inquisition dans le Midi de la France au XIIIe et au XIVe siècle* (Toulouse, 1880), p. 190. On the register's uniquely large size, see Pegg, *The Corruption of Angels*, p. 26.

remarkably complete record of the enquiry, in which even the unsuccessful interrogations are logged. These are short and to the point:

> Item, in the year and day as above, Hugh of Mamiros, sworn in as a witness, said that he never saw heretics, nor believed nor adored nor gave nor sent nor led them or had them led nor received nor heard their preaching.[57]

Sometimes they are terser still:

> Item, in the year and day as above, P[eter] Lapasse senior, sworn in as a witness, said the same in everything as the above Hugh of Mamiros.[58]

The terse formatting of the register obscures the reality of question-and-answer exchanges that made up the interrogation. In fact, the inquisitors had a series of pre-set questions for the deponent: 'did you see heretics?'; 'did you believe in them?'; 'did you "adore" them?', and so forth. It is more than likely that Hugh and Peter did no more in the basilica of Saint-Sernin than repeat a single word: 'no'.

Many depositions were not this fruitless, though, and whilst the style of MS 609 is on the whole rather terse, splashes of colour and the occasional more verbose story are scattered throughout. Individual histories tended to come in snatches sometimes separated by many years, and there is a clear sense that the constraints on the inquisitors' time set an upper limit on the length and detail. One thing for which the historian working with this register can be grateful, though, is the apparent concern of Bernard of Caux and Jean of Saint-Pierre that witnesses date with reasonable accuracy the events they described. Some episodes can be dated back to the late twelfth century, the register thus providing a unique portrait of Cathar life before persecution began.

Despite various attempts, the text has not yet been edited. The first twelve folios of the register were transcribed in the appendix to a southern-French scholarly journal in 1868; Mark Pegg judges this short edition to be 'close to useless'.[59] The original paper leaves were still considered to be 'généralement bien conservé' by Charles Molinier in 1880, an opinion which was echoed by Yves Dossat in 1959 and Pegg in 2001.[60] A copying attempt was begun by Walter Wakefield and Austin Evans in 1933. The transcription this produced has not been widely known about amongst historians working in the field,

57 MS 609, fol. 1r.

58 Ibid.

59 See Pegg, *The Corruption of Angels*, p. 26. The edition can be found in B. Dusan, 'De Manso Sanctarum Puellarum', *Revue Archéologique du Midi de la France: recueil de notes, mémoires, documents relatifs aux monuments de l'histoire et des beaux-arts dans les pays de langue d'Oc* 2 (1868), Appendix (separately paginated), 1–12.

60 Molinier, *Inquisition*, p. 164 n. 3; Dossat, *Crises*, p. 61; Pegg, *The Corruption of Angels*, pp. 27–8.

and I became aware of its location only after the research for this book was complete.[61] Here, therefore, I have made use of a photostat of the Toulouse manuscript, as well as a draft-quality transcription by Jean Duvernoy which has been generously made available online. As a number of folios of the photostat reproduction are illegible, this transcription has been invaluable.[62]

II–VII. The Doat collection

We jump forward now 600 years to the mid-seventeenth century, when the French crown sponsored a project by Jean de Doat to collect and collate documents from the south of the kingdom which bore upon 'the rights of the crown, and [which] can serve history'.[63] This massive copying project – held today in the Bibliothèque nationale de France under the name *Collection Doat* – took some interest in inquisitorial registers, and 'still represent[s] the largest and most complete source of information on Catharism'.[64] Of the 258 volumes, numbers 21–37 contain material bearing on the Cathar heresy and the work of the inquisition.[65] One of the results of the broad scope and geographical sweep of the Doat project is that the final work is a varied and

61 The MS is at New York, Columbia University Library, Butler Collection, BX4890.B47 1255g. The catalogue record notes that its seven volumes contain 'a typescript of a transcription of the text of the manuscript and a copy of the negative microfilm of the manuscript itself'. My thanks to Pete Biller for this reference. On the copying project, see Pegg, *The Corruption of Angels*, p. 26. The rear cover of Annette Pales-Gobilliard's 2002 edition of Bernard Gui's *Sentences* stated that the author was preparing a critical edition of MS 609. The author's death left the project stalled in its early stages and its status is uncertain. See Bernard Gui, *Le livre des sentences de Bernard Gui: 1308–1323*, ed. A. Pales-Gobilliard (Paris, 2002). Additional information provided by Peter Biller (personal conversation).

62 In three parts, see J. Duvernoy, *Le manuscrit 609 de la bibliothèque municipale de Toulouse: Lauragais 1245–1246, 1253 – Copie Jean Duvernoy* (PDF format, 3 parts), http://jean.duvernoy.free.fr/text/listetexte.htm (accessed November 1, 2006). A scanned copy of the register is now available at the website of the bibliothèque municipale, under the 'Manuscripts' tab: http://rosalis.bibliotheque.toulouse.fr (accessed September 10, 2013). This digital reproduction was not consulted for this book.

63 For a summary of material in the Doat Collection relating to the inquisition, see Molinier, *Inquisition*, pp. 34–40. A concise reiteration of this summary in list form is in C. Bruschi, '"Magna diligentia est habenda per inquisitorem": Precautions Before Reading Doat 21–26', in *Texts and the Repression of Medieval Heresy*, ed. C. Bruschi and P. Biller (York, 2003), pp. 92–3. On the copying project itself, and the collection as a whole, see J. Roche, *Une église cathare: l'évêché du Carcassès* (Cahors, 2005), pp. 50–4 and *Inquisitors and Heretics in Thirteenth-Century Languedoc: An Edition and Translation of Toulouse Inquisition Depositions, 1273–1282*, ed. and trans. P. Biller, C. Bruschi and S. Sneddon (Leiden, 2011), pp. 20–33. For an introduction and edition of some of the correspondence between Doat and his masters, see H. Omont, 'La Collection Doat à la Bibliothèque Nationale: Documents sur les recherches de Doat', *Bibliothèque de l' École des Chartes* 77 (1916), 287–93.

64 Bruschi, 'Precautions', p. 92.

65 See ibid. and Molinier, *Inquisition*, pp. 34–40.

diverse collection of different types of document and periods of inquiry. As well as the records from the trial process, they also contain extracts from and copies of normative texts – including Gui's *Practica* – as well as papal bulls, polemical treatises and various other documents.

Despite its impressive budget and the skill of its director, Doat's project was not entirely without problems.[66] It moved from archive to archive, selecting documents to copy, and transporting them to Doat's peripatetic scriptorium. In this sense, it followed the model of the inquisition itself, though encountering somewhat less local hostility (the only serious setbacks were at Narbonne and Carcassonne).[67] The documents' modern users might be particularly concerned to read in his letters of the difficulties encountered in finding, employing and retaining scribes of suitable skill.[68] Fortunately, Doat seems to have been able to find enough good-quality scribes, and the standard of the finished product is – with a few exceptions – very high.[69] The most important (or, at least, the most distinctive) methodological problem with these particular texts is caused not by sloppy scribes, but by the copying project itself, however, which imposes an additional layer of distance between the historian and the thirteenth-century deponent.[70]

For this book I have consulted a portion of volume 21 (the penances of Peter Sella), and volumes 22–26 in their entirety, thus covering a substantial portion of the deposition material in the collection. The material in volume 21 is of a somewhat different nature to the remainder of the register, and is therefore discussed separately below.

66 On his 'shrewdness' see Omont, 'La Collection Doat', p. 328. On expenses, see Documents I–IV in the same.

67 On the 'geographic principle' shared by inquisitors and Doat's team, see Bruschi, 'Precautions', p. 93. On the difficulties, Omont, 'La Collection Doat', p. 328. For a fuller account, see ibid., document IV.

68 In the detailed record of his expenses, dated 1 August 1669, he complained of the difficulty of getting good scribes, 'those who can read the old titles in Latin, Spanish and in the vulgar [languages] do not write very well, and those who write well do not know how to read [these texts]': Omont, 'La Collection Doat', p. 294. See also pp. 306, 312, 318.

69 For a rare example of sloppier work, see D24, fols. 54r–5v.

70 Mark Pegg contrasts the authenticity of MS 609 with the more compromised Doat collection: 'though invaluable … [Doat] is still a seventeenth-century copy written in a beautiful flourishing cursive with the Latin respelled *style classique* and the marginalia of the inquisitors left out', Pegg, *The Corruption of Angels*, p. 20. Elsewhere he has suggested that the 'apparent fact' that the Doat registers are the only inquisition documents to refer to the good men and good women as *perfecti* 'should suggest that the seventeenth-century copyists … perhaps took more transcribing liberties than is often realised': 'On Cathars, Albigenses, and Good Men of Languedoc', *Journal of Medieval History* 27 (2001), 192–3 n. 28. He gives as an example of such a reference, D26, fols. 258r–9r. Although they contain a controversial passage (concerning the reception of Castel Faure), these folios contain no use of the word 'perfectus', referring instead to 'heretici' and 'boni homines'.

Penances issued by Peter Sella: Doat 21

This collection documents 732 penances issued by Peter Sella to men and women from the diocese of Quercy in the years 1241–42.[71] Sella is of some historical interest: a man of substantial means and secular influence, he was one of the first to join the Dominican order in 1215, around which time the original residence of the inquisitorial tribunal at Toulouse was donated from his personal holdings. He was appointed inquisitor in 1233, performing the role with a zeal that former associates considered to verge on betrayal.[72] The penances are unlike most other trial records in the Doat collection. The blunt assessment of Célestin Douais was that they comprised 'only a statement or table of punishments with the name of each person affected'.[73] Most depositions did not in fact follow this pattern.[74] The following is a typical example from the register, quoted in its entirety:

> G. Lasvignes often received heretics, guided them, and heard the preaching of the heretics, he adored once. He will stay for a year in Constantinople, concerning the cross [that he should wear as punishment] and the route [of his 'pilgrimage', the same details] as the others, and he will support a pauper for a year.[75]

Length varied, but penances are much shorter than other material from the Doat collection. This is an unusually long example:

> Rainalde has been a receiver of heretics, and has heard their preaching many times, and in diverse places, and was present at a certain heretication and received a *placenta* [a type of bread, or plaice] from the heretics and has guided heretics, and often adored them, and held them at Christmas and has received a loan from the heretics. She will carry a cross in front for three years, for the rest, as the previous Raimonde.[76]

71 They are located at D21, fols. 185[bis]r–212v. See also Douais, ed., *Documents*, I, pp. cxlvij–cxlviij, from which the count is taken.

72 Sella is documented in the writings Jordan of Saxony, William Pelhisson and Bernard Gui, and in legal documents in the Paris archives – for a summary of some of this evidence, see M.-H. Vicaire, *Saint Dominic and His Times* (New York, 1964), p. 168. As Laurent Albaret points out, the bibliographical sources for Sella are incomparably rich amongst the inquisitors of his era. See Laurent Albaret, *Les inquisiteurs: portraits de defenseurs de la foi en Languedoc, XIIIe–XIVe siècles* (Toulouse, 2001), p. 43. On Sella and the inquisition at Quercy, see Jörg Feuchter, *Ketzer, Konsuln und Büsser: Die städtischen Eliten von Montauban vor dem Inquisitor Petrus Cellani (1236/1241)*, Spätmittelalter, Humanismus, Reformation 40 (Tübingen, 2007), chapter 5, pp. 257–305.

73 Douais, ed., *Documents*, II, 143.

74 D21, fols. 191r–6r give only the name and the penance issued, however.

75 D21, fol. 200v. *L'inquisition en Quercy: le registre des pénitences de Pierre Cellan, 1241–1242*, ed and trans. J. Duvernoy (Castelnaud la Chapelle, 2001), p. 62.

76 D21, fol. 201v; *L'inquisition en Quercy*, ed. Duvernoy, p. 64.

As can be seen, these deposition summaries are sparse in detail and make no attempt at chronological precision. Around one third of them deal with contact with Waldensian preachers, and a number record interactions with both Waldensians and Cathars. In fact, many have seen in them an example of religious pluralism amongst the laity in Quercy.[77] Though we can only speculate about the purpose of this collection, its brevity suggests that it was intended as quick-access reference material.[78] Though short, its entries are sometimes surprisingly revealing, occasionally allowing life stages and particular beliefs to be identified.

Depositions before various inquisitors: Doat 22–26

The form of the depositions copied into volumes 22–26 of the Doat collection is consistent throughout.[79] Using criteria unknown to us, Doat and his team made a selection from the documents available to them, rewriting each deposition in a uniform hand, 'correcting' original spelling and annotations, and giving each a title and summary in French. The copies made for Doat reveal rearrangement or removal of depositions; we do not know whether this was the decision of his own scribes or of those who had compiled the thirteenth-century 'originals' from which they worked. An important caveat for the historian working with groups of depositions from the Doat collection, therefore, is that they cannot be always be regarded as coherent and complete units.

The length and number of depositions given by individual deponents varied, as will be seen from the following list of material consulted:

> Depositions from 1243–44 given principally before Brother Ferrier,[80] also before Pons Gary and Peter Durand.[81] Taken from the inquisitorial archives at Carcassonne.
> *D22 106v–D24 237v 109 depositions of 84 deponents.*[82]

77 See tables of adherence (Cathar, Waldensian, and 'mixed') in *L'inquisition en Quercy*, ed. Duvernoy, p. 210, and Taylor, *Heresy, Crusade and Inquisition in Medieval Quercy*, pp. 160–5, which revisits this material. See also Y. Dossat, 'Les vaudois méridionaux d'après les documents de l'inquisition', *Cahiers de Fanjeux* 1 (1967), p. 25.

78 Albaret suggests two uses, either as a field-notebook for later inquisitors, or as a reference when drawing up letters of penance and other legal documents: *Inquisiteurs*, p. 53.

79 In researching this book, I have consulted microfilm copies of volumes 22, 23, 24 and 26. I was also generously allowed early access to transcriptions and translations of the material from the 1270s in volumes 25–26 prepared by Peter Biller, Caterina Bruschi and Shelagh Sneddon. This material has now been published as *Inquisitors and Heretics in Thirteenth-century Languedoc*.

80 Ferrier was the earliest Dominican inquisitor, first appointed to serve under the archbishop of Narbonne in 1229. On his career, see Walter L. Wakefield, 'Friar Ferrier, Inquisitor', *Heresis* 7 (1986), 33–41.

81 On these, see: Douais, ed., *Documents*, I, pp. cxxxviij–cxlvij.

82 D22 contains a significant amount of material events at Montsegur in the period before its capture in 1245.

Depositions from 1243–44 and 1246–47, given before Bernard of Caux and Jean of Saint-Pierre. Taken from the Dominican archives at Toulouse and inquisitorial archives at Carcassonne respectively.[83]
D22 1r–106r – 44 depositions of 39 deponents (1243–44).
D24 237v to end – 22 depositions of 14 deponents (1246–47).

Depositions from 1273–80, given before Pons of Parnac and Ranulph of Plassac.[84] Taken from the Dominican archives at Toulouse.
D25 fol. 1r–D26 fol. 79r – 183 depositions of 80 deponents.[85]

Depositions from the 1280s and early 1290s,[86] given principally at Carcassonne before the inquisitors Jean Galand[87] and (separately) William of Saint-Seine.[88] Taken from a compilation in the inquisitorial archives at Carcassonne, probably composed in 1303–04.[89]
D26 fols. 80r–316v – 71 depositions of 26 deponents.

The character of these records is not uniform: the material in volume 22 is relatively 'free' and emphasises narrative; that in volume 23 is more 'rigid and formulaic'; volumes 25 and the first part of 26 are 'extraordinarily rich sources of information'.[90]

Volume 26 has been the subject of some interest from historians. Conditions in the inquisitorial prison at Carcassonne under Jean Galand were the subject of complaints to the king of France.[91] He was a controversial figure

83 At the end of each set of extracts some details of the register consulted have been provided by Gratian Capot, who authenticated the copy, for example at ibid., fols. 106r–v: 'Extracted and collated from twenty cahiers of parchment fastened together, of which the first is marked N°2 [sic] and the second CLXVIII, found in the archives of the Brothers Preacher of Toulouse, by the order and in the person of monsieur Jean de Doat …'.

84 See Douais, ed., *Documents*, I, pp. clxxii–clxxxj. Peter Biller, when preparing the edition of this register, noted that 'Depositions before [Parnac and Plassac] … have a richness which it is tempting to attribute to special qualities in these less well-known inquisitors': 'The Common Woman', p. 143 n. 70. See also the brief comment in Dossat, *Crises*, p. 195.

85 These have been published in *Inquisitors and Heretics in Thirteenth-Century Languedoc*. For this book I consulted a draft of this edition, as well as microfilm copies of the original.

86 The eleventh deposition of Bernard Benedict of *Villardonello* before the inquisitor Nicholas d'Abbeville is dated 1301. See D26, fol. 312r. Dossat gives the dates 1284–89: see Dossat, *Crises*, p. 46.

87 Inquisitor of Carcassonne (1278–93), see Douais, ed., *Documents*, I, clxxxii–cxc.

88 Successor (1286–92) to Jean Galand at Carcassonne: see ibid., cxc–cxjc.

89 On the register as a whole, see Roche, *Une église cathare*, pp. 59–67.

90 Bruschi, 'Precautions,' pp. 105–6.

91 One of these – made in 1286 – still survives. The text of the appeal is printed in J. M. Vidal, *Un inquisiteur jugé par ses 'victims': Jean Galand et les Carcassonnais (1285–1286)* (Paris, 1903), pp. 39–44. It is also discussed in J. Given, *Inquisition and Medieval Society: Power, Discipline, and Resistance in Languedoc* (Ithaca, 1997), pp. 64–5, and at greater length in A. Friedlander, *The Hammer of the Inquisitors: Brother Bernard Délicieux and the Struggle against the Inquisition in Fourteenth-Century France* (Leiden, 2000), pp. 13–21. By way of contrast, it is interesting to note the contents of a 1282 memorandum concerning irregularities at the prison. That note, written by Galand, suggests that conditions at this

at the time, not least because he was engaged in a very public feud with the Carcassonnais elite. His register describes a plot led by members of that group to destroy the inquisitors' records, and contains evidence implicating some of the same men as committed adherents of Catharism.[92] The most detailed recent treatment of this material is that of Julien Roche, who concluded that whilst some of the register could be trusted (including that which described the plot), other testimony was 'manipulated' by Galand.[93] It is not my intention to critique or defend the material in question, but two points should be noted: first, if elements of the register had been altered in an attempt to deceive, this would have been done by men with experience of inquisitorial archives and knowledge of Cathar practice. They would have tried to make their falsifications plausible by matching the accounts as closely as possible to those in 'genuine' testimony. A reading of the register supports this claim: although those attending the *consolamenta* recorded in D26 were notable for their high social standing, descriptions of the events themselves are remarkably similar to testimony from other registers. Second, it should be emphasised that no part of this book relies wholly upon evidence from Galand's register.

As a whole, the Doat volumes are significantly longer and more detailed than all but the most prolix of those in MS 609. The most striking thing for the reader moving from that collection to the Doat material is the change in scope: the former reveals only snapshots of lives, whilst some depositions in the latter allow one to reconstruct day-to-day encounters over time. Even within those formulaic testimonies which repeat over and again the familiar tired series of meetings and rituals, there is material relevant to the life-cycle theme adopted here.

VIII. The register of Geoffroy d'Ablis

The deposition registers of Languedoc exhibit new richness in the work of the inquisitor of Carcassonne, Geoffroy d'Ablis.[94] Alongside his two lieutenants, Géraud of Blomac and Jean of Faugoux, d'Ablis conducted an inquiry in 1308–09 the records of which are contained in MS 4269 of the Bibliothèque nationale, and have been edited by Annette Pales-Gobilliard.[95] The manu-

earlier point were more favourable to at least some inmates, revealing that those with the means to do so could buy off the jailer, Raoul, in order to obtain considerable liberties – including dining with the latter and his wife. It can be found in Doat 32 fols. 125r–6r and has been published by Douais, ed., *Documents*, I, pp. clxxxix–cxc.

92 On the plot, see below, p. 137 n. 81.

93 Roche, *Une église cathare*, pp. 391–441.

94 Two sets of records from the intervening period have not been consulted here. See p. 11 n. 48 above.

95 The edition (with parallel translation into French) is *L'Inquisiteur Geoffroy d'Ablis et les Cathares du comté de Foix: (1308–1309)* (Paris, 1984), ed. and trans. A. Pales-Gobilliard;

script of d'Ablis's inquiries – held in Carcassonne – seems to have derived from an original containing at least 147 folios, but has itself been reduced in size by around one third, now comprising the testimony of seventeen witnesses, spread over fifty-five folios.

Less famous than his contemporaries Bernard Gui and Jacques Fournier, the Dominican Master of Theology Geoffroy d'Ablis was appointed inquisitor general of Carcassonne in 1303. D'Ablis came on the scene at a time of significant conflict between the local population and the inquisitors, in which he was to play an important role.[96] A portion of the inquiry records aspects of this conflict in the form of a plot to steal or destroy the inquisitors' records.

During the early stages of the inquiry, the lengthy depositions it gathered were heard not by the inquisitor himself, but by either or both of his two subordinates; d'Ablis only stepped in for second and/or subsequent hearings. The register shares with that of Fournier a high level of detail when compared to even the lengthiest of earlier deposition material, although d'Ablis's records are somewhat more formal and less flamboyant than those of the bishop of Pamiers. A unique and remarkable feature of this register, which should also be noted, is the appearance of two depositions submitted in writing by the deponents; these appear, apparently unaltered, in the first person singular.[97]

IX. The sentences of Bernard Gui

No original depositions remain from Bernard Gui, the contemporary and counterpart of Geoffroy d'Ablis at Toulouse.[98] Alongside the sizeable list of historical and other works that Gui composed, there is, however, a record of the penances and punishments handed down between 1308 and 1323 during his time as inquisitor of Toulouse.[99] Gui is, according to the modern editor

hereafter GA. For what follows, on d'Ablis and the text, see primarily Pales-Gobilliard's introduction (pp. 1–77), as well as Molinier, *Inquisition*, pp. 111–13, Douais, ed., *Documents*, I, 198–202, and Dossat, *Crises*, p. 47.

96 See Friedlander, *The Hammer of the Inquisitors* on this.

97 These are the depositions of Peter of Luzenac and Peter of Gaillac and are – according to the editor – 'sans aucun doute, les plus intéressantes du manuscrit': GA, p. 44. Their depositions are at ibid. pp. 332–61 (Gaillac) and pp. 368–93 (Luzenac).

98 First published by Philippe van Limborch in 1692, the Sentences were republished from the same (rediscovered) manuscript in 2002 by Annette Pales-Gobilliard: see Gui, *Sentences*. From the time of Limborch's edition until the 1970s, historians had thought all originals to be lost, but the manuscript had resided since 1756 in the British Museum. For its history, see M. A. E. Nickson, 'Locke and the Inquisition of Toulouse', *British Museum Quarterly* 36 (1971), 83–92, and Gui, *Sentences*, I, 14–24. The manuscript is now held in the British Library as Add. MS. 4697.

99 Gui was inquisitor from 1307–23; he became bishop of Tuy in December 1323, and died at the end of 1331. For a timeline of Gui's career see P. Armargier, 'Eléments pour un portrait de Bernard Gui', *Cahiers de Fanjeux* 16 (1981), pp. 34–7.

of his inquisitorial manual (the *Practica*), 'sans contredit le plus connu des inquisiteurs languedociens'.[100]

His sentences were given during 'sermons general': formal elements of the judicial process and public shows of inquisitorial strength generally held on Sundays at the cathedral church at Toulouse or the cemetery of St-Jean Martyr at Pamiers.[101] 938 sentences were handed down in the course of the twenty sermons recorded, to 636 men and women (the numerical discrepancy being caused by individuals who appeared more than once).[102] Of these, almost 500 were for crimes related to Catharism; the number of men and women affected was nearly equal.

The sermons were awe-inspiring public occasions –'public safety announcements' intended to educate as well as to punish.[103] After a series of oaths by the royal and consular officials, those who had impeded the inquisition were excommunicated. Next, men and women were released from prison or had their penance lightened in other ways. Then, those who had been convicted made a public abjuration. Finally, the convicted were called in order of the gravity of their penance: first the *crucesignati* – those given the 'lighter' punishment of wearing crosses; then those consigned to prison; those who had died in heresy; and finally the unrepentant. Before the sentences were given, the faults of each of the accused were read out in Occitan. Gui's register records the Latin originals on which these oral catalogues of guilt were based. Although these *culpae* always represent condensed forms of the original depositions, flashes of detail sometimes remain.

The sentences throw greater light than other collections on the process of inquisition itself. The manuscript of Gui's sentences was clearly intended to be an accessible document for the use of subsequent inquisitors: it is laid

100 Douais, ed., *Documents*, I, cciii. See also P. Biller, 'Umberto Eco et les interrogations de Bernard Gui', in *Inquisition et pouvoir*, ed. G. Audisio (Aix-en-Provence, 2004), pp. 257–68. Gui is generally seen as a rather sober inquisitor, concerned primarily with establishing the facts. Apparent evidence of a more credulous attitude to reports of scandalous night-time activity by Waldensians is discussed in P. Biller, 'Bernard Gui, Sex and Luciferanism', *Praedicatores inquisitores I: The Dominicans and the Mediaeval Inquisition. Acts of the 1st International Seminar on the Dominicans and the Inquisition*, Dissertationes Historicae 29 (Rome, 2004), 455–70.

101 On the form of the sermons see Gui, *Sentences*, pp. 25–8.

102 For statistics, see tables in Gui, *Sentences*, II, pp. 1645–707, and in J. Given, 'A Medieval Inquisitor at Work: Bernard Gui, 3 March 1308 to 19 June 1323', in *Portraits of Medieval and Renaissance Living: Essays in Memory of David Herlihy*, ed. S. K. Cohn and S. Epstein (Ann Arbor, 1996), pp. 207–32. Much of the latter is reproduced in chapter 3 of Given, *Inquisition and Medieval Society*, pp. 66–92. Figures are also given in H. C. Lea, *A History of the Inquisition of the Middle Ages*, 3 vols. (New York, 1887–88), I, 494–5. The figures given by these different authors differ slightly, but not to a significant degree.

103 L. J. Sackville, *Heresy and Heretics in the Thirteenth Century: The Textual Representations*, Heresy and Inquisition in the Middle Ages 1 (York, 2011), p. 133. On the records of (thirteenth-century) sermons in general, see pp. 133–4.

out methodically in chronological order, making use of running titles, and displaying some effort to situate its subjects within their network of family relationships.[104] It opens with an alphabetical list of place names, followed by the 'primary finding tool': an index of all people sentenced, arranged alphabetically by place, then in the order that names appeared in the register.[105] Both this index and the main text have been annotated with further information on those named and cross-reference to their appearance in other registers.

X. The register of Jacques Fournier

If Gui was the most famous inquisitor from Languedoc, the bishop-inquisitor Jacques Fournier of Pamiers created the most famous register. The records of depositions given before Fournier in the years 1318–25 survive in MS Lat. 4030 of the Vatican Library; this expensive copy was made at a later date by command of the former bishop, who had become pope.[106] When Pamiers had been created as a diocese in 1295, it was intended to be an inquisitorial seat like Toulouse and Carcassonne. However, the 'inquisition of Pamiers' ceased to exist when its first inquisitor, Arnold Déjean, stopped work around 1302.[107] According to Vidal, the tribunal which Fournier directed represents a successful application of the principles laid down in the Council of Vienne in 1312, which sought to avoid past problems between inquisitors and local populations by calling for 'mixed' tribunals, where responsibility was shared between Dominicans and others.[108] Fournier's inquisitorial zeal won papal praise, and he was selected as one of the judges in the trial of the celebrated Franciscan enemy-of-inquisition Bernard Délicieux, chosen – according to the

104 On this, see Given, *Inquisition and Medieval Society*, pp. 28–42.

105 Given, *Inquisition and Medieval Society*, p. 36. On the development of alphabetical indexes and other finding aids during the twelfth and thirteenth centuries, see R. H. Rouse and M. A. Rouse, '*Statim Invenire*: Schools, Preachers, and New Attitudes to the Page', in *Renaissance and Renewal in the Twelfth Century*, ed. R. L. Benson, G. Constable, and C. D. Lanham (Oxford, 1982), pp. 210–18. Note, though, that the authors are primarily concerned with academic and reference texts, not court records.

106 The most comprehensive study of this register is J. M. Vidal, *Le tribunal d'inquisition de Pamiers* (Toulouse, 1906), which collects the following three-part article: J. M. Vidal, 'Le tribunal d'inquisition de Pamiers: Notice sur le registre de l'évêque Jacques Fournier', *Annales de Saint-Louis-des Français* 8 (1903–04), 377–435, continued at vol. 9 (1904–05), 5–87, and vol. 10 (1905–06), 5–52. In his edition of the register, Jean Duvernoy suggests that its function was both as a personal reference, and for use in case of appeals to the papal see (occupied by Fournier from December 1334). See *Le registre d'inquisition de Jacques Fournier, 1318–1325*, ed. J. Duvernoy, 3 vols. (Toulouse, 1965), I, 15–16, hereafter JF.

107 On the history of inquisition in Pamiers, see: Vidal, *Tribunal*, pp. 59–75.

108 Technically, Fournier worked under the auspices of the inquisitor of Carcassonne, who was represented by his lieutenant Gaillard of Pomiés. In practice he seems to have been an independent operator. See ibid., pp. 1–6, 73.

latter's most recent biographer – for his 'moderation and tact'.[109] A former Master of Theology at Paris, Fournier was an extraordinary inquisitor with an eye for detail, as is evident from the length of the deposition he collected: 314 folios of this massive collection records the cases of just ninety-five people.[110]

The body of the inquiry deals with an interconnected group of people of mixed social status centred on two villages in the foothills of the Pyrenees.[111] Deponents appear to have been allowed to speak at length, points of doctrine and detail were followed up with careful questioning, and Fournier's scribes recorded a great deal of incidental material. Historians of inquisition have often seen this as the result of great skill, zeal or self-indulgent curiosity in the character of the bishop.[112] Yet, as John Arnold has argued, the difference between Fournier and his fourteenth-century colleagues has perhaps been exaggerated. Whilst Fournier's register is perceptibly richer and more 'colourful' than other contemporary collections, all are more detailed and 'personal' than those of their thirteenth-century predecessors.[113] It is impossible to know whether Fournier's court allowed deponents to speak at greater length than the others or whether it simply recorded more of what they said. The difference has two causes, one practical and the other ontological. First, Fournier simply had more time for each deponent than his predecessors; the 1245–46 inquest processed around 100 times the number of individuals in a much shorter time than Fournier. There was also a significant shift in the way that inquisitors saw deponents, from repositories of evidence about heretics, to confessing subjects in need of conversion.[114]

The depositions in the register have been published in full by Jean Duvernoy, first in Latin and subsequently in a partial translation which – somewhat misleadingly – rendered the depositions as first-person singular

109 Friedlander, *The Hammer of the Inquisitors*, p. 263.

110 Preceding this are four folios of copied letters containing papal bulls. The very first folio contains a list of depositions. See JF, I, 7–17. For a detailed index to the depositions, see Vidal, *Tribunal*, pp. 15–58.

111 See JF, I, 18–20. See also Vidal, *Tribunal*, esp. pp. 115–19 (an analysis of the Tribunal's activity) and pp. 141–203 (on the procedure followed).

112 Some examples of this sort of glowing appraisal: 'Inquisiteur incorruptible et compétent, Jacques Fournier est en effet avant tout consciencieux' (JF, I, 19); 'a bishop of the highest calibre, who had a taste for acquiring knowledge in minute detail ... a supreme, albeit idiosyncratic, inquisitor' (Lambert, *The Cathars*, p. 232); 'able in a few minutes to tell a heretic from a "proper" Catholic ... fanatical about detail ... the whole Pamiers Inquisition register bears the brand of his constant intervention. This is one of the reasons why it is such an extraordinary document' (Le Roy Ladurie, *Montaillou* (En), p. xiii). Le Roy Ladurie provides a particularly fine example of this position's circular logic. He surmises Fournier's character from the extraordinary register, and then explains the register's extraordinariness by that just-identified character.

113 On this, see Arnold, *Inquisition and Power*, pp. 164–5.

114 Ibid., in general, and especially pp. 74–110.

French. The latter work is useful primarily for its detailed notes which sometimes amplify those in the (earlier) Latin edition.[115]

Working with the products of persecution

As readers will realise, all the sources just described raise problems of interpretation. They offer a processed version of the records of private interviews conducted by (or under the auspices of) two inquisitors in the presence of ecclesiastical witnesses, and were written by a notary employed by the inquisition. This environment was unquestionably a hostile one. Whilst the production of knowledge about Languedocian heresy may have been among the inquisitors' main aims, their ultimate objective was that of active repression.[116] Indeed, their primary aim, as one inquisitor wrote in his early-fourteenth-century guide, was the destruction of heresy, to be achieved through the destruction of heretics and their supporters.[117] It is hardly surprising, then, that historians have had an uncomfortable relationship with the records.

These anxieties have stimulated a re-examination of the registers as historical sources. Caterina Bruschi has laid out the methodological problems posed by those depositions from Languedoc contained in the Doat collection, describing in detail the layers of 'filters' imposed by the process of questioning, narrating and recording on the dialogue between inquisitor and deponent, of which the historian must be aware.[118] A healthy scepticism has developed towards the stories recounted in inquisitorial registers. 'The inquisitors', wrote James Given, 'had perfected techniques by which the very fabric of reality itself could be altered.'[119] Taken to the extreme, such

115 *Le registre d'inquisition de Jacques Fournier, 1318–1325*, ed. and trans J. Duvernoy, 3 vols. (Paris, 1978), hereafter JFD. Duvernoy's edition of the Latin text in 1965 is notable for its many errors, as a collection of errata published in 1972 testifies: J. Duvernoy, *Le registre d'inquisition de Jacques Fournier, 1318–1325: corrections* (Toulouse, 1972). As Le Roy Ladurie noted, though, whilst the edition 'is not without its faults ... it has the great merit of existing': *Montaillou* (En), p. vii.

116 The most important recent study of inquisitors as agents of social control in Languedoc is Given, *Inquisition and Medieval Society*. For a generally more sympathetic account of how inquisition worked in the very different context of fifteenth-century England, see I. Forrest, *The Detection of Heresy in Late Medieval England* (Oxford, 2005). An interesting discussion on the separation (or rather the lack thereof) between inquisitors' persecutory and 'religious' functions can be found in C. C. Ames, 'Does Inquisition Belong to Religious History?', *American Historical Review* 110 (2005), 11–37. See also C. C. Ames, *Righteous Persecution: Inquisition, Dominicans, and Christianity in the Middle Ages* (Philadelphia, 2009).

117 Bernard Gui, *Practica inquisitionis heretice pravitatis*, ed. C. Douais (Paris, 1886), pp. 217–18.

118 See Bruschi, 'Precautions'.

119 Given, *Inquisition and Medieval Society*, p. 214.

scepticism has caused Mark Pegg not just to distrust the registers in specific instances, but to reject their claims at a much more fundamental level. In his *The Corruption of Angels*, Pegg argued that the inquisitors had recast unconnected encounters, fleeting village courtesies and temporary localised piety as patterns of adherence to an organised ecclesiastical hierarchy. Theirs was not the pedestrian business of documenting reality, he argued, but the rather grander project of 'taking apart ... a world and causing it to be remade'. Taking scepticism of the registers in a different direction, John Arnold has charted the development of inquisitorial attitudes towards those confessing and the effect this had on the sorts of evidence they produced. In the first part of his *Inquisition and Power* Arnold describes the changes in the discourse of the registers as the inquisitors moved from viewing the laity as an undifferentiated mass, out of which information about heretics was to be drawn, to cast them as individuals confessing personal guilt.[120]

All these studies make one thing very plain: the historian cannot – as Le Roy Ladurie did in *Montaillou* – treat deposition records as if they were direct and uncomplicated narrations of past reality. How, then, should one proceed in light of the methodological problems just described? One approach – that of Arnold in the second part of *Inquisition and Power* – is to put the dialogue of the depositions themselves in the foreground.[121] This approach is an extremely productive one, and confirms Bruschi's impression that the 'dialogical conflict' (her scare quotation marks) between inquisitor and deponent was more 'balanced' than is often supposed, even when the inquisitors were the ultimate victors.[122] Stimulating and useful though this way of dealing with deposition registers is, however, it is not – I believe – the only valid approach. I have proceeded instead from the position that, despite their flaws, the records compiled by inquisitors in Languedoc record a reality prior to their existence, a reality which their reader can reimagine.[123] My response to the debate above is to be frank about inquisitorial involvement in the material it uses, whilst parading its flaws for the reader as often as possible. I have striven not to adapt the depositions I quote, but rather to keep them in the third person, and to remind myself and my readers of the inquisitors'

120 Arnold, *Inquisition and Power*, pp. 1–110.

121 Ibid, pp. 111–229. Similar ground is also covered in idem, 'The Historian as Inquisitor: The Ethics of Interrogating Subaltern Voices', *Rethinking History* 2 (1998), 379–86.

122 Bruschi, 'Precautions', p. 110.

123 Cf. Arnold, *Inquisition and Power*, p. 110: 'it is a mistake to ignore the context of inquisition within which our evidence is produced, not because one must strip away the "veil" of inquisitorial language, but because one must recognise that we are caught in a false paradigm if we search for the subject prior to speech, for the deponent before he or she confesses'.

presence by including the more formal aspects of the registers.[124] It is also worth noting that much of the material of interest to the current study is found in 'surplus' features of the register: those incidental elements of testimony which had little bearing on the enquiry, but which somehow survived the processes of edition and abbreviation. Caterina Bruschi and others have argued that these elements are less problematic than those that bear directly upon the investigation, because no-one had any reason to manipulate them.[125]

The depositions that the inquisitors gathered reveal real historical phenomena: the expressions of religious sentiment that self-consciously fell outside the structures of the Church. Although they were partial and prejudiced, they sought to document this reality as accurately as possible. Whether or not one agrees with their conclusions is another question. But although the records they produced are problematic, it is my belief that these documents can still be used – with care – to reconstruct the past lives of the men and women who came to testify.

124 When quoting deponents' own reports of direct speech, however, I have sometimes translated more freely, especially when the phrase in question is an idiomatic one.

125 Bruschi, 'Precautions', p. 94. Also well worth reading on this is S. Justice, 'Inquisition, Speech and Writing: A Case from Late Medieval Norwich', in *Criticism and Dissent in the Middle Ages*, ed. R. Copeland (Cambridge, 1996), which offers a positive view (from a historian's perspective) of an inquisitorial scribe – a disinterested professional, reliable because he was non-partisan, and likely to record superfluous but now-interesting detail through curiosity and boredom.

1

Childhood

In 1234, the six-year-old Isarn of Villeneuve had his first encounter with the good men. He had gone with his mother to visit the house of his grandfather William, who was dying. Amongst the crowd of friends, family and neighbours who had gathered around the sickbed had been two men unfamiliar to the young boy. The strangers – whom Isarn would later identify as heretics – were performing a ritual blessing to purify William's spirit and guarantee it a place in paradise. Quite a crowd had gathered, though whether they had come to witness the rite or to pay their respects is not clear. In any case, all those present had 'adored' the two men, bending their knees before them and petitioning them to pray to God. In the account he later gave of that day, Isarn himself did not have much contact with the two – he could not in fact remember whether he had adored or not. Later that same year his contact with heretical preachers was briefly renewed: he was sent to them by his mother, bearing gifts of bread and wine. These two encounters, it seems, were the limit of his contact.[1]

Twelve years later, in March in 1246, Isarn was called to appear at Toulouse before the inquisitors Bernard of Caux and Jean of Saint-Pierre, and to recount his contact with the good men.[2] It was then that he described for his interrogators what they would probably have seen as tentative childhood steps into heresy. In these matters, as he told it, Isarn had been an obedient child. He had believed that the heretics were good men and that they could save souls, so he told the inquisitors, 'because his mother had taught and instructed him'. The scribe who copied Isarn's deposition even noted the strange qualification that 'from the age of discretion he did not believe heretics to be good men'.

Isarn's brief but evocative account forms an excellent starting-point for an exploration of the interactions between children and heretics. The two brief snapshots of his contact with the good men, the intertwining of family and faith, and Isarn's careful equivocations on the matter of belief and ritual

1 Isarn's deposition can be found in MS 609, fol. 168r.

2 It was not, in fact, the first time he had been called – he confessed to having given evidence to the inquisitor Ferrier some years before at Limous. The record of that earlier testimony appears not to have survived.

adherence all introduce themes that will re-emerge over and again in the pages that follow.

The theme of this chapter – childhood – has been explored extensively by medieval historians, many of whom were reacting to Philippe Ariès's supposed claim in 1960 that it did not exist in the Middle Ages.[3] In fact, whilst Ariès was undoubtedly incorrect in claiming that medieval people were 'indifferent' to children, or that they had 'no awareness of the particular nature of childhood', his exploration of childhood as an *historical* and *social* category has often been overlooked.[4] Far too many of his successors have treated childhood as an uncomplicated natural phenomenon, which it is not.[5] Historians of heresy, however, remained for a long time indifferent to these debates. When they considered it at all, they have viewed childhood as a straightforward period of religious acculturation. In this view, family connections provided one of the primary networks through which faith spread, and childhood was the period in which conversion was most readily achieved.[6] Around the beginning of the thirteenth century Languedoc was composed, we are told, of 'societies in which ... the young were unobtrusively initiated stage by stage into heretical beliefs and practices'.[7] Later, a 'tradition of cultural transmission' apparently operated, through which 'children took over their parents' ideology'.[8] Generally speaking, most modern historians seem more or less to follow Henry Charles Lea, who described 'the plastic period of childhood' during which future cult practice is set on a path from

3 P. Ariès, *L'enfant et la vie familiale sous l'ancien régime* (Paris, 1960). The work is best known in the English-speaking world as P. Ariès, *Centuries of Childhood*, trans. R. Baldick (London, 1962). The verdict of Adrian Wilson is that this English version of the text is 'not a scholarly translation': A. Wilson, 'The Infancy of the History of Childhood: An Appraisal of Philippe Ariès', *History and Theory* 19 (1980), 132–53 (p. 132 n. 5). For a survey of responses from historians, see L. Haas and J. Rosenthal, 'Historiographical Reflections and the Revolt of the Medievalists', in *Essays on Medieval Childhood: Responses to Recent Debates*, ed. J. Rosenthal (Donington, 2007), pp. 12–26.

4 For the quotations, see Ariès, *Centuries of Childhood*, pp. 38–9. James Schultz is of the opinion that Ariès's most important contribution was the historicising of childhood. See J. Schultz, *The Knowledge of Childhood in the German Middle Ages, 1100–1350* (Philadelphia, 1995), pp. 2–9.

5 Some examples from the 'affective' school of medieval childhood are: Shahar, *Childhood in the Middle Ages*; Jenny Swanson, 'Childhood and Childrearing in ad status Sermons by Later Thirteenth Century Friars', *Journal of Medieval History* 16 (1990), 309–31; Nicholas Orme, *Medieval Children* (New Haven, 2001).

6 See Arnold, *Inquisition and Power*, p. 149 for some examples.

7 Lambert, *The Cathars*, p. 74. See also Abels and Harrison, 'The Participation of Women in Languedocian Catharism', p. 246. Compare Bernard Hamilton's comment that 'membership of the Cathar Church was confined to adults': B. Hamilton, 'The Cathars and Christian Perfection', in *The Medieval Church: Universities, Heresy, and the Religious Life: Essays in Honour of Gordon Leff*, ed. P. Biller and B. Dobson, Studies in Church History, Subsidia 7 (Woodbridge, 1999), pp. 5–23 (p. 12).

8 Le Roy Ladurie, *Montaillou* (En), p. 231

which it will not later diverge.[9] The influence of family members upon an individual's religious adherence is certainly supported by deposition evidence.[10] However, the idea that this was a *childhood* process has not yet been proven. This chapter draws together a substantial body of deposition material about heresy and childhood, and so can address for the first time the place of children in the Cathar movement, and what heterodoxy actually meant to them.

The chapter has three principal sections. The first of these explores children's experience of religious practice in Languedoc, as well as their contact with heterodox ministers. This survey of childhood encounters considers all interactions, whether they were explicitly 'religious' or not. In its second main section, this chapter turns to examine a group that has not yet been comprehensively surveyed elsewhere: children who became members of the movement's ascetic elite. Concentrating on this phenomenon of heterodox child oblation might be seen as at odds with one of the broad aims of this book, namely the attempt to balance a historiography that is currently weighted towards the elite of heterodoxy by highlighting the under-appreciated role of ordinary followers and supporters. In fact, this is not the case. Most childhood entrants remained consoled only for a short period, before re-entering secular society, and 'childhood religion' had been part of the experience of the many lay members of the Cathar community. Its exploration is thus integral to any study of lived religion in that milieu. It also raises some important questions about childhood engagement with religion and the ways in which this was mediated by the community. These questions are dealt with at greater length in the third and final section, which draws from all of the preceding material and other deposition evidence to explore contemporary understandings of childhood and of the ways in which children could, and should, engage with religion. This treatment of 'knowledge' about childhood as a contingent historical phenomenon owes much to James Schultz, whose work on this area is deeply though provoking.[11] Interestingly, it will demon-

9 Childhood was, according to Lea, 'the time in which the future man or woman is to be moulded and trained into implicit obedience to ecclesiastical formulas and authority, and when the habits are to be formed which will render them docile and obedient subjects during life'. See H. C. Lea, *A History of Auricular Confession and Indulgences in the Latin Church*, 3 vols. (Philadelphia, 1896), I, 400.

10 See C. Taylor, *Heresy in Medieval France: Dualism in Aquitaine and the Agenais, 1000–1249* (Woodbridge, 2005), pp. 182–3. For discussion of the relationship between adherence, faith and 'family loyalty', see Arnold, *Inquisition and Power*, pp. 149–52. In contrast, Jacques Paul is of the opinion that the role of the family in this regard has often been overstated, and concludes that 'les réalités familiales proprement médiévales se combient avec le catharisme, d'une façon qui n'est peut-être pas complètement cohérente': 'Famille et hérésie', *Cahiers de Fanjeaux* 43 (2008), 349–72 (p. 371).

11 See Schultz, *The Knowledge of Childhood in the German Middle Ages*; and J. Schultz, 'No Girls, No Boys, No Families: On the Construction of Childhood in Texts of the German Middle Ages', *Journal of English and Germanic Philology* 94 (1995), 59–81.

strate that ordinary deponents' 'knowledge' about childhood and belief has a great deal in common with that of high churchmen and intellectuals.

Before plunging into this material, however, it is important to step back and examine the character of the deposition evidence about childhood. This material and its production were subject to additional constraints which affected most other testimony much less. What is more, those constraints themselves also bear upon some of the discussion about childhood as a culturally constructed phenomenon which develops throughout the chapter.

Material about childhood is not always easily found in the depositions, and evidence from third parties about encounters with children is particularly lacking. Occasionally the lists of names of people present at Cathar meetings include those who can be confidently identified as children.[12] Sometimes people remembered conversations about children too. However, these occurrences are rare – for the most part it seems either that deponents did not notice children, or that inquisitors were not interested in their behaviour. The reasons for these omissions will be discussed later.

What about more direct testimony: did children *themselves* give evidence to the inquisitors? The signs are not encouraging. Taking evidence from the young was not a usual part of medieval legal procedure. In the legal code of Toulouse published in 1286, courts were obliged to ensure that witnesses were over the age of legal puberty.[13] Girls testifying had to be older than twelve and boys fourteen; testimony was to be taken from their parents if doubts about a witness's age could not be satisfactorily resolved.[14] Canon law also regarded twelve and fourteen as turning-point ages. Gratian's *Decretum* specified that boys and girls below the ages of twelve and fourteen respectively could not swear oaths. Their evidence was thus inadmissible in legal cases, a bar that was extended up to the age of twenty in criminal trials.[15] However, the *Decretum* had also specifically named two crimes for which the usual legal incapacity of minors was to be waived: *lèse-majesté* and heresy.[16] Thus, whilst the first inquisitors' manual, prepared in the 1240s, enjoins inquisitors to summon men over fourteen and women over twelve, it also notes that 'if perchance they shall have been guilty of an offence', young people should also be summoned.[17]

12 See, for example for example 'filia quae parvula erat': D22, fol. 15r; MS 609, fol. 142r. These examples are discussed below.

13 The term 'legal puberty' is borrowed from R. Metz, 'L'Enfant dans le droit canonique médiévale: orientations de recherche', *Recueils de la Société Jean Bodin pour l'histoire comparative des institutions* 36 (1976), 9–97.

14 *Les coutumes de Toulouse (1286) et leur premier commentaire (1296)*, ed. H. Gilles (Toulouse, 1969), Article 31.

15 Metz, 'L'Enfant', pp. 74–80.

16 Ibid., pp. 74–80.

17 An English translation is Appendix 6 in W. L. Wakefield, *Heresy, Crusade and Inquisition in Southern France 1100–1250* (London, 1974), pp. 250–8.

In practice, it is impossible to ascertain exactly how many young people were interrogated, for the scribes did not habitually record the ages of those who gave testimony or received punishment. Age, we must therefore assume, was of little relevance to the tribunal. Yet, tellingly, those rare individuals whose ages *were* recorded were almost all young people.[18] It seems a reasonable conjecture that in such cases the scribe was noting an exception to normal procedure, in much the same way as they noted the few deponents who were lepers, but not those who were physically well.[19] In any event, it is plain from the personal histories recounted in the testimony of very many deponents that they were not below the age of majority, as the events they mention often date back many years.

There is some evidence that inquisitors had experience of dealing with the young. The early fourteenth-century inquisitors' manual, known as the *Practica* and written by Bernard Gui *c.* 1323–24, contains directions on the issuing of a lighter penance 'outside the [inquisitorial] sermon' to 'nine, ten, or eleven year-olds' in order to spare them from public shame.[20] The wording of the procedure implies that the lower limit for punishment (and, one might therefore assume, interrogation) was nine years old. Furthermore, even these rare young deponents were treated with leniency. Indeed, the register of sentences issued by Gui indicates that even adolescents in their late teenage years were considered to be unusually young subjects of inquisitorial justice.[21] Whilst not utterly conclusive, therefore, the evidence strongly suggests that children were not normally summoned.

The majority of surviving evidence about childhood engagement with Catharism comes neither from third parties nor directly from children themselves. Instead, it is found in the testimonies of adults reflecting back on childhood. Evidence of this kind is relatively easy to identify, in part because deponents were often eager that their young age be recorded when testifying about childhood transgressions. Some deponents gave exact ages at which certain events took place, yet too much trust should not be placed in these estimations. For the most part, though, people giving evidence did not attempt precision. The (vernacular) terms they used were translated into Latin by the inquisitors' scribes as 'puer' (boy) or 'puella' (girl), sometimes with the qualifying adjective 'parvus, parva' (small).[22]

18 For example, see the depositions of Arnald Olivarius, 'puer decem annorum', D22, fol. 238r; 'Joanna del Pas, fifteen years old', D23, fols. 273v–91v (on whom, see below pp. 48–51). A rare exception to this rule is the deposition of 'Pons Amiel, *senex*' (my emphasis), MS 609, fol. 198r.

19 E.g. the deposition of 'W[uillelmus]. Rigaut leprosus', MS 609, fols. 75v–6r

20 Gui, *Practica*, pp. 44–5. See below, pp. 87–9, for further discussion.

21 See below, p. 87.

22 On the vocabulary of childhood in Occitan, see L. M. Paterson, 'L'enfant dans la littérature occitane avant 1230', *Cahiers de civilisation médiévale, Xe–XIIe siècles* 32 (1989), 233–45 (pp. 237–8).

The meaning of such terms can be problematic. 'Infans' (infant) and 'iuvenis' (youth), for example, are used in the depositions both as terms to describe particular stages in the life cycle and as derogatory descriptors of older people.[23] Fortunately, this lack of clarity rarely causes serious problems. That deponents highlighted these encounters as specifically taking place during childhood, and that inquisitors thought this fact worth recording, is a significant matter to which we shall return at the end of this chapter. For the moment, though, we turn to the encounters themselves.

Children and the good men

For those who were children in the years before sustained persecution began in the 1230s, casual contact with the good men and good women was an unremarkable fact of life. Such contacts could take place independent of adult initiation or mediation. Many of the deponents who gave evidence relating to their childhood simply recalled having seen them living openly ('publice', publicly) amongst the other men and women in their town, village or castrum. Giving testimony in 1245, William of Lagrasse remembered the situation half a century earlier. 'He saw', reads his deposition, 'heretics at Montmaur and Mirepoix and at Laurac and in many other places in the land, residing as other men'. When they preached, he said, 'nearly all of the men of the land came together and came to hear their preaching' and to perform ritual adoration.[24] Peter of Puycalvel remembered in his deposition having seen 'William of Gourdon and many other male and female heretics publicly existing in their own houses' when he was a boy not yet five years old.[25] Since the good men still travelled around in plain sight, children naturally glimpsed them on their journeys; Raymond Adémar told the inquisitors that he had seen them in Roquemaur, Villemur, Rabastens and 'in all the land' as a boy.[26]

Like Peter and Raymond, most of those who gave testimony about having seen good men did not elaborate on these brief encounters. It seems that the

23 This was also a technique in Occitan-language literature, see ibid., p. 238. Even when they were used by deponents in a more technical way, the precise boundaries between the life stages such terms described is not always clear. See, for example, Raymond Hugh's description of 'quendam filium Pontii de Gomervilla, *multum iuvenem vel puerum*' (my emphasis), D25, fol. 107r; Raymond apparently saw Pons of Gomerville's son as straddling an age boundary, but where exactly that boundary lay he did not say.

24 'Item apud Montem Maurum et Mirapiscem et apud Lauracum et in multis aliis locis terre vidit hereticos publice stantes sicut ceteri homines, et predicantes, et fere omnes homines de terra conveniebant et veniebant audire predicationem eorum, et adorabant eos': MS 609, fol. 133v.

25 Ibid., fol. 175r (DT).

26 D22, fols. 70r–v.

good men were sufficiently integrated into society to have encountered children relatively often, but they were sufficiently impressive figures for those encounters to be memorable years later. In fact, the children who remembered the encounters knew who the good men were, sometimes by name. They must also have known something of what they were. Sometimes this knowledge was picked up through gossip, either amongst adults or children. Children like Raymond Jean assimilated some of the phraseology. Raymond confessed to having seen Raimonde Autier as a young boy, and remembered that at the time 'people said that she was a female heretic' ('dicebatur quod erat heretica').[27] Most children did not need telling that such people were unlike the other adults they encountered. Since the good men made their way of life a chief selling-point of the faith, their rejection of normality – including in the years before the war the adoption of distinctive clothing – was easily recognisable even by the young.

Sometimes the actions of the good men marked them out even more clearly to children. Indeed, some amongst them seem to have made a special effort to impress children they met.[28] Helis of Mazerolles confessed to the inquisitors that as a girl she had often enjoyed gifts of 'bread, wine, nuts and other fruits' from the good men.[29] This generosity stuck in the minds of other deponents too. William of Saint-Cogot had eaten the bread and nuts offered by good men whom he saw publicly as a child of only seven or eight. He remembered these trifles thirty-five years later; indeed, it is the sole incident recorded in his testimony.[30] Though they were memorable, the gifts to William, and to others like him, do not seem to have had a religious function: they were social, not sacramental. Given the context in which their memories were being recorded, this distinction would have been an important one for deponents. What these Cathar ministers were giving out was not symbolic food, as some of these deponents were keen to point out – it was just food.[31] Such good-neighbourliness was sometimes reciprocal. Young Bernard Gasc and his mother had lived next door to the good man William of Carlipa for a

27 MS 609, fol. 176r. It seems probable that this word 'heretica' really was the one that Raymond said he had heard, rather than being an imposition of the record. There were no doubt some circumstances in which the inquisitors would have wanted deponents to 'speak the words' and so internalise the definition 'heretic'. Here, however, if 'heretic' really was a substitution forced by the inquisitor or imposed by the scribe, the change would have completely altered the significance of what the unspecified 'they' had been saying about Raimonde (and also eradicated those speakers' crime in promoting heresy). Cf Arnold, *Inquisition and Power*, pp. 139–40.

28 Also noted in Pegg, *The Corruption of Angels*, p. 101.

29 D23, fol. 161r.

30 MS 609, fol. 181v.

31 William Julian noted that he 'ate of the *unblessed* bread of the heretics' ('pane ... *non benedicto*', my emphasis): MS 609, fol. 89r (DT). Pegg notes the case but does not mention this careful qualification: *The Corruption of Angels*, p. 101.

year in the latter half of the twelfth century, during which time they had often eaten in William's house and given him bread, wine and nuts.[32]

It seems that at a date around 1230, children encountered the good men in a variety of circumstances, many of them secular. Their depositions recount a level of casual, even friendly, contact which may at first seem surprising. It should not, for in the early thirteenth century, the good men led a movement that was both public and popular. They were often important figures in the community, who took part in commerce and were sometimes employers. They had a close relationship with their followers, and got along reasonably with the wider community. This easy-going relationship between secular community and religious leaders applied to children as well as adults.

During the opening decades of the thirteenth century, then, the good men were simply part of the background to everyday life. This comfortable state of affairs was disrupted for some after 1209 by the fear and the reality of war. Thereafter, deponents – especially those with military backgrounds – divided time into eras before and after 'the coming of the crusaders'.[33] Yet war did not signal immediate or universal change for good men and their secular supporters; it affected different places to different extents at different times.

The advent of the inquisitors in the 1230s marked more clearly the beginning of a new and enduring situation.[34] Once organised repression had begun in earnest, the public existence that had previously been reasonable became increasingly dangerous. In some places the inquisitors' summons triggered the withdrawal into hiding of prominent members or supporters of the sect. For others, the threat was less immediate. Yet everywhere there was a gradual increase in wariness. In all but the most isolated of communities, the social circle of the good men began to grow smaller, now including only a trusted few. The time when good men had lived publicly became a distant memory.[35]

32 MS 609, fol. 159r. This took place 'seventy years ago', according to his deposition – I have assumed from this, and from the event described, that he was a child at the time.

33 For example, Bertrand of Quiriès, knight, recounted a childhood encounter which took place 'ante primum adventum crucesignatorum'. See ibid., fol. 29v (DT).

34 Some deponents seem to have seen the 1229 Peace of Paris, which formally ended the Albigensian Crusade, as the turning-point; thus, after describing the good men whom he had seen living publicly, Peter of Puycalvel was careful to point out that 'all this was before the peace' ('hoc totum ante pacem'): MS 609, fol. 175r . Peter of Mazerolles, a secular lord, divided events almost into those 'citra pacem' and those 'tempore guerre' as often as he reckoned them in years: MS 609, fols. 124r–5v.

35 Giving evidence in October 1277, Raymond Arquier remembered that his aunt (with whom he lived), a consoled Cathar good woman and her companion were 'living in the town of Sorèze, and went about publicly in the streets, and to Church, and to the bakehouse, and they carried out their business publicly just like other women of Sorèze, with any of the people, and anyone with them'. This was, he reckoned 'sixty years ago, or thereabouts': D25, fols. 275v–6r. Raymond of Estanove told the inquisitors in 1274 that 'nunquam vidit hæreticos postquam publice morabantur': D25, fols. 151v–2r.

In parallel with this social shrinkage came a geographical widening of horizons. No longer safe in one place, and facing an ever-increasing crisis in staffing and recruitment, the Cathar Church turned peripatetic. Large gatherings became increasingly rare. Those few which did still take place were rarely held in public. Instead, they were private, secret and often nocturnal. The likelihood of contact between Cathar ministers and ordinary children – who were less mobile, less independent and probably less discreet than adults – was thus significantly reduced by this withdrawal from public life.

In records of later inquisitors (from the 1270s onwards), there are far fewer public childhood sightings. Older children, with more responsibility and independence, still had occasional chance contacts with good men and good women. Na Dyas,[36] a former good woman, recalled a hostile response from 'some infants who were looking after oxen' ('quidam infantes qui custodiebant boves') whom she and her companions had encountered whilst on the run from inquisitorial persecution.[37] Rather than showing the respect that Dyas and her companions had expected, these young cowherds had shooed them off with threats of denunciation.[38] The balance of power had shifted – no longer could locally powerful good men display their largesse in the distribution of sweet things to village children. The persecutory context also stripped some of these encounters of their religious significance. To some who now glimpsed the fugitive good men and good women, it was more striking, and perhaps more exciting, that these people were fugitives than that they were heretics. It is worth noting that the deponents who recounted encounters with the good men and women outside the home were usually men. This reflects the greater autonomy they enjoyed, as well as a more general trend in the deposition evidence of prioritising testimony by or about men.

In any case, all children's exposure to heresy was now increasingly governed by older relatives. A few children knew good men or good women directly through family ties. For some, good men and good women were also aunts, uncles and even parents. These were difficult relationships to manage, but whilst entry into the sect's ascetic elite made normal family life impossible, it did not usually lead to a complete severing of ties. Indeed, families often supported these entrants with gifts of food and money, and offered them shelter when it was needed.

36 *Na*, a contraction of the Occitan *domna* (lady), was originally an honorific for women of noble status. It was used indiscriminately for 'women of every social state' in charters dating from the period around the year 1200, according to John Mundy, see J. H. Mundy, *Studies in the Ecclesiastical and Social History of Toulouse in the Age of the Cathars* (Aldershot, 2006). Mark Pegg says, however, that 'only noblewomen' were called *Na* in MS 609: *The Corruption of Angels*, p. 96.

37 D23, fol. 57r.

38 It is thus possible that Na Dyas's was a pejorative use of 'infantes' to describe those who had humiliated her company.

In the main, families were more likely to remain in close contact with female converts to Cathar asceticism than they were with men. It is not always clear at whose behest this connection was maintained. Whether the women or their former families initiated the contact was probably irrelevant to the younger relatives who participated in these visits, though. Sometimes these heterodox aunts, mothers and grandmothers were encountered fleetingly and publicly. Bertrand of Montmaur saw his heretic aunt living publicly in his hometown. Like her co-religionists – but also like more conventional doting relatives – she had often handed out treats.[39] Others had a more sustained and overtly religious influence. Parents seem to have occasionally sent their children to stay with these pious relatives. Around 1209, the seven-year-old Maurina Bosc was sent to stay with her aunt Carcassona at the local 'house' of good women ('in domo hereticarum') for five months.[40] Likewise, Alazais of Toulouse stayed with her good-woman aunt for over a year as a child.[41] Although both were given some instruction in the faith by their aunts, there is little to suggest that this was the overt purpose of their visits.[42]

Children's experiences of Catharism within the family were not always positive. Sometimes one family member's religious fervour was a cause of tension with their relatives, because of either genuine religious disagreement, or the fear of capture. In 1229, for example, two daughters of the good woman Ayceline (along with two of their friends) attempted to convince her to leave the sect. The encounter was later narrated to the inquisitors by Ayceline's grandson, who was only ten years old at the time of the events he described.[43] Divisions like this were common. Whilst they must have put a strain on family life, their effects were not necessarily destructive, and many families divided in faith stayed united in other ways. For some, though, entry into the sect seems to have had a more disruptive effect on normal family life. This was the case for Alazais Augier who never saw her mother, who became a good woman when she was still 'in the cradle', and for Nomais Brun who last saw her good-woman mother as an eight-year-old in the late 1230s, before the woman was forced to flee.[44]

Personal knowledge of the sect and its members through family ties to good men and women – whether they were strong or severed – doubtless carried more emotional weight than the briefer public encounters described above. It also allowed some children a chance to gain an awareness of their relatives' faith. Such ties could serve to deepen the intensity of children's

39 MS 609, fol. 231v. Specifically, she had given him 'poma et nuces et alios fructus'.

40 Ibid., fols. 180v–1r.

41 Ibid., fol. 253v.

42 On this, see below, p. 53 n. 138.

43 MS 609, fol. 143v: deposition of Pons Faure.

44 MS 609, fol. 115v. Nomais's mother had taken flight after her companions were captured and burnt: ibid., fol. 180v.

experiences of the Cathar faith. This was particularly true as persecution drove Cathar ministers to become dependent on their secular supporters for food and shelter.

For host households of the fugitive good men and women their guests brought honour and peril in equal measures. Children in particular might be seen as a danger by increasingly anxious faith communities. Arnold Sicre and his young brother Peter were sent away by their mother as small children 'because', a member of her circle later told him, 'you were already talking, and we feared that you would reveal us'.[45] Yet whilst it could lead to such shunning, the other result of this atmosphere of increased secrecy was that the children of families deeply involved in the Cathar movement often had particularly close encounters with its leaders.

The story told by William of Baysses – a unusually vibrant narrative in Bernard Gui's *Sentences* – is evocative of this intimacy.[46] William first came into contact with the good men as an eight- or nine-year-old in 1303. The encounter began in the heart of the family home, where the Baysses family (William, his brother John and their parents) were warming in front of the hearth. William's father asked if he would like to see the 'good men'. 'Which men are those?' the child replied, not seeming to treat the question seriously enough, and receiving a slap from his mother. William, chastened, followed his brother and father to the upper floor of the house to meet the two strangers. When everyone was seated, the men welcomed him, saying, 'Don't be afraid, because we won't do you any harm!' Over the next few days, William had similarly prosaic encounters. They apparently comprised the sum of his contact with Catharism.

William's deposition, given eighteen years after the events described above, provides a vivid snapshot of his engagement with the good men and their faith. It is one whose character and boundaries are set by the fact that he was a child. His questioning of who it was he was about to see, which we might interpret as childish inquisitiveness, was demonstrably seen as inappropriate by his mother. Another evening when William had gone to the upper floor to see the two visitors, he was sent away to bed. Like those of their number who had dispensed treats to local children in earlier years, the two good men seem to have been more indulgent towards children than their parents were. In fact, they seem to have been trying to build a relationship. William remembered how another evening the men had come down into the main part of the house and, addressing him and his brother directly, said, 'children [maynada] we are good men. People call us heretics, but we are not.'

Perhaps because of the heightened danger and secrecy, this encounter seems to have imprinted itself deeply upon the mind of the young William,

45 JF, II, 28.

46 His deposition is found in Gui, *Sentences*, II, pp. 1456–8.

standing out more starkly than those of deponents from earlier years had for them. Then, good men had been an unremarkable part of everyday life, active and highly visible in towns and villages. In contrast, the men William had met were something new; they were unfamiliar and exotic. It was a new sense of glamour that allowed one young boy in the 1290s to imagine that the good men hiding in his father's attic were not ministers but forgers.[47]

Indeed, depositions from around this time show contact with the good men to have been embedded within the fabric of family life. Home life also shaped loyalties too, something which William of Baysses's deposition makes very clear. He was asked by his interrogators why he had not come to confess earlier, and the answer was filial obedience. When his father had first been summoned before the inquisitors, William told them, his parting words were 'My son, I don't know whether I'll see you again, but make sure that whilst your mother and I live you don't say anything about what you've seen concerning heresy.'[48] This plea was effective, and for eighteen years William kept those childhood meetings secret.[49]

Such encounters might be cited as evidence of cultural transmission of religion.[50] Yet William of Baysses's testimony implies that loyalty and conformity were the sentiments governing his silence, not religion. The appeal his father made was not to William's faith, but to family allegiance. Indeed, the father did not apparently ask his son to forswear confessing, only to withhold his confession until it would no longer endanger his parents. Although bonds of family and bonds of faith were closely entangled in the Baysses family, it is clear that ultimately the former were seen as more powerful.

So, children were aware of the good men's existence and had contacts with them throughout the period studied here, albeit in diminishing numbers and within a more tightly controlled context. Thus far, our gaze has been concentrated on the public sphere, and on encounters whose religious content was minimal. Discussion will shortly turn to the involvement of children in the ritual life of the Cathar movement. First, though, it will be useful to sketch orthodox attitudes towards children. Not only do these form the backcloth against which our understanding of Catharism must be set, but they also represent a sort of cultural baseline from which many unacknowledged assumptions were drawn by even the most ardently heterodox. Baptism is an obvious starting-point.

47 GA, p. 260.

48 William's father, mother and brother all gave depositions in 1310. See Gui, *Sentences*, I, pp. 572, 640. William perhaps escaped because he was still under fourteen when the summons was issued. William's father's injunction can be found in William's own deposition.

49 The father of eight-year-old Jacques Garsen extracted a similar promise from his son in the 1290s. William's father had sheltered members of the Autier circle. See GA, pp. 362–4.

50 See above, pp. 28–9.

Most people's first major contact with religion came in the baptismal rite, the formal marker of entry into the Christian community, and a necessary condition for salvation. As we shall shortly see, this was as much the case for heterodox families as it was for orthodox ones. Indeed, ensuring that one's offspring were baptised had been a fundamental parental obligation from the time of Augustine.[51] When exactly that obligation should be fulfilled was a more open question. The seasons of Pentecost and Easter alone had been reserved for baptism in the early Church. This custom had continued when infant baptism was introduced, but a number of concessions were made in the early Middle Ages to allow more rapid baptism in situations where this was expedient.[52] As baptism within days of birth gradually became the universal norm between the tenth and thirteenth centuries, the baptismal seasons fell into disuse. This process happened at different rates across Europe, but by the late thirteenth century the seasons were 'obsolete'.[53] It is difficult to know when things changed, but it is certain in any case that infants would have been baptised throughout the period examined in this book, whether immediately after birth or a few months later. Any Christian could perform the rite, for its power was drawn directly from the Trinity and did not need priestly mediation.[54] Baptised children were, like baptised adults, full members of the Church.[55]

Languedoc's ecclesiastical councils display some concern with baptism.[56] A particular concern was that sickly infants not die unbaptised. The council of Albi in 1230 exhorted parents to administer baptism *in extremis*, authorised them to pronounce it in the vernacular if they had no Latin, and instructed priests to remind them of the importance of confirmation.[57] Any abandoned

51 See Metz, 'L'Enfant', p. 59.

52 For example, baptism was allowed at any time for sickly infants, and in regions undergoing conversion. See P. Cramer, *Baptism and Change in the Early Middle Ages, c. 200–c. 1150* (Cambridge, 1993), pp. 137–40.

53 See J. D. C. Fisher, *Christian Initiation: Baptism in the Medieval West* (London, 1965), pp. 117 and 109–19 in general.

54 *Decrees of the Ecumenical Councils*, ed. and trans. N. Tanner, 2 vols. (London, 1990), I, 230–1.

55 Metz, 'L'Enfant', p. 59. See also Tanner and Watson, 'Least of the Laity', pp. 397–9.

56 Lateran IV had decreed in its sixth canon that diocesan synods should be held every year. See *Decrees*, ed. Tanner, I, 236–7. It was not custom, however, for every synod to publish statutes. On the form and function of local councils, see O. Pontal, *Les statuts synodaux* (Turnhout, 1975).

57 Albi 1230, [31, 30]: SS, 18. Some further evidence from east of the region: in 1260, the council of Arles instructed priests to explain to their parishioners 'qualiter & quibus verbis debeant uti dum parvulos in casu necessitatis baptizant'. Canon 3 of the same council, on confirmation, included a reference to 'parvulis'. See, on these, G. D. Mansi, ed., *Sacrorum conciliorum nova et amplissima collectio*, 53 vols. (1757–98), XXIII, col. 1004, hereafter Mansi. Bordeaux, to the west, exhorted that children 'qui etiam intelligere possunt' should go to be confirmed: Bordeaux 1234, [6]: SS, p. 48.

children were to be baptised when found, by laypeople if necessary.[58] The Church's determination that all infants be baptised no matter the circumstances required careful planning; when women died in childbirth, for example, their yet-unborn offspring were baptised by means of caesarian section.[59]

Most people would not have found themselves in such extreme situations. Deposition evidence provides an insight into the typical experience. Amblard Vassal of Arifat told the inquisitors that in around 1268, in his absence, his godmother had 'lifted a certain infant, the daughter of the same witness, from the holy font'.[60] In the early fourteenth century the Autiers told people that when one of them had 'carried a child to be baptised', the coldness of the water had proved fatal.[61]

Baptism was in fact a favourite target of the good men's preaching, and was therefore of keen interest to the inquisitors – so much so that a question on anti-baptism preaching was a standard part of the interrogation process. Some deponents went into some detail about the content of this preaching. In 1244, for example, Raymond Adémar testified that 'he had not … heard the errors [of the heretics], except that he had heard them saying that "when children die immediately after being baptized, they are lost"'.[62] Around sixty years later, baptism was of particular concern to Peter Autier, who sent it up to great effect. In the early 1300s, Peter Raymond Dominic of Born had been told by Autier that 'baptism of water made by the [Catholic] Church has no value for children, because they do not consent, but only wail'.[63] Around the same time, William Bélibaste used a similar *exemplum* in conversation with Arnold Sicre, saying that 'it displeases them [i.e. the infant recipients] when they are baptised, whence they even wail and cry when the priest splashes water on them'.[64] A version of this preaching remembered by Sybille Peter had even included elements from the baptismal rite itself: 'The child is asked,' Sybille remembered Autier telling her, '"do you want to be baptised" and the reply is made for him "I do" – but he does not want it and cries when he is baptised. He is also asked if he believes in this or that, and the reply is made for him "I believe". But he does not believe, because he does not have the use

58 Nîmes (etc.) 1252, [10–11]: SS, p. 276.

59 Nîmes (etc.) 1252 [19]: SS, p. 282; Albi 1230, [49]: SS, p. 26. See also Nîmes (etc.) 1252, [18]: SS, p. 280, which provided for baptism by a midwife during labour if the infant was thought to be in danger of death.

60 D25, fol. 188v.

61 The child's death in the story occurred 'when they wanted to return him to his mother.' See GA, p. 172.

62 'quando pueri moriebantur statim post baptismo perdebantur': D22, fol. 70v.

63 Gui, *Sentences*, II, p. 1476

64 JF, II, 52.

of reason.'[65] What is significant about this sort of detailed evangelistic satire is pre-existing knowledge it assumes about the event being mocked. In other words, the audience needed to be familiar with the baptismal rite in order to get the joke.

In fact, the good men's rejection of baptism was treated with severe scepticism amongst their followers, although some of the latter's beliefs about it were hardly orthodox. John Maury had heard the preaching, but himself believed that baptism made both adults and children Christians (which was orthodox), but that it did not remit the sins of infants because they did not have any (which was not).[66] John Roche believed that its effects were only provisional; its salvific power could be lost if the recipient later committed murder, for instance.[67] William Escaunier had been told that when a 'good chaplain' baptised a child, it would not be eaten by a wolf or drown.[68] During a conversation in a grain-store in around 1301, Jean Jaufre commended those who had children baptised, justifying his praise by citing (amongst other things) its cosmetic benefits.[69] Whether we see these beliefs as 'popular superstition', they are certainly evidence of strong lay support for the baptismal rite by the 1230s.[70]

Whilst all Christians were equal, after baptism children were still excluded from several sacraments. They could not be engaged for marriage until the age of seven, nor marry before twelve or fourteen. They were also excluded from the sacrament of penance and from the Eucharist. Confession became a yearly obligation for Christians of both sexes at the Fourth Lateran Council of 1215. The obligation applied, however, only to those 'above the age of discretion'.

This 'age of discretion' was interpreted by one influential commentator as seven, at which point children were able to make moral choices and could thus be held responsible for their actions.[71] Legislators in Languedoc, however, interpreted the term differently and thus took a more indulgent attitude which exempted most children from the need to confess.[72] The councils

65 Ibid., II, 410; the same story is recounted by Peter Maury, ibid., III, 228–9. For another comment on such preaching, see ibid., I, 282 n. 120.

66 JF, II, 48; II, 544 (no. XXXII). Note that the Latin noun 'puer' when used to signify 'child' does not specify sex. John Roche believed something similar: that unbaptised children of Christian parents would be saved 'propter etatem', even though they had done neither bad nor good: JF, II, 244–5.

67 Ibid.

68 Ibid., II, 16.

69 Ibid., II, 110.

70 The former assessment is that of the Fournier Register's editor, Jean Duvernoy: JF, II, 16 n. 205.

71 The commentator was Hostiensis, who reasoned that children were capable of sin (*doli capax*) at this age. Metz, 'L'Enfant', pp. 64–5.

72 On the variability of the term – which Hostiensis himself recognised – see ibid., p. 21.

of Narbonne in 1227 and Béziers in 1246 enjoined confession on those over fourteen.[73] The councils of Toulouse in 1229 and Albi in 1254 satisfied themselves with repeating formulation of the Lateran without further explanation, but it does not seem unreasonable to suppose that they would have followed the interpretation of their local colleagues.[74] Reception of the Eucharist was also linked to the 'age of discretion' – as mentioned in decrees of Toulouse 1229 and Albi 1254.[75]

Children did not take part in the sacraments, but their instruction was not entirely neglected by churchmen. For adults, the church building was one such site of instruction. The councils of Languedoc had long exhorted upper elements of society ('domini et dominae') to regular church attendance, but had displayed little interest in their children.[76] Around the middle of the thirteenth century, there were some efforts in this regard. Amongst the punitive heresy legislation of the 1246 council of Béziers one canon ordered the establishment of Sunday schools for those over the age of seven. The same canon exhorted priests to expound their sermons in simple language so that the congregation might understand more easily.[77] Similarly, the council at Albi in 1254 repeated a concern that 'very many have erred because of [their] ignorance of the articles of faith', and so ordered that children over seven years old should be led to church 'by their parents' to be taught these basic tenets.[78] The interest in education from legislators in Languedoc is perhaps best explained by their preoccupation with eradicating heresy; other regions did not concern themselves with the matter until much later.[79] The extent to which such injunctions were followed is difficult to ascertain, however, and deposition evidence reveals little about the matter.[80]

73 Narbonne 1227, [7]: Mansi, XXIII, col. 23; Béziers 1246, [46]: Mansi, XXIII, col. 704.

74 Toulouse 1229, [13]: Mansi, XXIII, col. 197; Albi 1254, [29]: Mansi, XXIII, col. 340.

75 This was drawn from Canon 21 of the Fourth Lateran Council; see *Decrees*, ed. Tanner, I, 245. On Eucharist, see Metz, 'L'Enfant', pp. 61–3.

76 On injunctions regarding adult attendance, see Toulouse 1219, [2]: Mansi, XXII, col. 1135; repeated at Toulouse 1229, [25]: Mansi, XXIII, col. 200.These canons are also concerned that the congregation remain for the entirety of the ceremony.

77 Béziers 1246, [7]: Mansi, XXIII, col. 693.

78 Albi 1254, [18]: Mansi, XXIII, col. 837. A similar statute was issued in Sisteron in 1249 [19], that children over seven were to be taught the Paternoster and the creed and to be led to church on Good Friday to kiss the cross and on Easter Sunday to receive the Eucharist: SS, p. 192.

79 In England, for example, the instruction of children was not required by bishops until the reformation: N. Orme, 'Children and the Church in Medieval England', *Journal of Ecclesiastical History* 45 (1994), 563–87, (pp. 565–6).

80 Deposition evidence does not shed the same light on this matter as it does on that of baptism. Some attempt was made, however, to ensure local enforcement of synodal statutes: parish priests were expected to copy them down into their own synodal books. This normative evidence reveals nothing of practical application of specific rules: Pontal, *Les statuts synodaux*, p. 68. It has also been suggested that older children formed part of the

The Church's attitude towards children was thus an ambivalent one. Once baptised, they were full members of the Christian community in a theological sense, but children could not participate in the annual rituals of confession and communion. There appears to have been an effort during the early thirteenth century to get children into church buildings, but such attempts are couched in language which suggests that this was an innovation only sparsely practised.

What of their status in the Cathar movement? We have already seen that the good men scorned baptism of infants because of their lack of understanding, but they did not entirely neglect the young. Good men and good women took the time to befriend children in their local communities. Before it became too dangerous, some children would have seen good men as they preached publicly in streets, fields and local cemeteries.[81] Others were taken along by adult relatives who attended the more select gatherings of those friendly to (or curious about) the good men.

The principal shared ritual of the Cathar community was a monthly ceremony referred to in Occitan as simply 'the service'.[82] Rainier Sacconi – Italian Cathar turned Dominican friar – records the details of the service, which he calls the *confessio venialium*: 'one says [the words] for all, speaking in a loud voice, with all bent to the ground in front of the prelate [who is] holding the Book in front of his chest'; the liturgy in question consisted of an interspersed series of confessions and requests for absolution.[83] Sacconi noted that the ritual was performed once a month when possible and that a 'deacon' officiated.[84] The service involved only consoled men and women of the elite; ordinary followers did not participate. They did, however, perform the customary genuflections when coming into the presence of the good men and perhaps throughout the service, and they sometimes received the kiss of peace at the end. Believers could thus benefit from the religious atmosphere, and from the preaching which sometimes accompanied it.[85]

inferred audience in some thirteenth-century sermon collections. Again, this is normative evidence with no direct link to Languedoc: Swanson, 'ad status sermons', *passim*.

81 Peter of Cabanil, for example, reported one such event in the cemetery of Saint-Julien in 1240: D24, fols. 28v–9r.

82 *Le Nouveau Testament: traduit au XIIIe siècle en langue provençale suivi d'un rituel cathare*, ed. L. Clédat, (Geneva, 1968), pp. ix–xi. For a formal description, see Duvernoy, *Religion des Cathares*, pp. 203–8, which also reproduces the relevant section of the Occitan Ritual, with translation.

83 For the text of Sacconi's polemical work, see F. Šanjek, 'Raynerius Sacconi O.P. Summa de Catharis', *Archivum Fratrum Praedicatorum* 44 (1974), 31–60 (p. 46). For the Provençal ritual, see *Rituel cathare*, ed. Clédat, pp. ix–xi.

84 'Item officium dycanorum est audire confessionem peccatorum venialium a subditis suis que fit semel in mense': Šanjek, 'Summa de Catharis', p. 48.

85 Mark Pegg has a different view: he presents the ritual as one where the believers themselves were far more active. It was 'a coming together; of *crezens* around some good men … [at which] the good men … remained determinedly passive, essentially motionless,

A question about presence at the monthly ritual was put by Bernard of Caux and Jean of Saint-Pierre during their enquiries in 1245–46, and found its way into the manual they wrote.[86] Deponents, however, often referred merely to 'preaching', and were unclear about whether that preaching was part of a service or not. In the years before effective organised repression, preaching often took place in private buildings. These meetings were sometimes very well attended, gathering in as many as forty or fifty people.[87] Whilst mentions of the ritual (referred to as the *apparelamentum*) are frequent in the early inquisitorial registers, their incidence decreases after 1275, and the ritual is not recorded in collections later than 1284.[88] As the danger increased the meetings became more select, moved into the homes of individual followers, and were attended by a smaller audience of trusted friends and potential converts.[89]

The format of the addresses given by good men varied. William Bernard recalled a small gathering sometime in 1225 at which two unnamed good men had been expounding passages read out by the local notary public, but things were rarely this formal.[90] After the preaching, the congregation

whilst the *crezens* in marked contrast, created a mood of feverish worship as they genuflected and bowed until a sustained sensation of holiness permeated the space in which everyone stood'. Pegg also argues that the genuflections required by this ritual were 'similar' to but 'distinct' from that of the *melioramentum*. This last point appears to be based on the deposition of William Garsias (MS 609, fol. 164r), which talks of a woman who fell during performing her 'venias et genuflexiones'. This seems slim evidence. Neither is it generally clear from the depositions whether the genuflections performed by believers happened before, during or after the ritual itself: the precise chronology of individual events being flattened, as a general rule: Pegg, *The Corruption of Angels*, pp. 98–100

86 The *Ordo* instructs inquisitors to ask a deponent about their participation in ritual life, including 'whether he was present at their *appareillamentis*': *Wakefield, Heresy, Crusade and Inquisition, p. 252.* One amongst many examples of the question being used is in Alazais den Poca's deposition, which records the following: 'Asked if she ever believed heretics to be good men, or adored, or gave or sent or received [anything from them] or accepted peace from the heretics or from their Book or was present at an *apparelamentum* or a *consolamentum* of the heretics, she said no': MS 609, fol. 95r (DT).

87 These gatherings were in 1193 (fifty people) and 1206 (forty); see the depositions of Raimonde of Saint Razano, D23, fol. 309r, and of William of Saint-Nazaire, MS 609, fol. 32r (DT). Further examples are given in Arnold, 'The Preaching of the Cathars,' p. 192 n. 37.

88 For Jean Duvernoy, this is explained by the absence of the Cathar hierarchy from Languedoc by this period; one might add that the evolution of the Cathar elite from static communities of moderate size to individual cells composed of two peripatetic good men would have rendered it very difficult – and dangerous – to organise, even if there had been a deacon to officiate: *Religion des Cathares*, p. 208. On the possible etymology of this term, see ibid., p. 207.

89 On the changing location of Cathar preaching, see Arnold, 'The Preaching of the Cathars', pp. 194–6.

90 MS 609, fols. 232v–3r.

filed out, bowing before the good men and asking for their prayers and petitions.[91]

These gatherings were, as we might expect, predominantly adult affairs, at which the presence of children was a noticeable rarity. John Vital, recounting a meeting twenty years earlier, remembered two little girls who had been present there, and noted that they had not performed the ritual *melioramentum* at the end of the ceremony like everyone else present.[92] Pons Aigra remembered that around 1236, when he had gone to a local vineyard to see the heretic Pons Faure, one of the women there had brought along her four-year-old granddaughter.[93] We do not know whether these children came because their parents saw their religious instruction as desirable; lack of alternative childcare is an equally plausible motive for their presence.

Sometimes the young were actively excluded. Raymond Aiffre recalled that once when he was young, in the time 'before the crusaders had come', he had been taken by his uncle to a place where the good men were preaching. Yet, once there, he was not allowed to go in to hear what they were saying because of his young age.[94] Bernarde Bederressa's 1246 testimony records that when good men were being entertained in her family home, her father had thrown her out 'because she was a girl, and young'.[95]

John Vital's testimony suggests that children were allowed access, but excluded from the *melioramentum*. In its full form, this ritual – referred to by inquisitors as *adoratio* – was a performance of three genuflections, made by believers upon meeting good men, and between good men themselves on certain occasions.[96] The supplicant knelt before the good man, with his or her hands on the ground, and bowed forward to kiss them, saying 'Benedicite, lord [or good Christian, or good lady], God's blessing and yours; pray to God for us.' On the third bow they would add 'Lord, pray to God for this sinner, that he will deliver him from an evil death and lead him to a good end', this last mention of 'a good end' perhaps being a reference to the *consolamentum*.[97] The good man would echo the supplicant's words on each repetition.

It is clear in the depositions, however, that the full *melioramentum* was not always performed. Practicality and the pressure of persecution meant

91 On early Cathar preaching, see Arnold, 'The Preaching of the Cathars', pp. 183–96. The remainder of the article deals with the content of sermons given by William Bélibaste in the 1300s.

92 D22, fol. 15r.

93 MS 609, fol. 142r.

94 'non intromittebat se quid dicebant quia parvulas erat': D23, fol. 80v.

95 No date was given for this incident. The wording hints that whilst Bernarde's youth was clearly a disqualifying factor in the eyes of her father, her sex might have been part of the problem too: MS 609, fol. 237r.

96 Duvernoy, *Religion des Cathares*, pp. 208–11.

97 Deposition references can be found in Duvernoy, *Religion des Cathares*, p. 208. The allusion to the *consolamentum* is suggested in Lambert, *The Cathars*, p. 142.

that good men were often greeted only with an inclination of the head. The significance of these greetings is disputed. Jean Duvernoy sees the same basic ritual underlying even the very short forms, whereas Mark Pegg has recently argued that the rite was merely 'pious cortesia': 'a style of highly contingent politeness' misinterpreted by the inquisitors.[98]

Participation in the *melioramentum* was one of the primary means by which inquisitors distinguished between those who they saw as 'believers' and those who merely lent support and aid. Whether or not this binary distinction was valid, inquisitorial attention ensured the survival of evidence about the rite.[99] Like the two little girls John Vital saw, children appear not to have participated in the rite. Bernard Mir, for example, attended a 1221 sermon in Saint-Martin and there – although he saw that the others knelt before the good men – he did not himself adore 'because he was a youth of fourteen'.[100] Likewise, Arnold Helias claimed not to have adored in around 1226 'because he was a boy', and other deponents recounted similar examples.[101] In 1240 Bernard of Villeneuve seems to have been of the impression that the young did not habitually adore: his deposition (given twenty-nine years later) reports a gathering in his parents' cellar and notes that everyone present adored, except for himself and his brother 'and Bernard Barra – of whom he doubted whether he adored, because he was young'.[102] Thirty years later, Peter Pictavin was of the same opinion.[103] These deponents might have been attempting to deceive the inquisitors by deploying a recognisable stereotype:

98 Duvernoy states that 'the *melioramentum* was not a trivial mark of respect': *Religion des Cathares*, p. 210. Compare with Pegg, *The Corruption of Angels*, pp. 92–103.

99 Pegg believes that the *melioramentum* was 'objectified' by the inquisitors into 'the classifiable form of *adoratio* so that it forced people to see their past and future nods as much more formulaic than they ever were'. See idem, *The Corruption of Angels*, p. 103 . Compare with the testimony of Peter of Cabanil (given in 1243) that in 1240 a group had forgone the *melioramentum* because they did not know they were amongst friends ('quia timebat sibi ad invicem quia non erant amici'): D24, fol. 28r. Joanna del Pas reported similar fears from *c.* 1243: D23, fol. 280r.

100 MS 609, fol. 187r–v.

101 D22, fol. 53r. Austorge of Rouzégas said that her daughter and another girl had been present when she performed the *melioramentum c.* 1237, but had not themselves adored. She later sent a gift of lettuces and a pike ('lactucas et quemdam lucium') with them to the heretics: D24, fol. 3r–v. Peter Ferroli of Trebons recounted a series of gatherings he had attended in the 1220s in Saint-Germain, but claimed not to have adored or seen others perform the ritual 'because he was very young': '... non adoravit eos nec vidit alios adorare – quando ipse testis erat multum iuvenis'. The incident is dated as 'tempore guerræ, ante prædictum tempus', where 'prædictum tempus' was fifty years ago: D26, fols. 64v–5r. Ten- or twelve-year-old William Raffard of Roquefort attended a *consolamentum* in the late 1220s, his deposition states, at which 'everyone but himself, who was a boy' adored: D26, fol. 37r.

102 The verb Bernard used – 'dubitare' – also carries the sense of 'to be unsure': D26, fol. 76r–v.

103 He reported a *consolamentum* of around forty-five years earlier, saying that all there

children did not participate in religious rituals. The benefits of such deception would have been at best marginal, however; many of the deponents had already confessed to having adored in other circumstances or would go on to do so.

Yet whilst some evidently thought that the *melioramentum* was not for children, other youngsters were actively encouraged to participate. Peter of Puycalvel told the inquisitors that he had been taught how to perform the rite by the local good men when he was not yet five, and 'did as they said'.[104] Gerald of Lautarz had adored 'two or three times' as an eight-year-old, according to Peter Sella's records.[105] Arnold Isarn, appearing before Bernard Gui in the early fourteenth century, claimed that as a child he had been taught to adore by his parents.[106] William of Baysses adored too, copying the actions of his father and brother, though, as he told the inquisitors, he did not really understand what he was doing.[107] Even Bernard Mir had apparently been made to 'bend the knee and say "bless"' before some heretics who gave him nuts in around 1215, when he was six years old. The problem of reconciling this evidence with Bernard's earlier testimony that when fourteen he had not adored 'because young' is something to which we shall return later (though it is perhaps worth noting that the scribe who wrote his deposition stops short of naming the earlier act as *adoratio*).[108] Some children were taught to adore as children by Cathar relatives.[109] The testimony of Peter of Auca goes even further in refuting the idea that children were excluded from the *melioramentum*. Peter had first encountered the good men at a sermon in 1215, when he was eight. Two years later, he said, he was in the presence of more good men, taken by his guardian Sicard. The ten-year-old Peter did not want to adore, he told the inquisitors, but Sicard instructed his charge to participate and gave him a sharp cuff to make sure he did.[110]

had adored except for a seven-year-old girl 'quae non erat aetatis [MS: alicuius] discretionis': D25, fol. 269v–70r.

104 MS 609, fol. 175r.

105 Duvernoy ed., *L'inquisition en Quercy*, p. 218 (D21, fol. 283v).

106 Gui, *Sentences*, I, pp. 216–18.

107 'Interrogatus de credencia hereticorum, respondit quod tunc ipse erat etatis octo vel novem annorum et nescebiat bene quid credere de eis, nec fidem habuit in secta ipsorum et illud quod fecit, fecit inductus per patrem et matrem.' Neither, he said, did he understand the words of the *melioramentum*: Gui, *Sentences*, II, p. 1458.

108 On other occasions the scribe did use the verb *adorare*. The text: 'cum ipse testis erat puer et hertici starent publice dicti heretici dabant ipsi testis nuces et faciebant ipsi testis flectere genua et dicere benedicite': MS 609, fol. 187v.

109 In *c.* 1210 *Domina* Geralda of Roqueville – then a 'puella parvula' – was taught to adore during an eight-day stay with her good-woman aunt: MS 609, fol. 66r (DT). Raymond Arquier's good-woman guardian had taught him how to adore around the same time: D25, fol. 276r.

110 D22, fol. 76r–v. Peter was apparently so upset by this incident that he left Sicard's care the next day 'et noluit postea cum eo manere'.

Many of the deponents who confessed to childhood participation in Cathar rituals were anxious to point out that they did so under instruction. Their depositions thus often explicitly state that they were following the example or command of adults. These adults played a crucial role in determining the opportunities and directing the behaviour of children who interacted with the good men. These decisions were not made in response to a clearly defined doctrinal framework, but on an apparently ad hoc basis. Some people expected that children would not take part in religious life until they had reached their majority. Yet others – including consoled Cathar religious – were keen to teach children their rituals. This realisation helps us to understand that the apparent contradiction between evidence of exclusion and that of participation is not in need of resolution. The deponents' accounts seem inconsistent for the simple reason that their experiences were inconsistent. Thus with Bernard Mir's childhood encounters. Whether we accept his division between 'bowing' and 'adoring' or see it as self-serving casuistry, it is entirely plausible that one group of adults might have expected him to perform ritual respect whilst in another context he was excluded.

The evidence surveyed suggests that the character of a child's experience of Catharism was influenced by a complex interplay of forces over which he or she had little control. Their own attitude and behaviour, family circumstance and the level of adult censure all played a part. Some good men and women were welcoming and friendly towards the young, whilst others were doubtless less interested; parents too could be either encouraging or censorious; some families had easy access to the good men, whilst others were more isolated. Children's experience of Catharism was thus mixed.[111] For some, it was more remarkable still. Let us now turn to a completely different sort of engagement with Catharism: childhood initiation as members of the ascetic elite.

Childhood religion

To begin, a story. Joanna del Pas became a good woman at the age of fourteen. She had first come into contact with the Cathar faith at the age of twelve when, following the death of her father, she went to live at Caragoudes with her aunt Joanna and uncle Arnold Bernard.[112] In 1241 or 1242 – she could not

111 Cf Taylor, *Heresy, Crusade and Inquisition in Medieval Quercy*, pp. 170–1. Taylor states that 'running errands' was the most usual context in which children encountered both Cathar and Waldensian heretics in Quercy, but notes that deponents may have been playing down the significance of their contact.

112 Joanna's deposition (given three years later) is at D23, fols. 273v–91v. It identifies her as

exactly remember – the good woman Bernarde of Bosc and her unnamed companion stayed in Arnold's house. Joanna, along with her aunt and uncle and their sons Arnold, Pons and William, performed the *melioramentum*. A few short years later, on 23 August 1244, Joanna gave evidence before the mendicant inquisitor brother Ferrier.[113] Unusually, and probably because she was a particularly young witness, Joanna's age was specifically stated.[114] Her deposition is thus a uniquely detailed first-hand account of life as a young good-woman-in-training, and a similarly unique account of the circumstances that led her to that position.

Back in the early 1240s Arnold Bernard's as-yet unremarkable niece had met other good women staying in her uncle's house. Two of these seem to have made a particular impression: the good woman Joanna and her companion, who had stayed there on and off for a year.[115] The family performed the ritual genuflections, the household and the good women sometimes ate together, and they were visited by various people who came to pay their respects to the guests.[116] Whilst they were there, the good women were also visited by the local Cathar deacon.[117]

After about a year – Joanna was not always precise about timing in her deposition – the two good women were led out of Arnold Bernard's house to a nearby wood, where they stayed with other good-woman companions.[118] One night, Joanna went to visit the good women; she stayed with them for a fortnight ('quindecim dies'), during which time they moved to stay on the land of Peter Faure of Caragoudes. At least some of the good women seem

'daughter of the late Isarn del Pas'. Isarn is not mentioned anywhere in the deposition itself, and I have thus assumed that his death predates the period covered. Caragoudes is some nineteen miles east of Toulouse.

113 The seventeenth-century scribe (or scribes) who copied Joanna's deposition into the Doat collection was particularly clumsy, and his work is liberally sprinkled with crossings-out, corrections, and half-finished sentences. There may also be some small omissions in the copy, perhaps where a line was missed in the copying.

114 Its opening words: 'Anno Domini millesimo ducentesimo quadragesimo quarto decimo kalendas septembris Johanna *quindecim annorum* filia quondam isarni del pas de bantieiras conversa de haeresi Diocesis Tholosanæ requisite de veritate dicenda' (my emphasis): D23, fol. 274r.

115 D23, fol. 276v: 'et steterunt dictae haereticae in dicta domo per uices per unum annum'. That three of its inhabitants shared the same name must occasionally have made things confusing in the household during their stays.

116 D23, fols. 274r–6v.

117 Ibid., fols. 276v–7r.

118 The dating by Joanna in her deposition is problematic for a number of reasons. The greatest level of precision she uses is the half-year, which – since all events she describes took place within a three-year time-span – makes determining chronological order very difficult. If followed rigidly, this dating sometimes orders events in a way that seems logically unlikely. Aside from some events dated quite precisely ('a year ago on the Pentecost past'), it thus seems reasonable to conclude that her dating was not meant to be anything more than the most vague of indicators.

to have worked for their bed and board, and young Joanna assisted them one day in mowing and harvesting corn.[119] A rare incidental detail for this time is provided later in Joanna's deposition: the young girl had made frequent visits with the good woman Guillemette Salamona to a supporter at Falgairac in order that his wife might apply a remedy to Guillemette's 'scabby' head.[120]

Around this time, Joanna made other visits to good women and good men who were also engaged in the harvest, and stayed with them for some days.[121] Once, she and her friend Bonasias took the makings of a fruit salad to the good woman Joanna and her companion, who were staying 'in a certain hut'.[122] Joanna was becoming a familiar face, but she was not yet trusted by everyone: two followers were unwilling to perform the *melioramentum* in front of her.[123] These visits had made a great impression on the girl, so much so that she soon told her aunt and uncle that 'she very much wanted to leave [them] and to go along with the heretics'.[124]

Her guardians consented – or at least conceded – and Joanna's aunt accompanied her niece (and her young fellow-traveller Bonasias) on the first part of their journey to the good women. After a night in the house of a Cathar supporter at Falgairac, Joanna was led early the next morning by two good men to a certain building in the field of another follower near *lengine vila*, where she stayed with five good women for around a month.[125] There seems to have been little hurry to receive the young neophytes, who stayed with a variety of good women over this time. In fact, Joanna waited the better part of four months for the *consolamentum* which would mark her entry into the ranks of the ascetic and sanctified good women.

119 D23, fol. 279r: 'et ibi per totam diem metebant siue colligebant spicas'.

120 Ibid., fol. 286r: 'et tunc Bernarda uxor Bernardi dayros aptabat caput suum praedictae Guillelmae salamone quae erat scabiosa': 'and then Bernarde wife of Bernard Dayros put a dressing on her, the aforesaid Guillemette Salmona's, head, which was scabby'. Joanna reckoned this encounter to have taken place 'two years ago and more', 'whilst she was staying in the said house with the other [female] heretic'. This comes after discussion of Joanna's time as a consoled good woman, and 'the said house' may have been one of the places she stayed during that time. The date given would, however, place the encounter *before* her reception. Joanna's (sometimes-unreliable) dating is perhaps supported in this instance by the description of the *melioramentum* that followed, as it implies that only Guillemette was the ritual's object, with Joanna an onlooker.

121 'et ibi inuenit dictos haereticos metentes': ibid., fols. 279v–80v.

122 They took, according to her deposition, 'Pira [pears] nespolas [medlars] et quasdam debanadiras [unidentified peeled fruit?]': ibid., fols. 277r–v.

123 'interrogatus dixit quod praedictus Arnaldus de Moirauila nec Bernardus frater eius non adorauit dictos haereticos quia Volebant [probably mistake for: nolebant] ipsos adorare quia ipsa testis videret': ibid., fol. 280r.

124 Ibid., fol. 280v: 'modis omnibus recedere uolebat et tenero [sic; mistake for tenere] uiam suam cum haereticis'.

125 Her deposition refers to a *batut*, which I have translated as 'building'.

After a fortnight's stay with Bonascas and her companion, Joanna was given the *consolamentum* by Raymond Fors, the Cathar deacon who had visited the good women in her uncle's house.[126] Little seems to have changed for Joanna after her reception. She still travelled around, staying with various good women in huts and cabins. She and her companions were escorted from place to place not by lay guides, but by pairs of good men. The young Joanna was now herself being 'adored' and served by faithful supporters. Her experience of life as a good woman was brief, however. After only three months, around the time of Pentecost, Joanna was captured along with her companions at the time, and taken to Toulouse to await the inquisitorial tribunal.[127] Before she could be interviewed, however, Joanna escaped.[128] The enthusiastic convert was re-consoled into the Cathar Church.[129] Her new-found freedom lasted only a brief four months, after which she was recaptured and led back to Toulouse.[130] Joanna's deposition thus ends where it began, with her appearance before the tribunal of inquisitor Ferrier.

Joanna's deposition is extraordinarily detailed, but the story it recounts is not unique. In fact, the appeal of heresy to young girls and their parents had been of concern to the Church for many years, and some attempts had been made to combat it. In 1207 Diego, bishop of Osma, and his companion Dominic had founded an abbey at Prouille, near Fanjeaux, in order to address the local problem.[131] According to Jordan of Saxony, Prouille was conceived as a place of reconciliation and re-education: its founder members were 'certain noble women, whose parents had been forced by poverty to entrust them to the heretics to be educated and brought up'.[132] Indeed, the abbey's founding

126 D23, fols. 283r–4r.

127 Ibid., fol. 285v.

128 Ibid., fol. 287v. When she was being held captive in the house of Sicard Alaman at Toulouse, Joanna was advised by one of her fellow-prisoners, a good man, to make her escape. Although this seems to have been easily effected, the two men with whom Joanna fled were quickly recaptured outside Toulouse. Joanna herself evaded recapture and retreated to her uncle's house, where she stayed for six weeks.

129 Ibid., fols. 288v–9r. Joanna was re-consoled in a woodland cabin (attended, despite the danger, by 'many male heretics and female heretics') following a three-day fast where no food or drink passed her lips. After her re-initiation, Joanna was told to fast for forty days ('per unam carantenam', fol. 289r). No mention of any such ritual cleansing is made for Joanna's first reception; it was perhaps necessary because of the close contact with members of the opposite sex which her capture must have entailed.

130 Ibid., fol. 289v: this was just six weeks after her second *consolamentum*.

131 On the foundation of Prouille see M.-H. Vicaire, 'L'action de saint Dominique sur la vie régulière des femmes en Languedoc', *Cahiers de Fanjeux* 23 (1988), 217–40 (especially pp. 217–22) See also the introduction to *Cartulaire de Notre-Dame de Prouille: précédé d'une étude sur l'albigéisme languedocien aux XIIe & XIIIe siècles*, ed. J. Guiraud (Paris, 1907).

132 Vicaire, 'L'action de saint Dominique,' p. 7. Bernard Gui quotes Jordan, but adds nothing beyond a brief (polemical) comment on the deficiencies of Cathar education programmes: *De fundatione*, pp. 7–8.

charters were addressed to the 'prioress and nuns, newly converted by the teaching and example of brother Dominic of Osma and his associates'.[133] Had she been born forty years earlier, Joanna del Pas might have been recruited as one of those first sisters.[134]

Jordan of Saxony's description of children who were 'handed over' is reminiscent of child oblation to mainstream religious houses. Orthodox contemporaries – and many later historians – have seized upon this similarity. Those who entered the order as children have been seen as little nuns, and those houses in which they stayed as the Cathar equivalent of nunneries, particularly in the years before the effects of persecution had really taken hold.[135] According to a common interpretation of a passage in Peter of Les Vaux-de-Cernay's contemporary chronicle (written in 1212–18), Count Raimond-Roger of Foix had established a sort of Cathar monastery for his wife and sisters at Pamiers before the crusade.[136]

In their seminal article on women in Languedocian Catharism, however, Abels and Harrison questioned this desire to equate the *domus* of the depositions with Catholic religious houses. 'It would seem', they suggested, 'that the orthodox parallel to these modest establishments should be sought not in the larger monasteries for women or men but instead in the contemporary reclusania [sic] and Humiliati and the later Beguines' – that is, in small,

133 See the grant by the archbishop of Narbonne in Bernard Gui, *De fundatione*, pp. 8–9.

134 Claire Taylor argues that the generally accepted account of female religiosity in the south – that they had no 'outlet in the monastic life' until the thirteenth century – is flawed, at least for Quercy. Families seem in fact to have made significant donations to religious houses in the region with a view to their daughters taking the veil. See Taylor, *Heresy, Crusade and Inquisition in Medieval Quercy*, p. 83.

135 An approach exemplified in G. Koch, *Frauenfrage und Ketzertum im Mittelalter* (Berlin, 1962). On the historiography, see Abels and Harrison, 'The Participation of Women in Languedocian Catharism', pp. 228–30.

136 Peter's actual words are more ambiguous: 'In castro preterea Apamiarum, quod erat proprium abbatis et canonicorum Beati Antonini, tenebat uxorem suam et duas sorores hereticas cum aliorum hereticorum multitudine copiosa … ipsis etiam sororibus suis et uxori in proprio allodio canonicorum hedificari domum fecerat dictus comes.' Whilst the count built 'a house' for his wife and sisters, whether or not it was conceived of as a *religious* house is less clear. See *Petri Vallium Sarnaii monachi hystoria albigensis*, ed. P. Guébin and E. Lyon, 3 vols. (Paris, 1926, 1930, 1939), I, 199–200. For an English translation, see *Peter of les Vaux-de-Cernay: The History of the Albigensian Crusade*, ed. and trans., W. A. Sibly and M. D. Sibly, (Woodbridge, 1998). On further links between the count and unorthodox belief, see pp. 27–8 n. 74 in the latter, and É. Griffe, *Le Languedoc cathare de 1190 à 1210* (Paris, 1971). Raimond Roger himself was linked to a Cathar-sympathising group in a deposition given in 1242, which is at D24, fols. 88v–109v. On the basis that there is no convincing contemporary evidence that the count was personally associated with heresy, Elaine Graham-Leigh argues that this deposition cannot be trusted. See E. Graham-Leigh, *The Southern French Nobility and the Albigensian Crusade* (Woodbridge, 2005), pp. 62–4.

often private houses with little formal organisational structure.[137] Mark Pegg followed a similar line when he argued that living with the good women was connected as much to a social rite of passage as to a religious vocation.[138] These arguments are untested: the further work called for by Abels and Harrison has not as yet been carried out.[139] Deposition evidence can shed some light on the experience of boys and girls who joined the sect as children, though.

Almost all of the evidence on young good men and good women – which for the most part comprises later recollections by them – is to be found in MS 609; the remainder is located in depositions from volumes 21–24 of the Doat register. Reports of childhood entry are thus confined to material gathered by inquisitors working in the 1240s. There is almost no evidence of child-consolation in the later enquiries copied by Doat's scribes, and nothing at all from the records of Gui and Fournier. This pattern suggests that the child-good-woman (or man) was a phenomenon that passed away with the appearance of the inquisitors. Even within the sixty-year coverage of the 1245–46 investigation, the evidence is strongly concentrated in the early years. The origins of the deponents were varied, the largest groups clustering around Le Mas-Saintes-Puelles (six deponents) and Fanjeaux (seven deponents).

A case study: Le Mas-Saintes-Puelles

The deposition record from Le Mas comprises the largest group of deponents from any one place in the register, and the material has been analysed in an article by Walter Wakefield.[140] 420 men and women from the village came to confess in Toulouse. Wakefield identified seventy-nine 'committed [Cathar] believers' amongst these individuals; he also found evidence in the depositions of a further thirty of their co-religionists who did not themselves give evidence. Of those identified as good men or good women by deponents from Le Mas, thirty-two had been residents of the town.[141]

Six women from Le Mas testified that they had been 'hereticated' (the inquisitors' term for reception of the *consolamentum*) when very young.[142] A further deponent had been told by her mother 'that she, when she was very little, often ate with the heretics and was with them for a long time', which

137 Abels and Harrison, 'The Participation of Women in Languedocian Catharism', p. 231.

138 Pegg argues that '… in many ways an infant's entering a house of *bonas femnas* was no different from the little migrations to live with an older woman … that all Lauragais girls seem to have undertaken in the years before their majority at twelve'. Pegg, *The Corruption of Angels*, p. 119.

139 Abels and Harrison, 'The Participation of Women in Languedocian Catharism', 230.

140 Wakefield, 'Heretics and Inquisitors: The Case of Le Mas-Saintes-Puelles'.

141 Ibid., pp. 210, 213–14.

142 These women were pointed out by Wakefield, ibid., p. 214.

Table 1.1. Child initiates from Le Mas-Saintes-Puelles

Name	Fol.	Status	Age	Date	Time as good man or good woman
Raimonde Germa	20r	W	'60 years ago'	1185	3 years
Ermengaud Aychard	20r, 22v	M	'50 years ago'	1195	6 weeks
Raimonde Gasc	22v	M	'50 years ago'	1195	2 years
Na Comdors Herma	20v	W	< 10	1199	9 months
Na Segura Vital	20r	M	10	1205	5 years
Ermengaud Boer	20v, 22r	M	'40 years ago'	1205	–
Pons Faure	29r–v, 42r	–	6	1240	n/a
Mother of Petron de N'Alixen	20v	M(?)	'very small [*parvulaI*]'	–	'a long while'

Key to status (given at time of deposition) – M: married; W: widow(er).
All references to Toulouse MS 609.

suggests that she too had received the *consolamentum*.[143] Only one boy can be identified: the good men attempted to recruit six-year-old Pons Faure. This attempt was aborted, however, by the child's objecting mother who dragged him away by the hair.[144]

All six of the women gave their testimony on either the nineteenth or twentieth of May 1245. They had been received in either the last decades of the twelfth century or the first of the thirteenth, and must therefore have formed a relatively high proportion of the twenty good men and good women residing in Le Mas before 1210.[145] Of the six women, five were linked.[146] Only Na Segura and Na Comdors estimated their ages for the inquisitors; Segura reckoned she had been 'a girl of around ten' when she lived as a good woman, and Comdors 'not yet ten' when she was received. The others can be assumed to have been young at reception due to the long periods of time (forty to sixty years) that had since passed.[147]

Little is revealed about the receptions of these women. Ermengaud Boer and Raimonde Gasc told the inquisitors that they had been inducted by the good man Isarn of Castres. Directly following the details of her own recep-

143 Petrona ux. P. de N'Alixen, MS 609, fol. 20v.

144 See testimony from him, his brother Bernard and mother *Na* Mateus: ibid., fols. 42r (DT) and 29r–v (DT).

145 Wakefield, 'Heretics and Inquisitors: The Case of Le Mas-Saintes-Puelles', p. 214.

146 The odd-one-out is *Na* Comdors, MS 609., fol. 20v. The five who can be more easily connected are Raimonde Germa (20r); Na Segura (20r–v); Ermengaud Boer (20v); Raimonde Gasc (22v); and Ermengaud Aychard (22v).

147 See table 1.1, above.

tion, Gasc identified in her deposition four other deponents from Le Mas as having been members of the ascetic Cathar elite. These testified that they likewise had been young entrants. Gasc's testimony raises some tantalising questions – had these girls entered the sect at the same time? Had they known each other whilst they were still members? Had they lived together, along with their older guardians? These possibilities are all intriguing, but unfortunately the brevity of the testimony leaves the questions unanswerable.

As they were all either young or very young, the girls from Le Mas are unlikely to have decided to become good women on their own. Na Comdors – who cannot be readily connected to the other women from Le Mas either before or after her reception – told the inquisitors a little more about the circumstances of her entry into the sect. Her mother had 'violently' ('violenter') made her become a heretic, she said.

All six women had eventually left the ranks of the good men and good women and returned to normal life. This figure is high: in total, only eight of the thirty-two known good men and good women from Le Mas had apostatised.[148] Periods spent as good men or good women varied greatly, from six weeks to five years. The women eventually abandoned the ascetic life. Raimonde Gasc told the inquisitors that she 'freely converted to the Catholic faith' after her time with the Cathars. She had been reconciled to the Church by no less than Dominic Guzman himself; Raimonde Germa and Na Segura confessed the same. Five of the women had been given the penance of wearing crosses sewn into the back and front of their garments – in most cases by Bishop Fulk of Toulouse. The social stigma attached to this seemingly light punishment could be severe, and it could have serious effects on both marriage prospects and employability.[149] Without exception their crosses soon disappeared from sight, either because the bearers hid them under other clothing when in public or because they destroyed them completely.

All six women married after abandoning the ascetic life. Some of their husbands had themselves been in contact with the good men.[150] Despite their conversions, most of the women remained active within the Cathar community. Ermengaud Boer and Na Segura entertained good men or good women in their houses. Ermengaud sheltered the good woman Rixende and her associate for about a year. Na Segura had sent bread and wine to the good men, and Raimonde Gasc– along with Ermengaud herself – 'adored' them around three times a week. Na Segura herself had the good man Bertrand Martin

148 Wakefield, 'Heretics and Inquisitors: The Case of Le Mas-Saintes-Puelles', p. 214. Whether or not this statistic includes these women is unclear.

149 On this matter, which was the subject of some inquisitorial hand-wringing, see below, pp. 85–9.

150 These were *Na* Segura, *Na* Comdors and Ermengaud Boer. The husband of the last of these, Peter Boer, is identified as visiting a good man in the deposition of *Na* Richa ('Narricha uxor den Azalbert'). See MS 609, fol. 21r.

and his associate in her house, where he was visited by Raimonde Gasc, along with members of Le Mas's ruling family. For these women, at least, the dichotomy between marriage and childhood Cathar asceticism was not a clear one – whilst their roles may have changed, they were still heavily involved in the movement.

Girls

Sixteen other women deponents can be identified as youthful Cathar initiates. A number of other women confessed that they had *lived* with good men or good women but had not been received into the sect.[151] Raimonde Jocglar (again, not counted as one of the sixteen) had followed groups of Cathars around in the 1240s, but was not consoled. Raimonde told the inquisitors that 'the said heretics did not want to receive her until she was well instructed in the customs and morals [*mores*] of the heretics and had first undertaken three forty-day fasts [lit: three Lents]'.[152] It is clear that these rigorous conditions were not always applied when the *consolamentum* was offered to young people.

Of the consoled, most were received in the years around 1200. Entry seems often to have been more a matter of compulsion than vocation. When she was ten or twelve, Coviens Mairanel was 'given to the heretics' by arrangement of her brother who was a believer.[153] She was not cut out for the religious life: after two years, she told the inquisitors, she recognised that she wanted to leave, take a husband 'and stay in the Catholic faith as a good Christian'. Arnalde of Frémiac was similarly 'compelled' in her youth, this time by her uncle; she held the course for longer, but left after only six years.[154] Alazais of Massabrac entered under highly charged circumstances – her mother had left her husband to join the heretics, and had crept back 'stealthily' one night to remove Alazais from the former family home.[155]

151 For example: Gauzia of *Na* Maria's deposition records that in *c.* 1205, when she was ten, 'she stayed with [the heretics] for half a year, but was not hereticated': MS 609, fol. 21r. 'Domina' Geralda, when a little girl, had stayed with her good-woman aunt for eight days *c.* 1210: ibid., fol. 66r.

152 Ibid., fol. 41r (DT): 'noluerunt ... hereticare donec bene esset instructa secundum mores hereticarum et fecisset primo tres quadragesimas'. See also Pegg, *The Corruption of Angels*, pp. 102–3 and index entry 'Raimonde Jocglar'. As Pegg notes, that she was not admitted into the sect did not deter those who captured Raimonde and her companions from attempting to burn her as a heretic. Her life was only spared by a last-minute conversion to orthodoxy 'from fear of the fire'.

153 MS 609, fol. 161v. Pegg notes this case in idem, *The Corruption of Angels*, p. 118.

154 MS 609, fol. 160v: '... avunculus i<psius> t<estis> compulit ipsam intrare sectam hereticorum'. Much of Arnalde's evidence concerns Fanjeaux, suggesting that this was where she lived.

155 For her deposition, see D23, fols. 203r–7v.

Table 1.2. Other child initiates: girls

Name	Fol.	status	Age	Date	Place	Time as good woman
Na Garsen Richolosa	189v	–	50 years ago	1196	Bram	2 years
Saura Bonet	143v	M	7	1197	Villeneuve	3 years
Gauzia of Na Maria	21r	M	10	1205	Saint-Felix	3 years
Audiardis Ebrarda	184r	–	(U)	1206	Villeneuve	1 year
Bernarde Vesiana	143v, 184v	M	8	1206	Villeneuve	1 year
Gairaude Vital	253r–v	M	parvula	1207	Lasbourdes	3 years
Guillemette den Ber.	114v	M	12	1207	Lasbourdes	3 years
Alazais of Massabrac	D24 fols. 309v–end	W	(U)	1208	Avellantelo	3½ years
Bernarde Gran	D22 fols. 1r–3r	M	(U)	1213	Villemur	3½ years
Coviens ux. B Mairanel	161v	M	10 or 12	1215	Fanjeaux	2 years
Bernarde Camelas	173v	M	puella parvula	1220	Montréal	2 years
Na Ava 'ux quon P Roca'	156v–157r	W	in iuventate sua	<1225	Fanjeaux(?)	2 years
Ermengaude	198v	–	(U)	1228	Fonterz	3 years
Raimonde Jocglar	40v–41r	U	(U)	1242	Laurac	6 months
Rixende ux. Andree	195v	M	–	–	Fanjeaux(?)	1 year
Arnalde of Frémiac	160v	W	dum erat iuvenis	–	Fanjeaux(?)	6 years

Key to status (given at time of deposition) – M: married; W: widow(er) U: unmarried.
All references to Toulouse MS 609.

None of the women revealed very much to the inquisitors about the pattern of their lives whilst consoled. Most, it seems, had lived not in a large community but with just two other good women. Some travelled often, though their depositions do not reveal why. Audiardis Ebrarda told the inquisitors that she had spent her year as a good woman 'praying, fasting, adoring heretics, listening to their preaching, and doing the other things that heretics do'.[156] Alazais of Massabrac gave a similar list of activities, adding the details that each day she ate bread blessed by the good men with them at their table,

[156] MS 609, fol. 184r.

repeating their ritual prayers each time, and that she performed the *melioramentum* daily.[157]

'After the aforesaid three and a half years were over', records Alazais's deposition, 'she left the heretics' sect and took Alzieu of Massabrac as a husband'. This 'desertion' to marry is echoed in the depositions of Guillemette den Ber and Audiardis Ebrarda.[158] Arnalde of Frémiac was given a penance by St Dominic himself; she was sentenced to wear crosses 'until she took a husband,' but in the end married after only a year.[159] In fact, almost all the women had married after they left the sect. Many had confessed to either Dominic or Bishop Fulk of Toulouse in the early years of the thirteenth century. Like the women from Le Mas, those who had to wear crosses had all prematurely abandoned this shameful penance.[160]

Some, like Coviens Mairanel, apparently broke off all contact with the Cathars after abandoning the religious life. Others kept their old faith whilst living more conventional lives. Na Ava – a good woman for two years in her youth – married after leaving the sect, but maintained her contact with the good men, and played host to them on various occasions. Her husband was to receive the *consolamentum* in his final hours, though he apparently died before the rite could be performed. Her son also guided the good men, and had been a believer for a while.[161]

Boys

The reception of children by the good men has often been considered to be an exclusively feminine phenomenon. Boys, however, make up roughly one third of the deponents who confessed to having been good men in their childhood. Whilst their numbers are small, it should be remembered the absolute number of women identified is similarly modest. Furthermore, it is unlikely that the inquisitors uncovered all the relevant cases, so both the men and the women identified here form part of a larger total. It should also be noted that

157 D24, fol. 205r.

158 MS 609, fols. 114v, 184r.

159 Ibid., fol. 160v. Jean Guiraud interpreted this condition as requiring Arnalde to prove by her marriage 'la sincérité et la solidité de sa conversion' before her punishment was lifted. See J. Guiraud, *Questions d'histoire et d'archéologie chrétienne* (Paris, 1906), p. 78. Guiraud's view that Catharism was inimical to both the family and society may have coloured his interpretation. In light of Bernard Gui's observation that the stigma of crosses could have a chilling effect on matrimonial prospects (on which, see p. 00 below), it seems equally plausible that this apparent requirement on Arnalde was in fact a *concession*, in order to improve her chances of marrying at all.

160 These were Audiardis Ebrada, Bernarde Vesiana and Gauzia of na Maria. See Table 1.2 above, p. 57, for manuscript references (all in MS 609).

161 MS 609, fol. 156v.

Table 1.3. Other child initiates: boys

Name	Fol.	Status	Age	Date	Place	Time as good man
William of Lagrasse	133v	–	'brought up by his father with the heretics'	1195	Lavaur	5 years
P[eter] Jocglar and his brother	120r	–	'raised by his father to become heretics'	1199	Labécède	6+ years
Raymond of l'Eglise	55v	–	10	1205	Montlaur	10 years
Stephen Scholar	70r	–	cum esset puer	1205	various	1y 2m
Pons Marcelli	189r	–	dum erat puer	1206	Fanjeaux(?)	2 years
William Aimeric	225r	–	10	1206	Montmaur	1 year
R[aymond] Richaut	118v	–	'30 years ago'	1215	Labécède	2 years
Matfred of Paulhac, Knight	D22 fols. 58r–62r	–	14	1221	Verfeil	4 years
Arnold Gerald	177r, 180r	M	11	–	Verdun	–

Key to status (given at time of deposition) – M: married; W: widow(er).
All references to Toulouse MS 609.

– as with their female counterparts – some boys had lived with the good men without apparently themselves receiving the *consolamentum*.

The earliest cases of boyhood reception date from the 1190s; they are Peter Jocglar and William of Lagrasse.[162] Both had fathers who were good men, who 'brought [them] up with the heretics' and had them 'hereticated'.[163] Peter's deposition named five good men and six good women who lived as good men and good women at Labécède, eight of them 'for as much time as he (the witness) and more'. Whether these were children too is unknown. One of those gave his own brief testimony.[164] Peter also said that he had heard that Ermengaud Bauga 'was with the heretics and had their clothes, but was not otherwise a heretic'. After around five or six years, both boys had left the sect. Both, too, had subsequently married. Indeed, Peter met his wife whilst a good man, for she too had been a 'vested' ascetic at the time. After meeting,

162 Peter: ibid., fol. 120r. William: ibid., fol. 133v.

163 The verb used in both cases is 'nutrire'.

164 Ibid., fol. 118v. Raymond Richaut said he had been 'hereticated' by them and had stayed for two years, mentioning no contact after. His estimate was that this was thirty years before his deposition, i.e. in 1215; that this dating does not match Peter's is less problematic than it might seem – all dates given in depositions are at best very rough estimates.

they remained in the sect for three years, although Peter's deposition disappointingly reveals no details of their courtship during this period.

At the arrangement of his brother, Raymond of l'Eglise was received during an illness when he was ten. He was carried to the good men by William Taylor and an associate around 1205, and after his recovery stayed there as a good-man-ascetic for ten years.[165] Stephen Scholar apparently travelled around with the good men for just over a year, after which time he 'freely' left them. Later than many of the other deponents, around the early to mid-1220s, Matfred of Paulhac was received at Verfeil 'in good health' but '[whilst he was] only a youth of fourteen'.[166] He told the inquisitors that the good men wanted him to study a course of *grammar*, and that they believed that he would be a great pillar of the Cathar Church. Their hopes proved vain, however, and after only four years he left the sect; he is identified as a knight in his deposition.

Arnold Gerald told the inquisitors that as an eleven-year-old, in 1205, he had stayed with two good men at Verdun who had taught him to sew. His wife, who gave testimony almost a year before him, however, had heard a different story.[167] Her testimony records that 'she had heard from her neighbours that her husband was a clothed heretic before he took her as his wife, but she did not know, nor had she ever heard it said by her husband that he had been a heretic'. In the highly sensitive religious climate of Languedoc, it does not seem probable that the neighbours had simply misunderstood things. Whilst they may have been engaging in malicious gossip, it is equally possible that both they and Arnold were telling the truth. His time as a 'clothed heretic' (i.e. a good man) may in fact have coincided with a sort of informal apprenticeship; this was a time when the good men lived publicly and engaged in commerce. Arnold was thus perhaps hoping that a half-truth would help cover up his heterodox past. Others told similar stories to the inquisitors. Peter Amiel had gone to stay with the good men at Laurac for two months in 1220 'but he was not a clothed heretic, and did not fast or pray or make those abstinences which they make'.[168] A few years earlier, in 1206, the ten-year-old William Aimeric had stayed 'as a messenger' with two good men at Montmaur, often adoring them and eating their blessed bread.[169] His brother and sister had also been heretics at this time, he later said. Other boys told similar stories during the 1245–46 enquiries. All said that they were secular employees or apprentices of Cathar ascetics in their

165 Ibid., fol. 55v.

166 D22, fols. 58r–v.

167 His deposition is at MS 609, fol. 180r, hers ('Ramunda uxor Arnaldi Gairaudi') at fol. 177r.

168 MS 609, fol. 13r. Peter does not give his age, but afterwards returned to his father's house, which suggests that he was at least unmarried, and probably also young.

169 Ibid., fol. 225r.

youth, but either specifically mentioned or implied by omission that they had not themselves lived a religious life.[170] Their claims are plausible, although – as we have seen – this distinction was not always perceived by their peers.[171]

The reception of children: a paradox?

The young entrants discussed above were of various ages when they received the *consolamentum*. The youngest were six or seven years old, the oldest near to or past their majority at fourteen. Reports of early reception in other depositions were less precise, placing the event 'in her youth', 'when he was a boy', 'when she was very small'. Some did not give their age at all – these have been included either because of circumstantial evidence or because the time which had elapsed since their reception was such that they seemed to fit the expected pattern. Whilst young female initiates outnumbered young male ones, young boys *were* consoled, perhaps in greater numbers than has sometimes been supposed. There is reason to believe that the practice may also have been current in thirteenth-century Italy.[172] It is important to remember, though, that the consolation of children was *not* a common feature of Occitan society. Even in Le Mas, where their numbers seem to have been relatively high, fewer than one in fifty of those interviewed confessed to childhood membership.

There is little evidence about the day-to-day lives of girls and boys who joined the ranks of the good women and good men. Even the longer depositions – like that of Joanna del Pas – tell us little about the communities in which young initiates stayed beyond the names of those who came to visit and sometimes those who lived there. The cause of frustration here will be a familiar problem for anyone who has worked with deposition records: our interests do not match those of their creators. Simply put, inquisitors were more concerned with mapping the Cathar social network – listing supporters and placing people at events – than with building up a picture of their day-

170 A possible exception is Pons Marcelli, who stayed for two years 'as a boy' with the good man William of Pexiora and his companion. Although Pons did not state that he became a good man, he did perform the *melioramentum* 'more times than he can recall'. The fact that, after leaving William, Pons had 'stayed with Saint Dominic for twelve years', suggests that his time with the good men had been more religious than secular. See ibid., fol. 189r.

171 For more on older apprentices to the good men, see pp. 00 below.

172 Rainier Sacconi – a former Cathar – compares two Cathar ascetics who must live according to the restrictions of their faith 'as if they were precepts of God'. The first is a sinful *senex*, the second 'a boy [*puer*] of ten years who never committed a single mortal sin before he became a Cathar'. See Šanjek, 'Summa de Catharis', p. 47.

to-day lives.[173] The terse lists of activities, which included praying, fasting, adoring and listening to sermons, are as detailed as the depositions get.

The groups in which the young initiates lived are somewhat easier to reconstruct. There may have been a community which drew in young girls at Le Mas before 1209, as five of the girls received there seem to have been connected. Yet this was an exception. Most of the young good men and good women had stayed in small single-sex groups. Many simply stayed with a pair of good men or good women: these appear something like a cross between foster children and religious apprentices, not as members of official communities. It may well have been that the five girls from Le Mas were distributed amongst pairs of good women after their *consolamenta*. Finally, it should be noted that whilst the establishment of Prouille suggests that the Church was seeking to combat like with like – Cathar 'nunneries' with a new Catholic foundation – neither official records nor monastic chroniclers ever made the parallel. It may well be, in fact, that the new foundation was simply addressing the absence of religious institutions for women in early thirteenth century Languedoc.[174]

Whatever the purpose of Prouille had been, the phenomenon of Cathar child oblation did begin to die off. If one were to plot the childhood receptions presented here by date, the graph's line would peak in the period before 1209, before falling away dramatically to maintain a very low level from the early 1220s; it would rally a little at its tail-end in the early 1240s, before quickly dwindling away completely. Neither the pre-crusade peak nor the subsequent drop-off is particularly surprising. Persecution evidently affected children's involvement in Catharism more heavily than that of adults. In times of active pursuit, slow-moving and vulnerable children would have become a dangerous burden for good men; if caught, they could well have been an easier source of information for the inquisitors than older witnesses. The risk for parents was double if their children were captured: not only would they suffer the loss of a child, but they might also be irrefutably linked to heresy.

The explanation for the revival in the 1240s can perhaps be found by examining the progress of persecution. Faced with increasing hostility and official intransigence in Toulouse, inquisition had been suspended in 1238. Although the official period of suspension was only three months, it was in reality three years before the tribunal resumed its activity.[175] The years of suspension and inactivity must have been something of a relief for the Cathars, which might have signalled the beginning of a return to the *status quo*, if not quite before

173 The 'social network' metaphor is borrowed from P. Ormerod and A. Roach, 'The Medieval Inquisition: Scale-Free Networks and the Suppression of Heresy', *Physica A* 339 (2004), 645–52.

174 L. M. Paterson, *The World of the Troubadours: Medieval Occitan Society, c. 1100–c. 1300* (Cambridge, 1993), p. 241.

175 Dossat, *Crises*, p. 143.

the war then at least before the inquisitors had begun their work. The resumption of the inquisitors' work in 1241 would not immediately have crushed this revival. It took the massacre of an inquisitorial party at Avignonet in May 1242 to trigger the rallying of the forces of persecution.[176] Even by 1243, conditions under which captured heretics were held at Toulouse were so lax that Joanna del Pas was able to escape with very little effort. Yet for reasons already discussed, the inquisitors' work must have had a chilling effect on participation of children in Catharism. It is not unreasonable to suppose that by the late 1240s their efforts had reduced that child participation almost to nothing.

What of the motivations of these young initiates and of those who offered them to be consoled? It is difficult to judge the accuracy of Jordan of Saxony's assertion that young female recruits to Catharism joined largely because of their parents' poverty. In some cases it is clear that the decision was one made by parents or other relatives alone, and in one case physical coercion seems to have been used. Yet this was not always true, as the case of Joanna del Pas has shown. Whilst her uncle may have welcomed the removal of a financial burden, there is no suggestion here either that poverty was a motivating factor or even that the decision was his to make. Joanna was a willing convert, and the key actor in her entry into the sect. No comparable evidence about motivations exists for the other young converts, though it is not hard to imagine that – for some at least – joining the ranks of those so obviously respected and revered by their families cannot have been entirely unattractive. Regarding the question of poverty, it should be noted that – according to evidence presented here – any parent who bet the value of a dowry on their prepubescent daughter remaining with the Cathars was liable to be disappointed.

It is not always clear why young girls or boys joined the Cathar elite. Many of those who joined when they were very young must have done so as a result of parental arrangement. Similarly, the young boys who were raised as heretics by their fathers cannot have had much say in the matter. The entry of some children was perhaps a matter of practicality, a concession by the good men to parents who would not otherwise themselves have been able to enter the sect.[177] Children taken into Cathar communities in this way were perhaps never really expected to become life-long good men or good women. Some, however, seem to have been specifically targeted as potential recruits. Good men actively attempted to recruit Pons Faure, in whom they

176 Ibid., pp. 145–51. On the 'turmoil and tension' of the period, see also Wakefield, 'Heretics and Inquisitors: The Case of Auriac and Cambiac'.

177 Frances Andrews has suggested something similar in Humiliati communities of the thirteenth century. See F. Andrews, 'A Safe-Haven for Children? The Early Humiliati and Provision for Children', in *Youth in the Middle Ages*, ed. P. J. P. Goldberg and F. Riddy (York, 2004), pp. 73–84.

found a willing convert, and they were enthusiastic in their encouragement of Matfred of Paulhac. This appears to have been unusual, however: the enthusiasm displayed by these two, and by Joanna del Pas, was not reflected in the testimony of other deponents, where the decision seems to have rested with adult relatives.

Knowledge about childhood, religion and belief

Having surveyed childhood experience within and without the Cathar sect, we now turn to the question of childhood belief. Here, it seems, adult influence was just as important as it was in regulating access to the good men or encouraging a vocation. A few of those who had childhood contacts with the good men gave direct evidence about their beliefs at that time. Isarn of Villeneuve Junior had been introduced to the good men around the age of six.[178] He ran errands to them on behalf of his mother, and had attended his uncle's deathbed *consolamentum*. When in 1246 the inquisitors asked the then-adolescent Isarn about his beliefs he confirmed that 'he had believed that they were good men and true and friends of God, and that they had a good faith, and that it was possible to be saved by them'. This much was standard inquisitorial formula, but Isarn went beyond mere confirmation; his deposition records that he had believed not out of love, logic or spiritual revelation, but rather through obedience. He had believed, he said, 'because his mother taught him to and told him to'.[179] 'I was a child,' we can almost hear Isarn saying, 'What else did you expect me to do?' In fact, Isarn was careful to point out that 'from the age of discretion' he had not believed the heretics to be good men.[180] The best part of a century later, the eleven-year-old Rixende *de More* confessed to having believed in the good men 'on account of the things which her mother had said about them'.[181] William of Baysses made a similar excuse: whatever he had done, he told the inquisitors, had followed the lead of his father and mother. On matters of doctrine, he pleaded ignorance. He was eight or nine at the time, and 'he did not well know what to believe of them [i.e. the heretics]', although he was certain that he had no faith in their sect.[182]

178 For what follows, see Isarn's testimony at MS 609, fol. 168r.

179 'quia mater ipsius dicebat et instruebat ipsum testis': ibid., fol. 168r.

180 'ab annis discretionis citra': ibid., fol. 168r.

181 Gui, *Sentences*, I, p. 886.

182 Gui, *Sentences*, II, 1456–8. Raymond Issaurat was another deponent who blamed his belief on childish obedience, saying that he held the faith 'quia parentes sui et dicti heretici dabant sibi intelligere et dicebant quod ita debebat credere et ita credidit'. See GA, p. 282.

According to these deponents, children could not be held responsible for their beliefs. Indeed, much testimony went even further. In answer to inquisitors' questions about the inception and duration of their belief, many said that they had believed *ab anno discretionis*, from the age of discretion.[183] In two depositions from the early 1230s, this crucial stage was 'after [the deponent] could distinguish between good and evil'.[184] As we shall see shortly, this referred to the ages of twelve and fourteen. The 'age of discretion' appears a number of times, but by no means frequently enough to suggest that deponents were simply echoing a standard inquisitorial question. Indeed, it was unusual for deponents to give an age rather than a date when asked about the beginnings of their belief.[185] Indeed, childhood and belief seem to have been mutually exclusive categories for most deponents. These men and women seem to have seen belief as a matter of discernment, and discernment a product of age.

Where did these ideas come from? We have already encountered the good men preaching scornfully against infant baptism. It is true that the teaching against baptism drew particular attention to children's inability to choose. Peter Autier's dictum that children carried to the font 'do not consent, but only wail' was a clever piece of sloganeering, which obviously stuck in the minds of those who heard it. The children (*pueri*) about whom Peter preached were evidently very young, and his meaning is clear: these baptised infants had failed to give consent because they were incapable of it. 'We, however,' he told Peter Maury, '[baptise] when a man is already twelve, and we are more greatly valued [sic] when he is eighteen, and already has the understanding of good and evil.'[186] The depositions reveal that the good men were

183 An example can be found in the deposition of Arnold Faure, at MS 609, fol. 195v. Some further examples: Saix of Montesquieu 'dicit se fuisse credentem haereticorum ab annis discretionis citra' (D24, fol. 134r); Phillipa of Mirapisce 'dixit se fuisse credentem haereticorum ex quo habuit discretionem' (ibid., fol. 202v). Peter of Luzenac wrote in his autograph deposition that he had 'always believed' as a good Catholic 'after I had *discretionem*': GA, p. 373. A rather poignant example is that of Arnold Sicre and his brother, who were told 'non habetis entendensa de be, quia illo tempore quo incepit mater vestra esse credens, vos duo eratis parvi'. This, and their propensity to talk, had led to the young boys' banishment (discussed above). On the other hand, Arnold was later told 'quia Bernardus [their older brother] iam habebat usum racionis et incipiebat habere entendenciam de be, dicta mater vestra retinuit eum secum et fuit unus de melioribus credentibus Comitatus Fuxi': JF, II, 28.

184 The deponents were William Faure – 'habuit fidem eorum primo postquam habuit discretionem boni et mali' (D22, fol. 5v) and B. Gralh – 'dixit etiam quod postquam habuit discretionem boni et mali habuit credulitatem haereticorum' (ibid., fol. 52r).

185 On the other hand, scribes may have been regularising more varied formulations – 'I believed from when I could understand', and so on – into a single piece of well-understood jargon.

186 'Nos autem quando homo est iam XII annorum, et magis appreciamur quando est XVIII annorum et iam potest habere intelligenciam boni et mali …': JF, III, 124.

conscientious about securing informed consent in practice, often refusing to administer the *consolamentum* to sick believers who had become unconscious or incoherent.[187] Children's lack of moral responsibility was one of the incidental arguments used to ridicule orthodox theology (in this case the idea that salvation could be affected by will) in the *Book of the Two Principles*, a theological treatise written by an unknown Italian good man in the mid-thirteenth century.[188]

As we have already discovered, though, Cathar preaching on baptism often failed to change the behaviour of those who heard it: even ardent supporters continued to take their children to the font. What is more, whilst Autier and his circle seem to have been more conscientious about receiving children than their predecessors had been, some amongst them were willing to administer their own 'baptism' to ailing infants with few apparent qualms.[189] In fact, ideas about the incapacity of children in the realm of belief did not originate with the good men, and were not limited to them.

The 'age of discretion' was a familiar concept in canon law, although it was not a singular and unmoving point.[190] Canonists used the term to describe the turning-points at which people were eligible to perform socially or spiritually important acts.[191] Sometimes this corresponded with the age of reason at seven.[192] Lack of reason – not having obtained discretion – was the rationale for children's exclusion from the sacrament of penance: only with understanding could a person be truly penitent. Thus the Fourth Lateran Council enjoined confession only upon those who had reached the age of discretion, interpreted by councils in Languedoc as at twelve or fourteen.[193] As we have seen, secular law also excluded those below these ages because of

187 See, for instance depositions of Peter Sicard (Gui, *Sentences*, I, p. 508) and Isarn Bosque (MS 609, fol. 235r).

188 *Livre des deux principes*, ed. C. Thouzellier (Paris, 1973), p. 348.

189 Jean Duvernoy draws a contrast between the fourteenth-century practice and that 'avant la Croisade', of receiving children 'dès l'âge de quatorze ans': JF, II, 410 n. 370. The comparison is certainly a helpful one, although the good men had received children much younger than fourteen both before and during the crusade, as we have seen in this chapter.

190 Indeed, the term was also known to the ancient philosophers and to medieval doctors. See L. Demaître, 'The Idea of Childhood and Child Care in Medical Writings of the Middle Ages', *Journal of Psychohistory* 4 (1977), 467–90.

191 Metz, 'L'Enfant', p. 21.

192 The Cathar author of the *Book of Two Principles* thought it came at four. He argues against judgement on the basis of free will, which, he says, would unfairly damn 'an innumerable multitude of children … four years of age or less … none of whom had from God in any way either the ability or the knowledge to do good': *Livre des deux principes*, ed. Thouzellier, pp. 402–4.

193 Thomas Aquinas was apparently alone in thinking that confession should be offered to all. His reasoning was that confession's object was not the body but the soul, and that the latter's life-cycle was not necessarily in sync with that of the former: Dove, *Perfect Age*, p. 48.

their inability to make sound judgements.[194] At the same time as this, mendicant friars had been writing sermons for mass consumption in which they criticised children for disobedience, emphasised their wax-like impressionability and laid the responsibility for their direction firmly with parents and teachers.[195] References to the inability of the young to tell right from wrong can also be found both in literature and political discourse.[196] In short, it was commonly understood in Languedoc that childhood was a period of moral incapacity.

Even inquisitors accepted that children could not be held to the same standard as adults when it came to discerning moral questions and matters of belief. The nominal age at which people became subject to the inquisitors' attentions was twelve or fourteen. The inquisitors tended not to summon young people, and were more lenient with them when they did. 'The crimes and ignorance of youth', wrote Bernard Gui in the section of his *Practica* dealing with extra-sermonal punishments for nine to eleven-year-olds, 'are more often pardoned in full, or for the most part.' 'The juvenile age', he continued, 'is easily twisted in its adolescence towards all manner of things, especially those around which it perceives the zealous desire of its parents (under whose command it is placed) to revolve.' Lacking as they did both 'fully prevailing' reason and the benefits of experience, children could not be judged as harshly as adults.[197] Jacques Fournier also thought that children could not be judged to have done good or to have sinned because they lacked reason.[198] No one, it seems, thought that children were capable of the discernment necessary to commit heresy.[199] Children were exempt from responsibility for participation, and childhood was thus a commonly employed justifica-

194 On the rights and responsibilities taken on at legal puberty, see p. 84 below.

195 Swanson, 'ad status sermons', pp. 322, 318 and throughout.

196 The *Song of the Albigensian Crusade* describes the pope absolving young Raymond VII because, at the time of the crusade, he was 'tant joves e tant innocent // Qu el pas no sabia ques era mals ni bes' – so young and innocent that he could not tell good from evil: Paterson, 'L'enfant', p. 236. Roger II Trencavel claimed in a treaty of 1179 that previous enmity had been stirred up 'Cum puer essem nec valens inter bonum et malum, utile et inutile decernere', and had fallen prey to evil counsel: Graham-Leigh, *The Southern French Nobility and the Albigensian Crusade*, p. 100.

197 Gui, *Practica*, pp. 44–5.

198 JF, I, 91–2.

199 Here are some examples. Austorgue of Gascou said that she had seen heretics publicly preaching at Sauveterre, but had at the time been 'infra annos', perhaps meaning 'within [i.e. below?] the years [of discretion]': Duvernoy, ed., *L'inquisition en Quercy*, p. 118; D21, fol. 227r–v. Raymond Hugh's penance reads that he had eaten with the Waldensians 'but he said that he was then ten years old': Duvernoy, ed., *L'inquisition en Quercy*, p. 168; D21, fol. 255r. Peter of Mazerolles confessed in 1246 that he had not eaten anything from the heretics 'apart from when he was a boy' ('nisi quando erat puer'); this may have been a reference to the evidence with which he had begun his confession (this was at MS 609, fol. 124r): ibid., fol. 125r.

tion for unorthodox behaviour. By appealing to this shared understanding, deponents hoped to persuade their interrogators to be more lenient.[200] The fact that inquisitors inscribed these excuses not just in depositions but also in the documents which recorded sentencing and punishment suggests that this was an effective tactic.[201] Those below the age of discretion could not be held responsible for their beliefs because they could not really believe in the first place.

The deposition records reveal varying experiences of religion amongst children and conflicting views about appropriate engagement amongst adults. How might this heterogeneity be synthesised? We can begin by pointing to a constant: for all children who formed part of the Cathar community, access was mediated by adults. Adults put children in situations where they might come into contact with the good men and women. Adults arranged and encouraged their children's initiation into the ascetic elite. Adults encouraged or proscribed certain behaviours and beliefs.

There was variety of opinion over what level of involvement was appropriate for children. At one extreme, some thought they should not even be spectators to public preaching; at the other, they were forcibly entered into communities whose daily life revolved around religious ritual. The difference here, it is important to understand, did not originate principally with the good men – who seem often to have been indifferent to the participation of children – but with secular members of the Cathar community. Parents, guardians and other relatives decided what level of involvement was appropriate for children under their care.

A clear chronological progression has also emerged. Before crusade and persecution made Catharism an underground movement, children had had greater opportunities to meet with good men and good women. It should be noted, though, that the setting for such meetings was not religious but almost exclusively social, and that few children attended preaching or other rituals unaccompanied. Later, as the good men and good women withdrew from public life, children's encounters with them began to depend almost entirely upon the connections and attitude of their elders. Within the select group within which they still occurred, these encounters became more intense, because they were now bound up with issues of love, danger and family loyalty.

200 Cf. Given, *Inquisition and Medieval Society*, pp. 108–9. Given argues that there was 'no shared normative universe' between inquisitors, good men and their supporters, and that these sorts of tactics cannot therefore have been effective.

201 The occasional, arch 'ut dixit' ('so he says') perhaps marks occasions when the childhood excuse was viewed with more cynicism. See, for example, the depositions of William de Cabanolas (D21, fol. 370r) and Rixende de More, wife of B[ernard] Durand d'Aurino (Gui, *Sentences*, I, p. 886).

About the more thorny topic of belief, there are two points to note. Firstly, many children were not being taught belief; rather they were taught obedience and loyalty to family values, family friends and family itself. Secondly, many deponents apparently understood that children under a certain age were not really capable of belief at all, or at least thought that the belief of children was somehow less significant than that which they as adults professed. This was a widely held opinion that was shared by inquisitors and good men alike. Thus, whilst we can say that children were sometimes taught that it was proper to participate in the rituals of the Cathars, or even to think of the Cathar clergy as 'good' men and women, it is more problematic to describe even these as 'Cathar believers'. Children may well have looked up to the good men. They may even have understood and accepted that they were representatives of the one true Church with the power to save souls. To many contemporaries, this was something other – something less – than religious faith.

In some deposition records, however, we read that children of twelve, ten and younger lived as good men and good women. Though we will probably never know very much about the daily existence of consoled children within the Cathar community, I suggest that their lives were not much different from those of their adult companions. This apparent equality should not be too surprising: to become a good man or good woman was to abandon previous distinctions and to take on a new role as a member of a sanctified elite. Some amongst the good men may have been convincing preachers or sympathetic pastors, but the Cathar community was split by a binary division. A person was either consoled or not; after that turning-point there was no progression, no learning, and no special devotion which could benefit the soul. In theory, the *consolamentum* washed away the world's distinctions. It seems that it washed away distinctions of age, too.

The practice of consoling healthy children was one which died out around the 1240s, as increasing danger made the maintenance of fixed dwellings and provision for young children completely impracticable. Peter Autier was thus largely correct when he claimed that his Church did not receive those below fourteen and preferred not to receive those below eighteen. Even before Autier, though, the reception of young children is puzzling. A scarcity of evidence does not help our understanding of the phenomenon in a logistical sense. It might be asked, for example, whether six-year-olds were capable of the three forty-day fasts which were apparently required before consolation, and what they did as an alternative if not. Yet the most important question is more fundamental: why did the good men receive children when it was against their own teaching? Perhaps the good men themselves had not developed a coherent theological justification for their reception of children. In religion, as in other areas of human life, practice often moves ahead of theory. The reception of children can be viewed as an experiment prematurely interrupted by external forces. Whether the practice would have continued in the absence of persecution, and thus developed a coherent theology, or whether it would have faded out of fashion, as it had begun to do in the Catholic Church, is impossible to know. Whatever the case, the participation of children would have continued to be mediated, shaped and proscribed by adult expectations and by adult understandings of the relationship between childhood and faith.

2

Youth

Dinner was not going well in the household of Peter Marty, blacksmith of Junac, and his two sons. 'Unless you shut up', Arnold Marty told his father, 'one of these days you're going to get your block knocked off.'[1] Enraged by this insolence, Peter picked up the salt cellar from the table and hurled it at his son. Restrained by his friend and dining companion, Arnold could only reply with more thinly veiled threats. 'You're no son of mine,' retorted the senior Marty, picking up the bench upon which he was sitting and throwing that too. Arnold beat a hasty retreat from the table and the house.

'Afterwards', recorded the scribe in 1323, as Peter's other son Bernard gave evidence before the tribunal of Pamiers, 'there was for a long time hatred between the witness's father and his brother.' The row had begun when Peter had challenged his adolescent sons about their late nights and early morning returns.[2] In fact, the younger men had been behaving conscientiously (if not safely or legally) as chaperones, guides and watchmen for Cathar ministers. Fiery tempers and generational religious conflict – would that all deposition records were as arresting.

In many ways, youth is a more problematic category than childhood, not least because it is harder to define and to identify. Our concern is primarily with the sociological phenomenon 'youth', rather than with the biological and legal period of adolescence, which is often defined more narrowly. As a life stage, youth is fluid, being defined in part by status (dependent, unmarried) rather than simply by age.[3] It is important to consider exactly what youth and adolescence meant to people in the Middle Ages, if anything at all. In doing so, this chapter takes three broad areas under examination. It firstly looks at encounters with heresy amongst young people in a set of easily identifiable social milieus – in the contexts of the family, as well as in three 'professional' categories, squire, apprentice and rural worker. Secondly, it discusses the effects on persecution, which, inquisitors recognised, could

1 'Nisi taceatis, capud vestrum ponetur ad pedes aliqua dierum' (literally, 'Unless you keep silent, one of <these> days your head will be placed at your feet') – my translation is rather free: JF, III, 261.

2 The case is also discussed in Given, *Inquisition and Medieval Society*, pp. 181–2.

3 E. James, 'Childhood and Youth in the Early Middle Ages', in *Youth in the Middle Ages*, ed. P. J. P. Goldberg and F. Riddy (York, 2004), p. 13.

fall particularly heavily on the young. Finally, the chapter turns to look at lived religion and belief.

Some historians would argue that the account of the Martys' flying furniture with which I began this chapter rests on a series of misrepresentations, amongst which is my use of the term 'adolescence'. The validity of medieval adolescence was first questioned by Philip Ariès.[4] 'Adolescence', it has been argued, 'is merely a product of our own culture … there is really no reason to expect to find it in any other time or place'.[5] Taking this assertion as his starting point, James Schultz has enumerated the three sorts of woolly thinking which he believes have plagued historical writing on the subject: lexical, physiological and psychological.[6] We do not in fact know his age, but it seems natural to associate Arnold Marty's outbursts with the emotional turmoil of adolescence; yet, as Schultz would have it, this would be to rely on 'a popular myth for which there is little scientific support'.[7]

Caution is thus surely sensible: whilst it may be our first instinct, labelling the Marty row as an 'adolescent episode' is speculative at best.[8] Yet whilst the ages of the protagonists are at no point explicitly discussed, we know that the sons were unmarried and still living in the family home. They were not children, but they had not taken on the full privileges and responsibilities of adult life either, and so their classification is difficult. Was their not-quite-adulthood a recognised life stage for contemporaries? Was it measured by age or by situation, or did both come into play? These are the sorts of questions we should ask when approaching our sources. The challenge – as Edward James has put it – is that of 'reconciling our own categories' with those of our historical subjects.[9] Most of the evidence about youth comes – like that about childhood – from depositions in which men and women narrated their own youthful experiences. The two primary questions that we should therefore ask are these: did these deponents use a category of youth/adolescence, and what did it mean to them if they did?

We must begin with words. Whilst it is tempting to dismiss questions of terminology as so much intellectual pedantry, they are important issues, for if the inquisitorial register does not identify young people we will be unable to discuss them.[10] Deponents did not use a precise vocabulary in their descriptions of young people. Most deponents used forms of the noun

4 Ariès, *Centuries of Childhood*, pp. 27–33.

5 J. A. Schultz, 'Medieval Adolescence: The Claims of History and the Silence of German Narrative', *Speculum* 66 (1991), 519–39 (p. 537).

6 Ibid.

7 Ibid., p. 526.

8 The term 'adolescent episode' is from Le Roy Ladurie, *Montaillou* (En), p. 263.

9 'Reconciliation' is an approach suggested in James, 'Childhood and Youth in the Early Middle Ages', p. 13.

10 Cf. B. Hanawalt, 'Historical Descriptions and Prescriptions for Adolescence', *Journal of Family History* 17 (1992), 341–51 (pp. 342–3).

'youth' (*iuvenis*) when describing persons between childhood and adulthood. Adolescent (*adolescens*), on the other hand, was only rarely used.[11] This is fortunate, because it allows us to sidestep the thorny subject of the latter term's translation.[12] The deponents' preferred term is thus often unproblematic for the reader: when a deponent describes the person leading the good men they saw as 'a certain youth', their meaning is reasonably clear. Adjectival usage, however, is more slippery. John Maury described a conversation he had with 'a certain man of Constans' in which the latter revealed that he was of the good faith of the heretic. Perhaps pressed for a more detailed description, Maury went on to describe the individual as 'a young man, and of little stature'.[13] It is not clear what this deponent means by this description, because we cannot know relative to what he considered his interlocutor 'young'.[14]

Similarly problematic is the mixing of terms denoting youth and childhood both by deponents and in the formal aspects of depositions themselves: something which has been described as a 'looseness of vocabulary'.[15] The noun *puer*, 'boy', was largely used by deponents to denote a child. Yet it could also refer to a semi-independent young person. Those students who testified during an investigation into alleged sodomy by Arnold of Verniolles alternated between *puer* ('boy'), *scholaris* ('scholar') and *studens* ('student') to denote themselves and their classmates, who ranged in age from fifteen to nineteen.[16] 'Youth' and 'boy' were similarly used interchangeably in depositions. Thus, Peter Aces – reported for careless speech in his mid-teens – was described by some as the former, but by others (and by himself) as the latter.[17] Even more difficult to interpret is the deposition attributed to 'Aldricus puer'. Is 'boy' here a description, that is to say, 'Aldric, a boy'? Or is it a nickname, 'the boy', Aldric? It is impossible to know. Similarly problematic are the deponents *Juvenis* of Lastroa and Stephen Coma *iuvenis* – in each case, 'the younger' or 'a youth'?[18]

11 Here are two examples. The Waldensian Raymond of Saint-Foy described the process for admitting a 'puer adolescens': JF, I, 59. Ermessenda of Cambiac described herself as 'adolescentula' at her first encounter with the Cathars: MS 609, fol. 239v.

12 Schultz argues that 'adolescence' is an anachronistic translation. See Schultz, 'Medieval Adolescence', pp. 530–3.

13 'Eodem etiam tempore ipse loquens invenit quendam hominem de Costanciano ... qui homo dixit ipsi loquenti quod ipse erat de illa bona de hereticorum, et erat homo iuvenis, et parve stature': JF, II, 476.

14 Not all young people can be classed as youths – if the man was a young husband, for example, he would fall outside the category as it is used here.

15 James, 'Childhood and Youth in the Early Middle Ages', p. 16.

16 See, for example, reports of a conversation between William Boer 'studens ... in gramaticalibus, etatis decem et octo annorum vel circa' and Arnold 'quidam puer in scholis': JF, III, 27.

17 Described as 'youth' (ibid., III, 455) and 'boy' (ibid., III, 495). See also ibid., I, 455–66.

18 D21, fol. 210v; MS 609, fol. 171r.

Even in simpler cases, we must ask what those deponents who related stories involving 'youths' were describing. Occitan society may well have recognised a period of 'biological' youth, between the onset of puberty and full adult maturity.[19] Puberty came at much the same point it does today: the early teens.[20] Legally, too, youth was recognised as a separate stage. The 1286 Customs of Toulouse carefully elaborated the rights and legal standing of those between fourteen and twenty-five, who remained under their father's authority whilst he lived.[21] Rights were afforded slowly. Its commentary (from 1296) notes that those below twenty could be litigants in civil trials, but should not be in admitted in criminal cases; they were, however, allowed to make criminal accusations.[22] Women, with their 'changeable and inconsistent hearts', were only able to participate in certain types of cases, whatever their age.[23] The same commentary provides as an example the case of 'a certain youth from Foix' – an apprentice baker – who was found in bed with his master's wife. In this legal document, the term *juvenis* is used with precision to designate a male between the ages of fourteen and twenty-five.[24] It is impossible to know how well understood such legal distinctions were. Given that the consuls' own officials did not always understand the rules, they may have passed laypeople by entirely.[25]

The lexical and legal definitions of youth from Languedoc share a common limitation: they deal primarily with men. The onset of puberty heralded a significant social change for girls, who tended to marry younger than their male counterparts, yet deponents did not speak very much of female youth. This fact is, of course, a serious limitation in terms of evidence-gathering.[26] It

19 This is Schultz's biological 'dictionary definition' of adolescence. See Schultz, 'Medieval Adolescence', pp. 526–30.

20 On the onset of puberty in the Middle Ages, see D. W. Amundsen and C. J. Diers, 'The Age of Menarche in Medieval Europe', *Human Biology; an International Record of Research* 45 (1973), 363–69. Monica Green cautions, however, that the writings upon which this and other studies have relied 'are formulaic and cannot be assumed to be historically reliable'. They are the result, she says, of numerological calculation rather than empirical observation, although this fact is apparently more evident in the discussion of menopause than that of menarche. See *The Trotula: A Medieval Compendium of Women's Medicine*, ed. and trans. M. Green, (Philadelphia, 2001), pp. 215–16 n. 85. However much they were reshaped to theoretical frameworks, though, it seems unlikely that the ages given can have deviated wildly from physical reality.

21 Articles nos. 7–8, *Coutumes*, ed. Gilles, pp. 87–8. See also the commentary on pp. 186–8.

22 The justification for this apparent double standard is that 'what is lacking in the minor is supplied by the authority of the tutor' ('deest minori etati suppletur per auctoritatem tutoris'): ibid., p. 217.

23 Ibid., p. 217.

24 Ibid, pp. 187–9.

25 In the case cited above, for example, the assessors had failed correctly to apply the rules on the treatment of *minores*.

26 Some girls spent a period of their youths as 'vested' Cathar good women. These are discussed above, in chapter 1.

is also, though, a stimulus for discussion: why were they under-represented? A possible answer to that question is discussed at the end of this chapter, but for the moment it must be sufficient to note that women are less well represented than men in this chapter.

Family life

For many young people, parents remained important guiding figures, influencing spiritual as well as secular matters. Gerald, one of the deponents sentenced by Bernard Gui in 1322, told the inquisitors that he had been accosted in the town square one day by a man who drew him aside and asked him if he was the son of Formond. The relationship was obviously important, and having ascertained that he was, the man began to preach to him, telling him that he should not do or say ill, or swear oaths, or lie.[27] Gerald cut off the conversation, telling the man that 'he had never taken anything of anyone else's, nor stolen anything'. Evidently the preacher had thought that receptiveness might run in the family: when Gerald recounted this tale, his father commended the man and his teachings to him. The interrelationship of kinship ties and religious adherence can be found even more explicitly in the testimony of the knight William Garsias. He told his interrogators in 1246 that it was 'because of the familiarity which his parents had with the said heretics [that] it seemed proper for him to do what he did with them, not on account of any faith or belief [of his own] that he had in them'.[28]

The mobility and lack of notoriety of young people made them particularly useful as guides, and so they often appear in the deposition record leading good men. A particularly colourful example is that of a youth called Peter (perhaps, the deponent thought, surnamed Montanié) from Coustaussa. Peter had met the twenty-year-old William Escaunier – who was hurrying to fetch a good man to console his dying mother – in a local drinking-house, and had promptly offered to go with him because of the journey's danger. Their travels, accompanied by Peter's grumbling brother, lasted three nights, one of which was spent awaiting the good man in the rain-soaked cemetery at Ax. To be able to leave at such short notice Peter must have been unattached and free; here again, it seems as if it was youth which enabled his involvement.[29]

Those who lived in the parental home sometimes encountered the good men through it. Like children, these young people were bound to obey the

27 Gui, *Sentences*, II, pp. 1578–80. As the content of this homily suggests, the preacher was a Waldensian.

28 MS 609, fol. 164v: 'licet pluries adoravit eos sed propter familiaritatem quod parentes ipsius testis habebant cum dictis hereticis oportebant ipsum facere ea quod fecit cum hereticis non propter fidem nec credulitatem quod haberet cum eis'.

29 For more on this story, see below, pp. 123–4.

parents under whose roof they still lived, but their greater independence often seems to have led to involvement that was deeper and – in the eyes of the inquisitors – more compromising. Leading good men was a task to which they seem to have been well suited. Bertrand Salès, his wife Vidalie and his children Peter (twenty) and Sybille (fifteen) were all sentenced by Gui in 1310.[30] Although the family shared a strong allegiance to the good men, Bertrand was by some way the most active and enthusiastic. He had, however, once sent his son out. Peter was charged with guiding the good men away from his house because, Bertrand's *culpa* records, 'he [Bertrand] had heard a rumour that those who had confessed to heresy had been cited in the inquisitorial sermon'. We might suppose that it was Peter's youth that particularly fitted him for this task, because it meant that he was unknown to the inquisitors. Pons of Latour's father may have had the same idea when he sent his son to lead some good men in the 1220s.[31] The deposition evidence does not allow us to be exhaustive, but it is clear that whilst families certainly did not always agree about matters of religion, violent inter-generation conflict of the type with which this chapter opened was rare.

While parents still had a strong influence on behaviour (of which more later), youths did have greater freedom – and thus more chance of independent interaction – than children. For some young males, this freedom came in the form of employment outside the home. One of the key differences between these (male) youths and younger children was that of mobility. Those who were older were no longer as tightly bound to their parents as they once had been. Although the new-found freedom was not itself religious in nature, it did provide greater opportunities for interaction, and made them useful members of the Cathar movement.[32]

Squirehood

Squires are perhaps amongst the most easily recognisable groups of medieval youths. Indeed, Barbara Hanawalt has identified squirehood alongside apprenticeship as one of the available 'mechanisms ... noting [adolescence's] existence as a life phase' in medieval Europe.[33] Such people do in fact appear in depositions, as 'domicelli' and 'scutiferi'. Since they often acted as general-purpose servants, those squires from Languedoc whose knightly masters were

30 Bertrand: Gui, *Sentences*, I, pp. 392–4 ; Vidalie: ibid., pp. 394–6. For Peter and Sybille see Table 2.1 on p. 86 below.

31 MS 609, fol. 71v.

32 The importance of mobility in the operation of the Cathar Church is discussed in Bruschi, *The Wandering Heretics of Languedoc*, especially chapter 2, pp. 50–99, 'Catharism and its Mobility'.

33 Hanawalt, 'Historical Descriptions and Prescriptions for Adolescence', p. 342.

friendly with the good men might easily have come into contact with them. One such example is provided by the squire Peter William of Roqueville, who had gone with his uncle to see some fugitive good men in a wood in the 1250s, but was unable to adore 'because he was holding his said uncle's hawk, and was standing apart with the dogs'.[34] A number of other squires can be found in the deposition records, appearing either in the stories of knightly deponents, or as deponents themselves. Only rarely, though, do we find out much about these squires beyond the fact of their occupation and we almost never find out about their age.

Faced with this lack of evidence, therefore, we must proceed with caution: it cannot simply be assumed that the squires encountered in the deposition evidence were young people. Literary sources surveyed by Linda Paterson suggest that Occitan squires did not fit the typically imagined model of knightly apprentice, and that in any case not all squires were young.[35] The words translated as squire in those sources often described a range of tasks and statuses, which changed over the course of the twelfth and thirteenth centuries. Paterson distinguishes between the Occitan terms 'donzel' – a young aristocrat in service, perhaps to a relative – and 'escudier' – originally a more menial servant.[36] In practice, the distinction seems to have been less clear. Peter William of Roqueville, for instance, sounds like a cross between a twelfth-century *escudier*, 'simply [a servant] performing a rather menial job'[37] and a *donzel*. Language is also a problem. Whilst the Occitan terms have Latin parallels (*domicellus* and *scutifer*), our sources were spontaneously translated into Latin by scribes who were not always local, and in practice the two seem to have been used interchangeably. Neither is it always clear that squires are young. Older people could also be squires and even those who started young might, for economic reasons, have retained their status well into their adulthood. Given the uncertain status of the Occitan squire as youth, and the lack of evidence in the depositions, little can be said here about them, beyond observing that for young men who were squires – as for youths with other occupations – duty sometimes involved them in religious as well as secular matters.

34 D25, fols. 134v–5r. Since Peter had already implicated himself, and had admitted to having adored on other occasions, this excuse may well have been genuine.

35 Paterson, *The World of the Troubadours*, pp. 82–4. See also L. Paterson, 'The Occitan Squire in the Twelfth and Thirteenth Centuries', in *The Ideals and Practice of Medieval Knighthood I*, ed. C. Harper-Bill and R. Harvey (Woodbridge, 1986), pp. 133–49.

36 Paterson, 'The Occitan Squire in the Twelfth and Thirteenth Centuries'.

37 Paterson, *The World of the Troubadours*, p. 82.

Apprenticeship

A more fruitful search can be carried out in the towns. Here, where there were more opportunities for independent and semi-independent employment, young people were beginning to form new networks of their own. Apprentices were one group that had become increasingly common in urban communities. Some of these were the product of formal legal arrangements, of the type that Kathryn Reyerson documented in her study of employment contracts in Montpellier.[38] Most deponents did not tell the inquisitors about the details of their contracts, although information about pay sometimes came up anecdotally. Arnold of Verniolles, for instance, told the inquisitors in 1323 of a conversation he had recently had with an apprentice cobbler. The youth – whom Arnold reckoned to be around eighteen years old – had told him that he did not think he would be able to provide for himself in the trade, and would happily give it up to be employed as a servant.[39] Whatever their economic situation, however, apprentices had an increased level of independence, and whilst family networks could be important in securing apprenticeships, recipients were freed from family influence in their daily lives.[40] Living away from their family home under the guardianship of a master, these boys (and sometimes girls) formed relationships entirely separate from those of their parents, which sometimes exposed them to new ways of thinking. An apprentice-master had an important and influential role in the development of his charges, for as well as craft-based training, apprenticeships helped to integrate these young people into social and economic communities.

In some cases, the training and advice took on a religious element.[41] Such was the case for Peter Pictavin, apprenticed at the age of twelve to Raymond Peter, a tailor from Sorèze.[42] Pictavin was introduced to the good men through his master, being taken in 1230 to a sermon given by the Cathar deacon Arnold Hugh.[43] Though he did not live with his master, over the following ten years of his training and employ, the young apprentice's close

38 See K. L. Reyerson, 'The Adolescent Apprentice/Worker in Medieval Montpellier', *Journal of Family History* 17 (1992), 353–70. It may be helpful here to note Goldberg's suggestions about arrangements for English servants which, he says, may frequently have been verbal, with 'much of what was expected between servant and employer … probably understood as customary'; P. J. P. Goldberg, 'What was a servant?', in *Concepts and Patterns of Service in the Later Middle Ages*, ed. A. Curry and E. Matthew (Woodbridge, 2000), p. 11.

39 JF, III, 45.

40 Reyerson, 'The Adolescent Apprentice/Worker in Medieval Montpellier', pp. 357–9.

41 See ibid. In the English context, too, Jeremy Goldberg has suggested that the socialising role of masters may have included direct religious instruction; Goldberg, *Women, Work and Life Cycle in a Medieval Economy*, p. 242.

42 D25, fols. 248v–71r.

43 Ibid., fols. 268v–9v.

relationship with his master brought him into further contact with the good men. He and two co-apprentices[44] were taken to sermons and summoned to offer charity and companionship at the bedsides of the Raymond Peter's dying friends.[45]

The relationship between Pictavin and Raymond Peter seems to have become close: years later, the tailor and his former apprentice would stroll in the gardens of Sorèze together, sharing the comical story of a nearly botched *consolamentum*.[46] The apprentice's story echoes many of the elements of young people's working lives which have been made familiar by the work of Jeremy Goldberg. He worked for a master who apparently stood *in loco parentis*, was closely integrated within the household, and was quite independent from his natal family. [47]

Raymond Peter was standing in for Pictavin's parents in a religious sense too, it seems, as he introduced his young charge to the teaching and important rituals of his faith. Given the close bond formed between master and apprentice, and the cost involved in supporting the apprentice's position, it seems reasonable to assume that these family members would have taken some interest in their choice of employer. Pictavin came from a family with connections to Catharism, and his apprenticeship may have been arranged with both economic and spiritual needs in mind.[48] That first gathering he attended in 1230 certainly made an impression, as he remembered the preacher's theme nearly fifty years later. Indeed, it was the beginning of a life-long association with the faith and its followers. Pictavin's contact with Catharism seems to have built outward from work-place associations, and whilst he claimed to have abandoned his Cathar beliefs after the massacre at Avignonet in 1242, this did not have any discernible effect upon his practical observance or his social network.

44 Ibid., fols. 256r–v. Another *condiscipulus* had died earlier: fols. 253r–4v.

45 Ibid., fols. 252r–3r, 253r–4r, 256r–v, 261v–2r.

46 Raymond Peter had been guiding two good men to a dying knight, when one of them realised that they had forgotten a gospel-book necessary for the ritual. Raymond Peter was sent back to fetch it: ibid., fols. 257v–8v.

47 See, for example, the following: P. J. P. Goldberg, 'Masters and Men in Later Medieval England', in *Masculinity in Medieval Europe*, ed. D. Hadley (New York, 1998), pp. 56–70; Goldberg, 'What was a servant?', pp. 1–20; P. J. P. Goldberg, 'Orphans and Servants: The Socialisation of Young People Living away from Home in the English Later Middle Ages', in *Adoption et fosterage*, ed. M. Corbier (Paris, 1999), pp. 231–46; Goldberg, *Women, Work and Life Cycle in a Medieval Economy*. In his 'Orphans and Servants', p. 232, Goldberg notes the contrast between the English life-cycle model and a southern or Mediterranean European pattern.

48 The death-bed *consolamentum* of Peter's uncle Arnold had been attended by Raymond Peter and various members of the Pictavin family: D25, fols. 268v–70r. As Peter Pictavin at no point mentions his father in his testimony, it may well be that Arnold arranged his apprenticeship in the knowledge that Raymond Peter was a right-thinking sort, who would be able to connect his nephew with the Cathar community.

Pictavin was not the only young man whose apprenticeship left such a mark. Close-knit commercial and professional networks provided important pathways through which beliefs and social practices were shared and spread. If nothing else, the apprentice or servant's integration into their master's household as an (obedient) dependant could result in their involvement in the logistical side of Catharism. It may for some have been an involvement in which they took little interest, simply seeing it as another of their duties. Raymond Dominic may have been hoping to give this impression in his deposition of 1246 which recounts that 'when he was a boy, and staying in the house of Arnold Sans, he saw heretics there whose names he does not know, and at the command of the said Arnold Sans, master of the said house … he led the said heretics outside the town one night'.[49]

Some women can be observed amongst the wage-earning youths in the depositions. Raimonde Arsen, a deponent from the village of Montaillou, was living as a servant and seems even to have negotiated her own conditions of employment.[50] These young women were also sometimes brought into contact with unorthodox faith through their work. Joanna of Proault had been living 'as a girl, as though a servant' in the house of Raymond Gasc.[51] She had encountered heretics in Raymond's house, although she claimed that her involvement had been minimal. In one exceptional case, the good men themselves had even intervened in the appointment of a maidservant for one of their followers, Guillemette Morlana, so that she 'could have a person … in whom she could trust on the matter of heresy'.[52] The sympathetic soul whom Guillemette employed was not a girl but a married woman.

In her study of fourteenth-century Montpellier, Kathryn Reyerson found that female apprentices were significantly fewer in number than their male counterparts, and worked in less prestigious trades.[53] Reyerson suggests that this discrepancy may have been partly due to the unwillingness of families to invest a second time in daughters whom they would later have to provide with a dowry.[54] In fact, married women appear more often as servants in the depositions than unmarried ones, suggesting that female service was a life-long rather than life-stage-specific occupation.

As we have seen, the close interest displayed by inquisitors in the lives of former apprentices was often justified. It may have been first focussed in this area by a contemporary perception amongst orthodox polemicists that

49 MS 609, fol. 207v.

50 JF, I, 370.

51 Gui, *Sentences*, I, p. 838: 'cum quo morabatur puella quasi pro ancilla'.

52 D25, fol. 122r.

53 Reyerson, 'The Adolescent Apprentice/Worker in Medieval Montpellier', p. 355. It is interesting to note that these included textile work, which was an occupation particularly associated with heresy.

54 Ibid., p. 360.

textile trades were closely linked to heresy. In the 1160s, Eckbert of Schönau informed his audience in a sermon directed against heretics discovered at Cologne that in (northern) France, 'Gallia', the heretics whom he knew as Cathars ('Catharos') were called weavers ('texerant'). The name was derived – as he rather unnecessarily pointed out – 'from the practice of weaving'.[55] As Malcolm Lambert notes, the connotations here were pejorative – the weaving trade was a suspect one, and was carried out in hidden places.[56]

Nowhere in the deposition records from Languedoc is 'weaver' used as a synonym for 'good man'. Yet the inquisitors may have been justified in associating heresy with particular trades. The investigation by Bernard of Caux and Jean of Saint-Pierre in 1245–46 uncovered the testimony of many youths who had been employed in the workshops of good men. These inquisitors' interest in apprentices was no doubt sustained by the reality they discovered. In the 1230s, Arnold of Terré from Fanjeaux – along with other trainees ('alios scolares') – had stayed for a year with the good man Peter Colomb, who taught him to sew.[57] Another of Peter's young students – Bernard of Puycalvel –was employed by the good man for two years, in order to learn the art of skinning.[58] Apparently this was a bustling commercial hub, his testimony reveals, with 'many people buying and selling [there]'.[59]

As well as being apprentices, deponents were also employed by heretic tradesmen for piecework in their youths. Peter Gari, who was to be a merchant in later life, was employed in a workshop 'of certain heretics' at Fanjeaux in his youth in the 1220s, and had earned money doing it 'whenever he was able'.[60] Finding employment in these workshops was common for local youths, he noted. In the late twelfth century, Peter of Terré had 'once helped them prepare lambskins' at the tender age of eight, and Peter of Garmassia had worked there in around 1215.[61] In 1205 Bernard of Villeneuve had been taught to sew for a year in Laurac, a little to the north. The split between apprentice and employee is not clear, and the boys who undertook paid work doubtless acquired new abilities whether or not there was a formal tutoring arrangement. In the case of Peter of Garmassia, these seem to have been profitable: his deposition finds him earning money using his skills some years after his initial employment had ceased.

55 Migne, ed. *Patrologiae: cursus completus series Latina*, 221 vols. (Paris, 1844–64), 195, 13. Twelfth-century writers' emphasis on regional variation in these names is discussed in H. Grundmann, *Religious Movements in the Middle Ages*, trans. S. Rowan (Notre Dame and London, 1995), pp. 14–15 and 260–1.

56 Lambert, *The Cathars*, p. 43. For other polemical uses see Duvernoy, *Religion des Cathares*, pp. 307–8.

57 MS 609, fols. 153v–4r.

58 Ibid., fol. 150v.

59 Ibid., fol. 150v.

60 Ibid., fol. 159v.

61 Ibid., fols. 168r, 157r.

The connection between good men and the weaving trade has been subject to some scrutiny by historians.[62] Charles Schmidt saw the good men's trade as nothing more than useful cover; their 'workshop' at Cordes, for instance, merely the facade for a Cathar seminary. The border between apprentice and acolyte may have been one that was easily crossed. It was certainly blurred in the popular imagination, as the case of Arnold Gerald demonstrates. Arnold told the inquisitors that he had only been taught to sew by the heretics with whom he had been sent to stay, whilst his neighbours later told his wife that he had been a fully fledged good man.[63] It was not only weavers who provoked such associations in people's minds: a similar overlap between craft and cult is clear in the evidence of Peter Roger of Les Cassès, who recalled that his brother had gone to Toulouse in 1230 'to learn the art of skinning, and there made himself a heretic'.[64]

Yet whilst there was clearly sometimes a path from apprenticeship to *consolamentum*, I would not agree with Schmidt that tailoring was only a front for the good men. Exposure to their life and preaching during an apprenticeship clearly informed a religious vocation for some, but the workshop need not have been a theological college for this to be the case. The testimonies collected by inquisitors seem to support the view that the good men were engaged in producing the goods of their professed trade, whatever conversations they may have had whilst doing it. Cordes, for example, was not just a hotbed of heresy, but also a commercial centre for weaving.[65] Neither was it the only place where good men were said to occupy themselves with that trade. The evidence given by deponents about their time working for heretics is convincing, not least because these men actually used their artisan training. The inquisitors were right to be interested in their time with the good men, though. Close-knit commercial and professional networks provided important pathways through which the beliefs and social practices were shared and spread. If nothing else, the integration of apprentices and servants into a master's household could lead to increased contact with the good men. For some apprentices, attendance at services and active engagement with the movement as guides and supporters was not so much a choice as an obligation to their employer.

Like the bonds formed between Peter Pictavin and his master, social connections and religious affiliations made during this formative stage of the young tradesmen's lives often endured. Peter Gari, for example, claimed to have abandoned his Cathar faith after only four years, but had nevertheless

62 The historiography of this is covered in a lengthy footnote in Koch, *Frauenfrage*, p. 18 n. 23.

63 On Arnold see p. 60 above.

64 MS 609, fol. 227r.

65 Koch, *Frauenfrage*, p. 18 n. 23.

continued to pay his respects to the good men.[66] The religious links forged in the workplace provided commercial opportunities for one apprentice: the skinner – and former employee of good men – Peter of Garmassia counted good men amongst his customers in later life.[67] To draw a clear distinction between the religious experiences and the day-to-day lives of these deponents is thus an impossible task; the two had become inextricably bound up together.

Rural occupations

Beyond the towns and the trades associated with them, young people found other employment opportunities as casual labourers and farm hands. As with apprentice networks, initial parental approval remained important. Bernard Marty told Ermengaud of Concenac that he would willingly come and stay with her and her husband as their shepherd, but only 'if his mother and father wanted it'.[68] Rural employers, too, could be good men, as evidenced by Arnold William, who told the inquisitors that in his youth he had stayed at Lantar for six months with a good man called Raymond, and had 'ploughed there daily'.[69] The availability of work varied with location and season, and so rural men and women often travelled around to find it; Le Roy Ladurie has given an evocative account of this peripatetic lifestyle for the shepherds of Montaillou.[70] Travel, of course, provided further opportunities for exposure to unorthodox beliefs. In his youth, the frail Bernard Agasse had travelled with his parents to work the harvest at Moustajou, and had come across the good men there in the 1240s.[71] At that time, an inquisitive young man could still happen upon the good men unexpectedly. This situation was not to last. A powerful example of how much things had changed by the early fourteenth century – as well as some insight into the world of agricultural work – is provided by the testimony of Peter Aces.

Peter was thirteen years old when he had the encounter that would eventually lead to his appearance before the inquisitorial tribunal at Pamiers. With

66 MS 609, fol. 159v.

67 E.g. 'Item, in villa de Velveder scidit duabus hereticabus unam camisiam et unam capam. Et sunt eodem tempore vel circa' (i.e. around 1220): ibid., fol. 157r.

68 JFD, III, 279–80. Le Roy Ladurie describes Bernard's story as a 'long, fascinating and pitiable' one, and says he came from a family ruined by the inquisition: *Montaillou* (En), p. 112; *Montaillou* (Fr), p. 72.

69 MS 609, fol. 207r.

70 See Le Roy Ladurie, *Montaillou* (En), chapters 4, 6 and 7, pp. 69–88, 103–35; *Montaillou* (Fr), pp. 108–32, 150–96.

71 D26, fol. 203v: 'ipse testis iuuenis existens iverat cum parentibus suis apud Villa Mostancionem in messibus, et ipse testis remanebat in villa quia non poterat ire ad campos cum aliis'. See also below, pp. 124–5.

two or three other boys he was guarding cattle and pigs at Esplas de Sérou, when – during a meal – one of the boys held up a turnip that they were eating and proclaimed that it was just like the stuff which priests held up during the mass.[72] Apparently – and doubtless to his eventual regret – this image stuck with the young Peter. Some four years later, in 1324, he found employment and lodgings with Peter Bernard as a cowherd and general servant.[73] According to the latter, Peter Aces was now a perfectly stereotypical youth, which is to say that he was a blabbermouth who did not take life seriously.[74] For the July harvest, four others were employed by Peter's master to reap millet.[75] The workers slept together in a single room, two to a bed, an unremarkable practice, even amongst married adults. One evening, whilst they were sleeping, Peter Aces burst in and began to cavort around the room, singing the Paternoster and irreverently poking fun at the clergy. When the workers asked him to stop and finally tried to eject him, he held up his hands as if officiating at a mass and as a parting shot asked them, 'Why do you say this? [Is it] on account of a turnip skin that the priests hold up like this at the mass?'

Apparently scandalised by Peter's behaviour, one of the workers – Bernard Maiestre – approached Peter's master the next day and related the story, telling him that no man should put up with such words, which he, Bernard, was going to report to the bishop (that is, to the bishop-inquisitor Jacques Fournier). Peter's master was initially happy with this outcome – he thought it might knock some sense into the young boy. Yet the master was also worried because he knew that the taint of heresy could all too easily stick to him, too. He told Bernard that Peter had been nothing but trouble to him, and that he could not put up with him any longer. By dismissing the boy almost straight away, he hoped to close the matter. After a day or two, he took the boy with him to the market at Foix, handed him some money, and released him from his employ.

The master's intuition – that he should distance himself as quickly as possible from the young troublemaker – was correct, but his hope to put an end to the matter was not fulfilled. The interfering Bernard sought advice about what to do about Peter from a priest with whom he was travelling. The priest quickly relayed a report to Fournier and all those involved (Peter, his master, Bernard, the other three boys and the priest) were hauled up before the tribunal.[76] Peter's master was not immediately forthcoming with his evidence, and he was held in prison. His silence was counter-productive,

72 JF, III, 462–3.

73 He is described both as 'boerio' and 'famulo': ibid., III, 455–6, 459.

74 Ibid., III, 460: 'erat lusor et loquax'.

75 Ibid., III, 455: 'ad messes iulii'.

76 The testimony of these six deponents can be found in JF, III, 455–66.

and it is clear that Fournier suspected him of taking Peter to Foix to escape the inquisitors.

The effects of persecution

When Peter Aces' story is compared with those of the young servants and apprentices, the changes brought about by persecution are evident. Indeed, the entire story is a testament to the success of persecution in Languedoc. Those who testified saw Peter more as a hapless fool than as a seditious heretic, yet his outburst had severe consequences for himself and those around him. His employer was thrown in prison; Bernard – because he was unwilling to reveal his own name – was threatened with a knife; and Peter himself was captured at Foix by the inquisitors' agents. For this adolescent, the new-found freedom of youth, coupled with his irreverent character, had led to catastrophe. Was this experience common? Did youths often come into contact and conflict with the machinery of inquisitorial justice?

Young people in Languedoc were certainly subject to the proscriptions of heresy law. Following the formal end of the crusade in 1229, the council of Toulouse had ordered that all, 'whether men or women', should publicly abjure heresy every two years, 'men from fourteen years and above, women from twelve'. It had also decreed that all those over fourteen (perhaps, therefore, implying only men) should swear to serve the peace.[77] The statutes of Toulouse were restated in a general sense at Albi in 1230.[78] Here, the ecclesiastical authorities seem to have been appropriating for their own purposes a familiar practice in Occitan society of beginning oaths of allegiance at the age of puberty.[79] Thus, the council of Albi in 1254 once again renewed the obligations of the statutes of Toulouse for those 'from the age of puberty', expanding the oath to include a promise to reveal 'believers, protectors, defenders and receivers' of heretics (as well as the heretics themselves, of course) to inquisitors or 'dioecesanis' (bishops). It was to be renewed every three years.[80]

As the enforced oath-swearing suggests, anyone over the age of twelve or fourteen could be summoned by the inquisitors.[81] Whether or not they

77 Toulouse 1229 [12] and [28]: Mansi, XXIII, cols. 196, 201.

78 Albi 1230, [63]: SS, p. 32.

79 See W. L. Wakefield, 'The Family of Niort in the Albigensian Crusade and Before the Inqusition', *Names: Journal of the American Name Society* 18 (1970), 97–117 and 286–303 (p. 101 n. 14).

80 Albi 1254, [11–13]: Mansi, XXIII, col. 835. 'Puberty' here clearly refers to legal puberty at twelve and fourteen, as is in fact spelled-out. See also Béziers 1246, [16]: Mansi, XXIII, col. 995. Here age is not specified. On the origin of these categories at the council of Tarragona in 1242, see Arnold, *Inquisition and Power*, pp. 42–3.

81 For discussion of this point, see above, pp. 30–1.

Table 2.1. Young deponents before Bernard Gui

Name	Age	Punishment	Inquisitorial Comment	Page(s)
Jacques Mercadier	18	Earlier given grace, then crosses	[Marginal note:] '… fiat ei gracia de crucibus in primo sermone quia minor erat quando conmisit'. (p. 216)	216–18, 224
Peter Guilabert	–	Double crosses (given 1309, lifted 1322)	[Marginal note:] 'Juvenis erat tunc et ideo mitius actum fuit cum eo et habuit cruces.' (p. 214)	214, 226, 1438
Arnold Isarn	15	Earlier given grace, then crosses	[Marginal note:] '… fiat ei gracia de crucibus in primo sermone propter etatem'. (p. 216)	216, 224
Peter Salès	20	Crosses (given 1310, lifted 1312)	–	346, 568
Sybille Salès	15	Crosses (given 1310, lifted 1312)	–	346–7, 568
Brulhes Capus	18	Spared crosses	[Comment in sentencing:] 'parcimus a crucibus intuitu pietatis'	622, 630
Maurande Maurand	17	Spared crosses	[Comment in sentencing:] 'parcimus a crucibus intuitu pietatis'	622, 630
Na Neus Sanchès	20	Prison	714, 770	
Johanna of Proault	–*	Pilgrimage	[Comment in sentencing:] 'parcentes tibi Johanne a penitencia confusibili ampliori ratione etatis in qua tunc eras'	838–40, 840

* 'puella quasi pro ancilla'

Page references to *Le livre des sentences de Bernard Gui: 1308–1323*, ed. Annette Pales-Gobilliard (Paris, 2002). All to vol. I.

were actually summoned is another question which it is for the most part difficult to answer. Bernard Gui is the only inquisitor whose thinking and practice can be examined in detail. Scattered throughout the sentences issued by his court in the 1320s can be found nine deponents whose youth was specifically mentioned: four boys and five girls ranging in age from fifteen to twenty. The very fact that information about these deponents' ages was recorded suggests that they were exceptional and deserving of special treatment. In fact, all but two were given a reduced punishment, and in most cases it was specifically noted that this was because of their young age. Jacques Mercadier was given grace the first time he was sentenced 'because he was a minor when he committed [these offences]'.[82] Similarly, when Johanna of Proault was ordered to go on pilgrimages in 1312, the inquisitor noted that 'we have spared you, Johanna, from a greater and more shameful penance, for reason of the age which you were then [i.e. at the time she had committed the offences for which he was sentencing her]'.[83] This principle of leniency towards youth was applied also to Peter Guilabert, who had strayed when he was a youth, and to fifteen-year-old Arnold Isarn, who had hidden things in his confession 'from fear and cowardliness, being then fifteen years old'.[84] Sybille Salès and her brother Peter were apparently not deserving of special consideration initially, but it is worth noting that their punishments were removed after only two years.[85]

Gui later codified the lenient attitude towards the young that these cases demonstrate.[86] His *Practica inquisitionis* contains a formula for assigning lighter punishments to the young 'outside the [inquisitorial] sermon', in order to spare them from a crippling burden of shame.[87] This provision was explicitly targeted at 'nine, ten and eleven year-olds', and it is therefore not surprising that children of these ages do not appear in the record of Gui's sentences. Yet the *Practica* also refers to them as 'youths' ('juveni') and describes their life stage as 'the juvenile age' ('etas juvenilis') or 'adolescence' ('adolescentia'), terms we might expect to refer mainly to older youths. The cases surveyed above indicate that Gui may have operated a sliding scale of leniency, dealing with children outside the sermon, but still showing consideration for older youths when they were publicly summoned. Whether or not Gui was an innovator in this regard is impossible to determine, because his is the only extensive record of punishments from Languedoc that survives.[88] Most surviving inquisitorial texts consist of material from the earlier stages of

82 Gui, *Sentences*, I, pp. 216–18.

83 Ibid., pp. 838–40: 'parcentes tibi Johanne a penitencia confusibili amplari ratione etatis in qua tunc eras'.

84 Ibid., pp. 216 (Arnold); ibid., 214 (Peter). The quotation is from Peter's second sentencing by Gui for failure to wear the crosses he was given; see on this Gui, *Sentences*, II, pp. 1484–8.

85 Ibid., p. 568.

86 Such is the opinion of the *Sentences*' most recent editor: ibid., p. 13.

87 Gui, *Practica*, ii.8, ed. Douais, pp. 44–5. See above, p. 67. See also the provisions for young people planning to marry, discussed p. 121 below.

88 The penitences issued by Peter Sella from D21 represent little more than a list of names and sentences. The sentences issued by Bernard of Caux and Jean of Saint-Pierre, published by Célestin Douais (in Douais, ed., *Documents*, II, 1–89) are more detailed, but are still limited in comparison with the detail and scale of Gui's register. A brief survey suggests that the sentences from Caux and Saint-Pierre do not contain material bearing upon this question. An interesting demonstration of leniency in that register, however, is that of Raymond Sabbatier, who in 1246 was given liberty from prison to live with his father 'qui valitudinarius est et catholicus et pauper', as long as the father lived: ibid., II, 10.

the trial process, before inquisitors had had an opportunity to display either leniency or harshness.

Inquisitorial punishments could certainly be very damaging to their recipients. Many individuals were sentenced to be 'signed with the cross', to wear large yellow crosses on their clothing at all times as a mark of penance.[89] Arnold Isarn, for example, was given crosses by Gui in 1309. This was in fact a lenient punishment, in concession to a deponent who was only fifteen when he first testified, but the young man was unable to bear the punishment for more than a year.[90] He told Gui that this was because he did not see 'where or with whom he could earn his living whilst carrying crosses'.[91] Arnold would have been far better off had he taken the punishment; his abandonment of the crosses was seen by Gui as the result of 'will and temerity'. His ongoing attempts to evade justice resulted in summonses, excommunication and, finally, imprisonment.[92] A similar story was told by Berengar Sevarelh. He had been forced to leave his own country thanks to inquisitorially imposed poverty, and had subsequently given up his penitential crosses 'because no-one wanted to employ him for work'.[93]

The problems these people experienced were part of the punishment, aimed at imposing stigma and shame. Marking out sinners from the broader community was their express purpose.[94] In the early years it was easy for deponents to throw off their crosses with only the slowest of inquisitorial

89 For a description of the punishment, see Given, *Inquisition and Medieval Society*, pp. 85–6.

90 See table above, p. 00.

91 Gui, *Sentences*, II, pp. 1484–8.

92 Arnold was imprisoned in 1322. For guidelines on the escalation of punishment in such cases, see Gui, *Practica*, i.2, 5, 14, 15, ed. Douais, pp. 2–4, 6, 12–14. Gui notes that 'crescente contumacia crescere debet pena': i.14, ed. Douais, p. 12.

93 It should be noted that Berengar does not fit the definition of a youth that I have adopted here: JF, II, 447, 449.

94 James Given sees the inquisitorial punishment system as having an educative function – 'part of a struggle to impose a cultural and spiritual hegemony on the masses of Languedoc' – as well as a social one – the creation of an 'out-group': *Inquisition and Medieval Society*, pp. 72–3, 90. Note also Arnold, *Inquisition and Power*, pp. 69–71. Arnold argues that the inquisitorial system of punishments was more nuanced, not simply creating a binary division between heresy and orthodoxy, but a 'set[ting] out before the eyes of the people a charcoal spray of transgression'. He also suggested that *crosses* specifically were chosen as the form of punishment in order to demonstrate 'the Church's ability to determine how these sights [of piety] were read'. A more sympathetic view of the inquisitors' aims in imposing this punishment is given in A. Roach, 'Penance and the Making of the Inquisition in Languedoc', *Journal of Ecclesiastical History* 52 (2001), 409–33 (especially pp. 422–5). Roach argues that – after a brief and ineffective flirtation with more violent methods– the inquisitors' punishments were intended as penitential and that cross-wearing in particular was about 'the inclusion of the penitent in the community' (p. 423). Cross-wearing became 'a very effective oppressive penance' (p. 424), and along with other non-custodial punishments, 'cross wearers saw their status decline as penance became notorious as a way of avoiding prison' (p. 433).

responses. A woman from Fanjeaux who had entered the sect as a girl was asked by Bernard of Caux in 1246 why she had given up her crosses, and she answered that 'all those signed with the cross were giving up their crosses, and because of this she the witness gave up [her] crosses'.[95] Jörg Feuchter has argued that the social stigma of inquisitorial punishments was minimal in one particular milieu – Montauban during the 1240s – where he suggests that local society banded together and thus remained largely unaffected.[96] Things may have changed by the 1250s, when Peter Pictavin told a friend that he *wished* that he (the friend) could give up his crosses, the implication being that this was not possible.[97] (The friend, however, had seen wearing crosses as a sort of martyrdom, saying that he would rather bear crosses and have 'those on whose account I wear them' staying in the land.) By the fourteenth century, the stigma of crosses was perhaps becoming too powerful. Gui's *Practica* included a formula for releasing penitent parents from the burden of wearing the crosses in cases where the infamy thus conferred was making it impossible for their children to find a marriage partner.[98] In the 1320s, men and women signed with the cross were so reviled and derided that the archbishop of Narbonne had to issue a warning to his flock not to harass them.[99]

The stigma of association with heresy did not stop young people from engaging with good men and their followers entirely, but it is clear that persecution reduced the chance that contact would extend beyond networks of which they were already part. Montauban is a case in point: whilst persecution did not result in a great deal of hardship in the town, it served there to tighten up a social network and to turn its members inward. Outside such networks, fear of inquisition and its agents created tension for anyone linked to the Cathar movement. The pressures were economic as well as social, a fact discovered by those from Cathar-sympathising families who sought employment outside the network of co-religionists. This must have been an increasingly common problem for any members of the movement. Lacking as they were in well-developed networks, youths would have felt the constricting effects of persecution more strongly than their elders as they tried to make their way in the world.

95 Note that the word used here to refer to those who wore crosses under compulsion – 'crucesignati' – is the same one that is translated in other contexts as 'crusaders': MS 609, fol. 160v. See also p. 00 above.

96 J. Feuchter, 'Le pouvoir de l'inquisition à travers ses peines: Le cas de Montauban (1241)', in *Inquisition et Pouvoir*, ed. G. Audisio (Aix-en-Provence, 2004), pp. 236–55.

97 D25, fol 267v. See also the comments of Pales-Gobilliard who says that 'Plus que la peine de prison, ces croix ont été abhorées': Gui, *Sentences*, I, p. 27.

98 Gui, *Practica*, ii.20, ed. Douais, p. 53.

99 Given, *Inquisition and Medieval Society*, p. 85.

Youths and faith

We have already seen that increasing independence could give young people new opportunities for interaction with heretics. The extent to which young people actually engaged in the community is less clear, however. William Chester Jordan has suggested that young male Jews in the Middle Ages may have felt compelled to convert to Christianity at an age when they were on the verge of assuming new adult identities and developing their autonomy. In other words, the liminal period of adolescence was one where crossing over from one world into another was easier.[100] Unlike Jewish converts, young converts to Catharism would not find stability or security, but youth may still have been a time where new identities and communities seemed particularly appealing. Lack of interest in the Church may have fuelled this desire.

There was no obvious place for young people in the calendar of Church life, although preachers took some interest in them.[101] All those beyond puberty were – in theory – equal, and whilst the transition from child to more fully involved youth may have been significant for some, there was no formal recognition of separate status. Confirmation was more closely linked to baptism than to coming-of-age in the thirteenth century.[102] Yet things do not seem to have been much better amongst the good men. Indeed, beyond those exceptional young people who had received the *consolamentum* as children and lived a life ascetic purity, there is little evidence in the depositions about the lived religion of youths. It seems that inquisitors and good men alike were uninterested in young people. The *consolamentum* was available to all who could make the requisite promises – and from some ministers even to those who could not – and youth was certainly no barrier, but no formal Cathar rituals marked the transition from childhood to youth, or youth to adulthood. Lifestyle and life stage were entirely irrelevant to the good men – even more so since most people received their 'spiritual baptism' only moments before death.

Young people were rarely received as good men or good women, and nor do they seem to have played a particularly significant role as lay followers. When youths were active in the community, their age drew comment. Such is the case in the deposition of Philip of Larnat, who saw 'a certain youth, [a heretic,] who, he believes, was the son of the said Peter Autier, heretic,

100 See W. C. Jordan, 'Adolescence and Conversion in the Middle Ages: a Research Agenda', in *Jews and Christians in Twelfth-century Europe*, ed. M. A. Signer and J. Van Engen, Notre Dame Conferences in Medieval Studies 10 (Notre Dame, 2001), pp. 77–93.

101 Young girls were a category to which *ad status* sermons might be addressed, for example. See Biller, 'Abundance and Scarcity of Food in the Inquisition Records of Languedoc', p. 276.

102 For legislation from Languedoc, see above, p. 39 n. 57.

and was called Jacques'.[103] Around the same time, Peter of Gaillac had heard gossip that Jordan of Ravat had been received by 'a certain young heretic who was not known in the region'.[104]

Young deponents were no more or less vocal about their beliefs than their older contemporaries, and it is thus difficult to single out any features of belief particular to young people. It is occasionally possible to discern something of adult attitudes towards the young, though. The mother and brother of Guillemette Clergue of Montaillou were quick to associate youth with ignorance and naivety, at least in order to win an argument. Guillemette recalled in her deposition a conversation she had had with those two about faith, during which they had praised and commended the good men to her. When she proved resistant they branded her silly and uninformed, her mother telling her 'it is obvious that you are young, and ignorant'.[105] Out shopping one day in around 1302, Alazais Adémar's son Raymond was commended to her. Rixende Palharesa told her that 'she very much loved her, because she had such a good son, who had so much grace [*gratia*] – although he was only a youth – that he should go with the good Christian William Autier'.[106] Alazais's son was exceptional, a praiseworthy anomaly and a real-life embodiment of the *puer senex* trope.[107] *Gratia* and, more broadly, an interest in religious matters were clearly not thought by Rixende to be characteristics of youth.

It is no accident that the chapter on youth is this book's most brief. Youths are – quite frankly – hard to find in the depositions. This is not because the men and women who gave them had no concept of youth, nor that it went unrecognised in the court. There can be little doubt that 'youth' had a distinctive meaning to the people of thirteenth-century Languedoc. Young people identified with others similar to them, and many older deponents distinguished between themselves and youths. Indeed, some stereotypes of the young – foolish, ignorant, and apathetic – seem remarkably similar to those held today. Yet religious leaders exhibited little interest in young adults; all those old enough to understand were subject to the same rights and responsibilities. Good men did not single the young out in their preaching, and young people were expected to show little interest in religious matters.

For many young men linked to the Cathar movement, youth was a time of discovery. For such people, the independence and responsibility associated

103 GA, p. 112.

104 He had also heard that the heretic 'went publicly by day', which unusual occurrence by the fourteenth century might be explained by the good man's youth and lack of notoriety: ibid., p. 354.

105 'bene apparet quod iuvenis es et nescia': JF, II, 335.

106 'dicta Ramunda dixit quod multum diligebat eam, quia habebat ita bonum filium, qui habebat tantam gratiam, cum adhuc iuvenis esset, quod cum Guillelmo Auterii, qui erat bonus christianus, iret': ibid., I, 313.

107 Burrow, *The Ages of Man*, chapter 3.

with employment offered new opportunities and obligations, religious as well as secular. Their interactions with people outside their family circle were no longer as passive as in childhood. Young men served, guided, worked alongside and debated with the good men. Youth remained a period of reduced independence, and so deponents were doubtless careful to emphasise to inquisitors that these associations were often formed on their parents' or their master's instruction. Yet whoever initiated them, links formed during this period would often last for many years.

Adolescence, then, was a time of increased freedom for boys – released from the obedience of childhood and as yet unbound by the responsibilities of matrimony. Girls – particularly noble girls – may have been less likely to experience this freedom, for it seems that they tended to marry young.[108] Yet the deposition record tells us little about their lives, and so this chapter has concentrated on young men. To understand why the evidence is weighted in this way, we must return briefly to Guillemette Clergue. Reading on from the jibes of her family, one discovers that this philistine and foolish young girl was also a wife. Her deposition reveals that Guillemette warned her mother and brother not to tell her husband about their conversation, saying he would kill her if he knew of it.[109] Indeed, it seems that Guillemette's self-perception reflected this dual identity as both wife and youth. She related a visit to attend mass at Prades (a visit for which she asked her husband's permission). There, she dined in her uncle's house, and after the meal 'played and danced' with the 'other youths and girls' of the town.[110] This is a tantalising glimpse into medieval 'youth culture' of which Guillemette formed a natural part, and it highlights a striking shift between carefree adolescent and controlled young wife.[111] Guilemette's tale does not indicate conflict between these two identities, though, for both she and her contemporaries accepted both. Like her, many young women were probably seen by their contemporaries as both immature adults and wives. Of these overlapping identities it was the latter which defined them, though. Whilst many of the wives described in the depositions were likely young women, it is almost always impossible to identify them as such, and so their stories remain untold.

In fact, 'youth' was only ever one of a set of interweaving identities for the deponents in this chapter. It always existed in parallel with other more

108 See pp. 96–8, below.

109 JF, II, 335.

110 Ibid., II, 338: '… et post prandium ipsa que loquitur cum aliis iuvenibus et puellis dicti loci de Pradis luserunt et duxerunt coreas'.

111 Le Roy Ladurie may have been referring to Guillemette's testimony when he wrote that 'In Prades d'Allion … young people of fifteen and over formed a specific age group, with their own dances and games at festival times': *Montaillou* (En), p. 216. He suggests that these groups may have existed in Montaillou, but argues that marriage patterns and 'the stifling *domus* system' meant that these groups were relatively powerless and short-lived.

powerful identities: apprentice, squire, pupil, servant, son or daughter. Adolescence was a liminal stage that bridged the gap between childhood and full maturity. Young people were given some adult responsibilities and could take a more active role than children, yet they were not really fully independent and were treated with leniency by inquisitors because of this. Opportunities increased for young people, but conflicting expectations and insecure statuses limited their role within the community.

3

Marriage

Picture the scene. It is some time in the late twelfth century, and we are in the French Pyrenees. In the spa town of Ax-les-Thermes, Arnold Weaver, a doctor and sometime notary from nearby Lordat, is in the square. He is approached by an older man, who looks to be in his fifties.[1] It is his father-in-law Peter, another notary. There is tension in the air. 'Arnold,' Peter says, 'you are not on good terms with me, or with your wife Guillemette, my daughter. You are harsh and cruel [to her], and you're doing this against Scripture, which teaches that a man should be peaceful, gentle and agreeable.' Arnold will have none of this: 'It's usually your daughter's fault,' he tells Peter. 'She is bad-tempered and a gossip.' Peter seems to have no answer, and the conversation takes a surprising lurch. 'Arnold,' Peter interjects, 'it says this in the Gospel of St John, "In the beginning was the word" …'. The subsequent exchange on the interpretation of scripture and the quality of each other's Latin is entertaining, but Guillemette does not come up again, and so we shall leave them as they walk on out of the town.[2]

This brief story, which began Arnold's testimony before bishop-inquisitor Jacques Fournier in December 1321, offers a glimpse into the workings of a fourteenth-century marriage.[3] The exchange reveals that, in Peter's mind at least, a married couple should be on good terms, live peaceably and that a husband should be gentle and kind. Arnold, for his part, expected his wife to be quiet and obedient and to accept his authority without question. The two men were well versed in scripture, and they would have found little there to contradict any of these ideas. Both would no doubt have agreed with Church teaching that a husband could legitimately chastise his wife if necessary, and with its censure of 'excessive' cruelty.[4] It was universally accepted that marriage was an unequal partnership in which the husband was in a position of superiority. Peter and Arnold probably did not differ in

1 See Lambert, *The Cathars*, p. 234.

2 The encounter can be found at JF, II, 213.

3 For another treatment see Le Roy Ladurie, *Montaillou* (En), p. 193; *Montaillou* (Fr), p. 281.

4 On separation from abusive partners, see J. A. Brundage, 'Domestic Violence, Medieval and Modern', in *Violence in Medieval Society*, ed. R. W. Kaeuper (Woodbridge, 2000), pp. 183–97; R. Schnell and A. Shields, 'The Discourse on Marriage in the Middle Ages', *Speculum* 73 (1998), 771–86.

their fundamental beliefs about marriage, but they had different interpretations of Arnold's actions. Arnold asserted his right to punish proportionately, whilst Peter was opposed to what he saw as excessive cruelty.[5] The latter's concern challenges some of our preconceptions about medieval relations between husband and wife; not least that domestic abuse was commonplace and universally accepted.

Peter and Arnold's brief encounter has thus far been presented as a simple exchange between a parent and his son-in-law. The two men's family relationship is an entirely valid framework within which the conversation gains meaning, but there is more here than meets the eye. At the time of their conversation, Peter (surname Autier) was only a few years away from leading the last and most successful revival of the Cathar faith in Languedoc since the fall of Montségur.[6] As we shall see below, he would be deeply critical of the institution of marriage in this new career, speaking of it with open disgust. Although matters of faith bore heavily on his mind even during this conversation with his son-in-law, he remained concerned with his married daughter's welfare, and sought to enforce his ideas about what her marriage should be like.

It does not seem far-fetched to imagine that there was some conflict between Peter's personal feelings and his developing Cathar ethics during his encounter with Arnold. Amongst ordinary followers of the good men the conflict between Catholicism, Catharism and conventional morality was, if anything, more pronounced. Yet married couples were among some of the strongest and most stable supporters that the good men ever found.

The complex and sometimes conflicted experiences of marriage and married life for those within the Cathar community are explored in this chapter in three sections. The first examines the social and cultural contexts of marriage, looking both at demographics – who got married, and to whom – and at the wedding ceremony itself. The second section investigates teaching about marriage by both the Catholic Church and the good men, asking what men and women in Languedoc knew about this and how they responded to it. The last considers the ways in which religious affiliation affected the lives of married men and women in a practical sense, looking first at those who hosted the good men in their homes and the impact on their lives this could have, and then at those for whom marriage and religious belief became irreconcilable.

Sexual relations are one thing that is not discussed in this chapter. Readers of *Montaillou* may be surprised at this omission; did not Le Roy Ladurie demonstrate that the deposition registers are brimming with juicy details? In fact, he did not. There is not much on the subject in Fournier's register

5 On this point Arnold's mind was not changed by the exchange with Peter. For further violence towards his wife after this conversation, see JF, II, 197.

6 See Lambert, *The Cathars*, pp. 230–71.

beyond testimonies about William Bélibaste and Peter Clergue, and even if we were to accept the rather leery accounts of their exploits at face value, it would be misguided to conclude that their adventures were inspired by religious sentiment. As Christopher Brooke has pointed out, 'there are more authentic things in *Montaillou* than [Peter Clergue's self-serving ideas about sex]'.[7] In earlier registers, there is even less to go on. Although the good men talked about it quite a lot, the deponents themselves were entirely silent about sex, and so, therefore, shall I be.

Social and cultural contexts

'God of Abraham, God of Isaac and God of Jacob,' reads one of the standard medieval marriage benedictions known as the Blessing of Tobias, 'bless these adolescents.'[8] Statutes issued at the synod of Nîmes in 1252 stated that children could be engaged to marry after the age of seven, though they could be promised by their parents at an even earlier age.[9] The statutes also note that the legal ages of marriage were twelve 'for a girl' ('in puella') and fourteen 'for a male' ('in masculo').[10] Yet such legislation can describe only the limits of a phenomenon, and benedictions reveal more about ideal than reality. One need only compare the modern legal minimum age for marriage in UK law – sixteen (with parental consent) – with the actual average age at marriage – around thirty – to see that normative evidence has the potential to mislead.[11]

Modern marriage is characterised by increasingly late marriage for both girls and boys, with a high proportion of both sexes never marrying. This 'European' marriage pattern emerged at some point following the end of the fourteenth century.[12] Things were very different in the Middle Ages. Work

7 See C. Brooke, *The Medieval Idea of Marriage* (Oxford, 1989), pp. 157–62. Note, however, that the term *amasia* (lover, or mistress) regularly occurs in MS 609.

8 On the origin of this, see J.-B. Molin and P. Mutembe, *Le rituel du mariage en France du XIIe au XVIe siècle*, Theologie historique 26 (Paris, 1974), pp. 265–6.

9 Nîmes (etc.), 1252 [141]: SS, p. 378.

10 Nîmes (etc.), 1252 [142]: ibid., p. 378. As we have already seen (above, pp. 65–8), the ages of majority at twelve and fourteen were well known in the social and legal traditions of Languedoc.

11 Data from the Office of National Statistics puts the average (mean) age of first marriage in England and Wales in 2011 as 32.1 for men and 30.1 for women. See http://www.ons.gov.uk/ons/publications/re-reference-tables.html?edition=tcm%3A77–292280: accessed 24 July 2013.

12 The seminal article is J. Hajnal, 'European Marriage Patterns in Perspective', in *Population in History: Essays in Historical Demography*, ed. D. V. Glass and D. E. Eversley (London, 1965), pp. 100–43. For problems with Hajnal's statistical methods, see R. M. Smith, 'Some Reflections on the Evidence for the Origins of the "European Marriage Pattern" in England', in *The Sociology of the Family: New Directions for Britain*, ed. C. Harris (Keele, 1979), pp. 74–112.

on a fifteenth-century census from Tuscany has revealed a 'Mediterranean' pattern of marriage in which almost all of the female population married in the mid-teens, whilst men married later, many remaining life-long bachelors.[13] Men and women in northern Europe, by contrast, both seem to have married significantly later.[14] In both regions, relative economic and social freedom allowed city dwellers to delay marriage for longer than their urban counterparts.[15]

The evidence for marriage patterns in Languedoc itself is 'pitifully sparse'.[16] Le Roy Ladurie concluded that Montaillou and its region followed the 'Mediterranean' pattern.[17] A study of fourteenth- and fifteenth-century marriage contracts from the city of Toulouse confirms that girls married earlier than boys, at around fifteen or sixteen, whilst John Mundy found evidence to suggest that in 'the age of the Cathars', Toulousan 'wives were smaller and younger at marriage than their husbands'.[18] The inquisitors' registers contain some incidental evidence on the realities of marriage. In 1246, Blanche, widow of a knight from Montesquieu, told the inquisitors that she had left her father's home in Laurac at the age of fourteen.[19] Aude Faure told Jacques Fournier that she was seventeen or eighteen years old when she married in 1310.[20] Raimonde, who had grown up in the village of Prades

13 D. Herlihy and C. Klapisch-Zuber, *Tuscans and their Families: A Study of the Florentine Catasto of 1427* (New Haven, 1985). The English edition is an abridged translation of D. Herlihy and C. Klapisch-Zuber, *Toscans et leurs familles: une étude du catasto florentin de 1427* (Paris, 1978). See also, R. M. Smith, 'The People of Tuscany and Their Families in the Fifteenth Century: Medieval or Mediterranean?', *Journal of Family History* 6 (1981), 107–26.

14 On the thirteenth and fourteenth centuries see R. M. Smith, 'Hypothèses sur la nuptialité en Angleterre aux XIIIe–XIVe siècles', *Annales: ESC* 38 (1983), 107–36. On the later fourteenth and fifteenth centuries: Goldberg, *Women, Work and Life Cycle in a Medieval Economy*, chapter 5, pp. 203–79.

15 This is only a rough caricature of a much more nuanced argument. In particular it is important to note that the sexes were not always affected equally. Urban and rural patterns in Tuscany are discussed in Herlihy and Klapisch-Zuber, *Tuscans and their Families*, pp. 215–18. Rural models are contrasted with urban in Goldberg, *Women, Work and Life Cycle in a Medieval Economy*, pp. 243–51.

16 J. H. Mundy, *Men and Women at Toulouse in the Age of the Cathars* (Toronto, 1990), p. 81.

17 Le Roy Ladurie, *Montaillou* (Fr), p. 277 n. 3. For his conclusions in general, see Le Roy Ladurie, *Montaillou* (Fr), pp. 275–8; *Montaillou* (En), pp. 189–91.

18 G. Laribière, 'Le mariage à Toulouse au XIVe–XVe siècles', *Annales du Midi* 79 (1967), 335–61 (at p. 350); J. H. Mundy, 'Le mariage et les femmes à Toulouse au temps des Cathares', *Annales ESC* 42 (1987), 117–34. Much of this material is explored at greater length in chapters 4 and 5 of Mundy, *Men and Women at Toulouse in the Age of the Cathars*.

19 MS 609, fol. 108v; cited in Mundy, *Men and Women at Toulouse in the Age of the Cathars*, p. 82. Mundy states that she had left in order to marry; the deposition does not say this.

20 This was of relevance only because at this age she had not yet received communion. She told her husband that it was not local custom for young men and women to receive: JF, II, 82–3.

d'Alion at the close of the thirteenth century, told the inquisitors that she had left the house of her mother when she was fourteen or fifteen years old in order to marry.[21] Exceptionally young wives did not always cohabit with their partners straight away. One of the deponents before the inquiry of 1245–46 told her interrogators that she had not seen her first husband receive the *consolamentum* when he died because she was young then, 'and did not yet live with [him]'.[22]

Not all marriages were first marriages; indeed, second and subsequent unions were common. They were frowned upon by the Church, and even the most celebratory of works about matrimony took care to explain their spiritual deficiencies.[23] A papal decree of 1234 forbade priests from blessing second marriages.[24] It is worth noting that this prohibition was not much repeated by local councils and is not mentioned in contemporary marriage liturgies.[25] Indeed, there still existed a variety of regional practices in the thirteenth century.[26] It has been suggested that young age at first marriage and a relatively short male life expectancy often led women to remarry.[27] This too is borne out by the number of female deponents who testified about their deceased first husbands.

The inquisitorial archives are rich, and we may learn much more about marriage patterns in Languedoc when evidence about them is mined with statistical rigour.[28] I have not conducted a quantitative survey of deposition evidence about marriage for this book, however, for my primary interest is lived experience, not demography. As Cynthia Johnson has noted, 'it was not

21 She married in 1304: ibid., 2.399.

22 The deponent was 'Pictavina uxor Ramundi Hysarni de Alborenx', whose deposition can be found in MS 609, fol. 191v; cited in Mundy, *Men and Women at Toulouse in the Age of the Cathars*, p. 82.

23 In the *Rationale divinorum officiorum*, discussed below, second marriages were seen as inferior because they did not promote unity, one of the threefold spiritual virtues of marriage: William Durand, *Rationale divinorum officiorum I–IV*, ed. A. Davril and T. M. Thibodeau, vol. 140, Corpus Christianorum, Continuatio Medievalis 140 (Turnholt, 1995), i.IX.13.

24 D. L d'Avray, *Medieval Marriage: Symbolism and Society* (Oxford, 2005), pp. 142–8.

25 Sisteron [51]: SS, p. 208. Of those published by Molin and Mutembe, it appears only in the ritual from late fourteenth-century Avignon: Molin and Mutembe, *Le rituel du mariage*, pp. 30–1.

26 In his *Rationale*, William Durand noted that some allowed a blessing to be given in certain circumstances, for instance, if the woman was a virgin, or if neither of the couple had previously received a nuptial blessing: Durand, *Rationale divinorum officiorum*, ed. D'avril and Thibodeau, i, ix, 15.

27 Mundy, *Men and Women at Toulouse in the Age of the Cathars*, pp. 84–5. Some demographic data can be found ibid., pp. 84–5.

28 It may be, for instance, that some quantitative conclusions about proportions marrying (and perhaps from that marriage ages) can be wrung out from the particularly complete evidence gathered either in Toulouse MS 609 and the Fournier investigations, or in some of the more coherent sets of regionally grouped depositions in the Doat collection.

so much legal rules or documents that restrained people's behaviour as the interests of individuals within a complex web of social relationships'.[29]

Factors affecting choice of partner

How did men and women make their marriage choices? There were various matters to take into account, including financial considerations. In Toulouse, although both parties brought money to a marriage, the share brought by the bride was much larger than that brought by her bridegroom.[30] The duty of male relatives to provide dowries could be a heavy burden, especially for those of higher status but little wealth, but it must also have given those relatives significant influence in the planning of the marriage itself. Indeed, economic concerns on both sides often resulted in the subordination of individual to family will for both parties in the marriage.[31]

This is not to say that personal choice was an unknown concept in the formation of medieval marriages. Free choice and 'marital affection' had become pillars of the Church's ideal marriage in the twelfth century.[32] Liturgies required the priest to establish the free consent of both parties – and even sometimes their love for each other – at the opening of the wedding ceremony. It is impossible to judge the effect of either theological or literary notions on real people's attitudes and practices, but most were probably aware of them to some degree. At the very least, Church law had established an outer boundary to coercion in marrying: explicit or violent compulsion was beyond the pale, and was sometimes accepted as grounds for annulment.[33] One recent study has suggested 'a significant level of personal agency' amongst both men and women marrying in twelfth-century Occitania.[34] Family pressures could still be brought to bear. Yet to say that third parties were deeply involved in the planning of marriages is not to say that the wishes of the couple themselves were summarily ignored, especially beyond the high-stakes marriage market of the nobility. Many may have resented the marriage choices imposed on them, but it may equally have been the case that a couple and their relatives would have had similar tastes or worked out compromises.

One area in which marriage choice certainly could cause problems was that of religion. For members of the Cathar movement there were obvious benefits to keeping marriage within the group, and this seems to be what

29 C. Johnson, 'Marriage Agreements from Twelfth-Century Southern France', in *To Have and to Hold: Marrying and its Documentation*, ed. P. L. Reynolds and J. Witte Jr (Cambridge, 2007), pp. 235, 248–9.

30 See Mundy, *Men and Women at Toulouse in the Age of the Cathars*, chapter 5, pp. 88–112.

31 Ibid., p. 103.

32 J. T. Noonan, 'Marriage in the Middle Ages 1: Power to Choose', *Viator* 4 (1973), 419–32.

33 Ibid., pp. 433–4.

34 Johnson, 'Marriage Agreements from Twelfth-Century Southern France', pp. 243, 248.

they attempted to do. In Le Mas-Saintes-Puelles during the early thirteenth century 'heretical proclivities [led] to the marriage of like to like' – that is to say, followers of the good men tended to marry their co-religionists.[35] A similar kind of 'endogamy of conscience' held sway a century later amongst the villagers of Montaillou. For them the 'understanding of good' was an important factor in marriage choice.[36] People did not always manage to keep relationships within the community, however, and those who 'married out' can be found in the depositions bemoaning their unfortunate circumstances. Thus, Guillemette of Saint-Flour told the inquisitors that she had heard her neighbour complaining in the early 1270s that 'she would be happy for it to have cost her an ear from her head' for her husband to have had as strong a faith as the staunch Cathar supporter Pons of Gomerville. Indeed, she told Guillemette, had she known in the first place that he did not share her faith, 'she would never have been with him'.[37] Similarly, in the early fourteenth century, Bernard of Taix had wept when he told Blanche of Rodes of how he had been 'greatly deceived in the wife whom he had accepted'.[38] He later explained the source of his grief to another fellow-spirit, saying that 'he was not able to talk with her of his secrets and to confide [in her] that which he wished'.[39] The interplay between faith and marriage partnership is a theme which we shall revisit throughout this chapter.

Marriage and Church law

It has often been assumed that marriage in the Middle Ages was very much the Church's business, but for much of the medieval period clerics struggled to exert meaningful influence. Substantial progress came with the Church reform movement of the eleventh and twelfth centuries, whose leaders sought to ensure that the Church had exclusive control over matrimony so that they might bring order and moral rigour to its legislation.[40] Amongst the key principles of their 'ecclesiastical model' of marriage were monogamy, indissolubility, free consent and exogamy (marrying outside kinship groups).[41] Progress on these issues was neither rapid nor uniform, and it is impossible to date the reformers' success precisely, but most commentators agree that by the middle of the twelfth century 'Church courts settled … the issue of marriage, its validity and its qualities.' In France, this monopoly may have

35 Wakefield, 'Heretics and Inquisitors: The Case of Le Mas-Saintes-Puelles', p. 219.
36 Le Roy Ladurie, *Montaillou* (En), p. 184; *Montaillou* (Fr), pp. 263–4.
37 D25, fol. 42v.
38 JF, III, 322.
39 Ibid., 3.326.
40 J. A. Brundage, *Law, Sex, and Christian Society in Medieval Europe* (Chicago, 1987), p. 183.
41 For a summary of this see ibid., pp. 183–4

been achieved even earlier.[42] As a result of this intervention in the policing of marriage, the period saw a massive contribution by canonists to the Church's body of theory about marriage, much of which was technically precise.[43]

During the thirteenth century, the local ecclesiastical councils of Languedoc took great interest in the policing of marriage. 'We decree', declared Durand of Beaucaire, bishop of Albi, in 1230, 'that when anyone is to be joined in matrimony, the priest should announce it three times to the people, saying the names of those to be joined, so that if anyone knows of an impediment, he can say it then, because afterwards he will not be heard. And [we decree] that this should be done on three Sundays or feast-days.'[44] This statute repeats almost to the letter the instructions of the fifty-first canon of the Fourth Lateran Council, which had instituted this practice of reading banns.[45] In Languedoc, the statute was quickly picked up. By the time Peter of Sampson was asked by the archbishop of Nîmes to draft a set of statutes in 1252, banns were so well established that he found it necessary to respond to some previously overlooked practical complexities.[46] He thus set down procedures for their reading in the case of a marriage between a man and woman from different parishes and in those cases where one or other of the parties had recently moved.[47]

Alongside the introduction of banns, clandestine marriage had been forbidden by the Lateran council and local legislators. Marriage should not be contracted, instructed the statutes of Albi, 'unless in the presence of the priest and other ministers'.[48] Whilst the theological basis on which the sacramental theory of marriage was built put great emphasis on the consent of the parties concerned, and thus did not allow clandestine marriages to be dismissed as invalid, they were nevertheless strongly discouraged.[49] In some places those

42 See ibid., pp. 183–4, and Brooke, *The Medieval Idea of Marriage*, pp. 127–8.

43 For a recent survey of canonistic thought on marriage (focussing on the twelfth and thirteenth centuries), see I. P. Wei, *Intellectual Culture in Medieval Paris: Theologians and the University, c. 1100–1330* (Cambridge, 2012), chapter 5, 'Sex and marriage', pp. 247–92. P. Biller, *The Measure of Multitude: Population in Medieval Thought* (Oxford, 2000), chapter 2, pp. 19–59 also covers much of this material. On France, see A. Esmein, *Le Mariage en droit canonique*, 2 vols. (1891), pp. 25–31; Esmein suggests that the Church's dominance may have come as early as the tenth century there.

44 Albi, 1230 [55]: SS, p. 28.

45 In canon 51: *Decrees*, ed. Tanner, p. 258.

46 Peter of Sampson's statutes formed a model for the region. From Nîmes in the north-eastern corner of Languedoc to Arles and Uzès, they also spread west to the centre of the region in Béziers and Lodève: SS, pp. 237–41.

47 In each case, banns were to be read in both parishes. See Nîmes (etc.), 1252 [170], [171]: ibid., p. 392.

48 Albi, 1230 [56]: SS, p. 28.

49 There was much debate in the Middle Ages over whether it was consent or consummation that made a marriage. In either case, though, the initiative was with the couple, not the

who had contracted such unions were subject to fine or punishment.[50] These also stated that those who had married clandestinely could legitimise their marriage with a ceremony 'in front of the church'.[51]

There were several reasons behind the Church's desire to formalise and control marriage. If priests were given oversight of a pairing, they would be able to ensure that it was compliant with canon law; to ensure – as one legislator put it – that 'diverse perils' be avoided.[52] Twenty-five of Pierre de Sampson's statutes dealt with such 'perils', concentrating especially on prohibited degrees of relationship.[53] These were degrees of relationship by blood ('consanguinity') and also of 'affinity', the spiritual bond formed at the baptismal font or during confirmation, or the affinity formed during adult life through sexual intercourse.[54]

All of this relied, however, on the co-operation of couples and their families. Banns were essentially passive tools, and this was not without its problems. So whilst some people knew enough about the laws of prohibited degrees of relationship to exploit them for their own purposes – of which more later – it is not clear that the legislative intricacies of ecclesiastically valid marriage were widely understood.[55] Indeed, even some legislators judged that it would be too long-winded to list all the rules in their statutes.[56] So it was perhaps with the possibility of lay indifference in mind that the statutes of Nîmes did not just mandate banns, but also directed priests to investigate the validity of any prospective marriage.[57]

Church. See I. M. Resnick, 'Marriage in Medieval Culture: Consent Theory and the Case of Joseph and Mary', *Church History* 69 (2000), 350–71.

50 In the case of Albi the punishment was a fine of 10 Raimondin sous: Albi, 1230 [56]: SS, p. 28. In those dioceses which adopted the Nîmes statutes it was 'a suitable penance': Nîmes (etc.), 1252 [144]: ibid, p. 380.

51 Nîmes (etc.), 1252 [167]: ibid., p. 390.

52 Nîmes (etc.), 1252 [143]: ibid., pp. 378–80.

53 Nîmes (etc.), [145–71]: ibid., pp. 380–92.

54 On sex, see Nîmes (etc.), [147]: SS, pp. 380–2, which stated that marriages were to be disallowed and separated if the husband had had previous sexual relations with a woman to whom his wife was related in a prohibited degree. On godparents, see Nîmes (etc.), [152–60]: SS, pp. 384–6.

55 It is interesting to note that the statutes of Sisteron in 1249 ordered priests to teach their parishioners how to calculate the degrees of consanguinity. The caveats are that Sisteron is a little to the east of our region of interest, and that the statute was not apparently repeated in Languedoc: Sisteron [48]: SS, p. 206.

56 Bordeaux 1234 [50]: ibid., p. 68.

57 They were instructed to err on the side of caution and to forbid dubious cases until a fuller investigation had been made: Nîmes (etc.), [143]: ibid., pp. 378–80.

The ceremony

If two people were deemed capable of marriage, according to the Church the best place to hold the ceremony was on its property. In much of Europe, a blessing of marriage was given before the mass in a doorway built onto the side of a church specifically for this purpose. This is the cause of some confusion for historians, as it is not clear whether a marriage described as 'in facie ecclesie' took place 'in front of the church building', that is to say, at a church door, or 'in front of the Church', that is to say, under the auspices of the institution. In Languedoc, though, proceedings took place inside the church itself.[58]

Wedding liturgies from the region employed a common format: exchange of vows, blessing, mass and 'bedchamber blessing' – although there were variations on the order in which these elements fell.[59] The ceremony began with further questions.[60] 'On the day of the wedding', began a twelfth-century liturgy from Cahors, 'they should come at the third hour [i.e. at around nine o'clock] to the church.' 'The priest should dress himself in holy vestments and enquire robustly about relationships'; in particular he would have sought to ensure that no kinship ties between the parties could later invalidate the marriage.[61]

There followed the blessing by the priest of the rings and of the coins which symbolised the marriage contract.[62] After the exchange of rings, the bride was handed over to the groom by a close relative. The groom then gave his bride a ring, saying according to one ritual as he did it, 'With this ring I marry you, with this gold I honour you, and with this dowry I endow you.'[63] Then came the mass, during which the couple received another blessing and

58 This was the case south of a dividing line which ran from Bordeaux-Périgueux to Grenoble. See Molin and Mutembe, *Le rituel du mariage*, pp. 40–4.

59 For an in-depth study of wedding liturgies from the Midi, see Molin and Mutembe, *Le rituel du mariage*. The appendix of that work contains the text of a number of liturgies. Of particular interest are:
- Ordo VI: Cahors, second quarter of the twelfth century (pp. 291–2)
- Ordo VII: Arles, second quarter of the twelfth century (pp. 292–3)
- Ordo XII: Arles, first half of the fourteenth century (pp. 300–1)
- Ordo XVI: Avignon, 1360s (pp. 308–10)
- Ordo XVI bis: Rodez, 1513 (pp. 310–11)

(Ordo XVI bis is an expansion of XVI with the addition of a 'typically *méridional*' blessing for the nuptial chamber.)

60 E.g. Ordo VII, (B), where the questions were about impediments and consent: Molin and Mutembe, *Le rituel du mariage*, p. 293.

61 See Ordo VI, ibid., p. 291.

62 Sometimes the latter was blessed later on in the service. See Ordo VI D.a, D.b, Ordo VII D, ibid., pp. 291–2, 293.

63 Ordo VI E, ibid., pp. 291–2.

took communion. Next, the wedding party processed from the church with the priest, who ceremonially returned the bride to her husband.[64]

The final part of the marriage was the 'nuptial visit'.[65] The priest entered the bedroom of the couple, performing various actions including sprinkling holy water and burning incense, and saying prayers for the couple. During these proceedings, the couple sat together on the bed or even lay in it.[66] This portion of the ceremony bound together the spiritual and the corporeal elements of marriage, and has been seen as evidence that the Church was not as embarrassed about sexuality as is often supposed.[67] It was – to borrow a phrase – a 'balancing [of] the requirements of the sacred and the profane'.[68]

How many weddings followed these liturgical frameworks is impossible to say. Marriage agreements from twelfth-century southern France showed 'little evidence' of ecclesiastical presence, according to one recent study.[69] It has been argued that Occitan marriage in this period was 'a social process, composed of several phases … rather than a discrete act'. It was marked by a social ritual, not a religious one: the man leading his bride to their new home.[70] By the thirteenth century things had perhaps changed, and rowdy congregations at weddings were beginning to draw the attention of legislators. The statutes of Nîmes bemoaned their tendency to say 'useless words and inconvenient things' during the blessings.[71] They also complained that the bride and groom often arrived at the church late – after the mass was over – in order to ask for the nuptial blessing.[72] This suggests that ecclesiastical involvement was considered important even if families wanted it on their own terms. Similarly, legislation which forbade priests to charge a fee for marriages 'even under the pretext of custom' indicates that clerical involvement had financial value to some.[73] The inquisitors' registers provide little further evidence. A deponent before Bishop Fournier mentioned a marriage that had taken place 'in facie ecclesie', whilst another spoke of a conversation

64 Ordo VII H, ibid., p. 293.

65 See Ordo VII, ibid., p. 293, Ordo XII, ibid., p. 300, Ordo XVI bis, ibid., pp. 310–11.

66 Ordo XV (I), ibid., p. 308.

67 See ibid., p. 255.

68 J. Bossy, *Christianity in the West, 1400–1700* (Oxford, 1985), p. 19; see pp. 23–4 for a discussion of the nuptial blessing as a sort of exorcism. See also Molin and Mutembe, *Le rituel du mariage*, p. 269, where it is argued that the dropping of the nuptial blessing in the early modern period was part of a de-sacralisation of everyday life: a move towards the separation of the sacred and the profane 'which the Middle Ages never separated'.

69 Johnson, 'Marriage Agreements from Twelfth-Century Southern France', pp. 237, 248.

70 Ibid., p. 227.

71 Nîmes (etc.), [172]: SS, p. 392.

72 Nîmes [173]: SS, p. 394.

73 Nîmes (etc), [168]: ibid., p. 390.

'on the first or second evening' of a wedding, but there is almost nothing about marriage ceremonies in earlier testimony.[74]

Theologians and canonists took a pragmatic view. Any declaration of marriage exchanged between a man and a woman established a valid union; this was the case whatever form of words they used, wherever they spoke them, and whether there were witnesses present or not.[75] As one Occitan canonist noted, marriage was the only sacrament to depend on will alone.[76] By the late twelfth century, there was agreement: it was 'present consent' that made a marriage, not priestly involvement.[77] We cannot know for certain how many marriages the Church was directly involved in, but it may have been a minority. Indeed it has been argued that it was through preaching, not ritual, that most people in this period would have experienced a link between marriage and religion.[78]

Marriage in religious doctrine

Catholicism

'It is better to marry than to burn,' St Paul had written to the Corinthians, and the Church had adopted a similar position ever since: marriage was a compromise to human weakness, but it was better than the alternative.[79] Marriage had only two legitimate ends: procreation and the avoidance of promiscuity. Yet whilst there was disagreement about the role of women and the sinfulness of marital sex, the canonists and theologians of this period wrote about marriage more positively than has often been imagined.[80] Thanks to the Church's increased involvement in marriage litigation, they began to consider seriously practical problems affecting married people, 'acknowl-

74 For an example of a marriage 'in facie ecclesie', see JF, III, 56. Gaillarde, the widow of Peter Autier, told the inquisitors of a conversation she had had 'on the first or second evening' of the wedding of Bernard Belot and Guillemette Benet: JF, I, 293.

75 See Goldberg, *Women, Work and Life Cycle in a Medieval Economy*, pp. 233–43. He argues that the Church's broad definition of marriage 'was out of step with the needs and sentiments of lay society', because it made binding contracts out of what may have been far more casual arrangements: ibid., p. 241.

76 The others combinations were: necessity alone (baptism); necessity and dignity (confirmation); necessity and order (penance, Eucharist, extreme-unction); dignity and will (holy orders – i.e. the priesthood). See Durand, *Rationale divinorum officiorum*, ed. Davril, and Thibodeau, i.IX.1–7.

77 There had been some debate over whether it was consent or consummation that made a marriage. For an overview, see Wei, *Intellectual Culture in Medieval Paris*, pp. 254–8.

78 d'Avray, *Medieval Marriage: Symbolism and Society*, p. 65.

79 1 Corinthians 7:9.

80 Ian Wei argues that scholars were not 'rabid misogynists', in his *Intellectual Culture in Medieval Paris*, p. 247. See also his discussion of the canonists' views on 'marital affection', ibid., pp. 258–60.

edging the significance of personality and custom in actual situations'.[81] Some liturgies also reflect this positive attitude. In twelfth-century Cahors, for example, the priest had to enquire not just about consanguinity, but also 'si est amor inter illos' – 'whether there is any love between [the couple]'. 'If they have love,' the celebrant was instructed, 'and are not discovered to be related, they should be joined.'[82] In Avignon – as well as five questions about impediments – priests were to ask the couple in turn if they were prepared to serve and be faithful to their spouse, 'give up his/her heart and body … now and always' and not to relinquish the other whilst they lived.[83]

A thirteenth-century liturgical commentary written by a native of Languedoc goes even further than this. The *Rationale divinorum officiorum* was written at the end of the thirteenth century by William Durand, who was born in 1230 near Béziers.[84] His view of marriage was celebratory. Within the section of the *Rationale* dealing with the sacraments, for instance, one finds a passage devoted to an extraordinarily romanticised discussion of the significance of marriage liturgy, and particularly to the giving of rings.[85] The ring was given, began Durand, 'as a sign of mutual love' ('dilectionis'). It was placed on the bride's fourth finger because 'from there, so it is said, a certain vein of blood runs all the way to the heart'. The custom of wearing rings began with Prometheus, he explained, whose ring was made of iron and set with an adamant. Just as iron is the strongest metal, he said, 'so love conquers all', and just as an adamant is unbreakable, so love is unconquerable even by death. Indeed, Durand believed the symbolism of marriage to be superior to that of all the other sacraments.[86] Florid as they might seem, these are not the musings of an unworldly mystic: their author had enjoyed a highly successful career as a university lecturer, member of the papal curia and bishop of Mende.

Such visions of romantic love seem to belong to the genre of troubadour poetry, not orthodox liturgy, but the bishop of Mende was not alone in his celebration of the role of marriage. Sermons on marriage celebrated the insti-

81 Ibid., p. 291 and chapter 5, pp. 247–92, generally.

82 Molin and Mutembe, *Le rituel du mariage*, pp. 291–2 (Ordo VI). The section on preliminaries reads, in full: 'Die qua sponsus et sponsa iungendi sunt, hora IIIa veniant ad ecclesiam; et induat se sacerdos vestimentis sacris, et inquirat de parentela fortiter, et si est amor inter illos. Et si aliquam parentelam invenerit, non iungantur. Si autem amorem habent, et in parentela non inveniuntur, iungantur.'

83 Ibid., p. 309 (Ordo XVI). In a more severe part of the preparation, priests also enjoined those whom they married to remain continent (i.e. not to have sex) until the third day after their marriage.

84 For a brief sketch of his life and career, see the introduction to Durand, *Rationale divinorum officiorum*, ed. Davril and Thibodeau, pp. xvii–xxviii.

85 For what follows, ibid., i.IX.10–12.

86 This comes in a discussion of different scales against which to judge the merit of sacraments. Alongside symbolism, the others were efficacy (which placed baptism highest), sanctity (Eucharist), and conferment (confirmation, orders): ibid., i.IX.16.

tution itself, and the equality of both partners.[87] Not all clerics and scholars shared these positive views, and whilst the popular image of a misogynistic medieval Church is overstated, it is not entirely baseless. Yet whilst some within the Church continued to see marriage as a necessary evil, there was clear theological, intellectual and institutional support for a more celebratory approach.[88] Whilst some equivocated about it, the Church supported and valued marriage as an institution in theory and in practice. For those who followed the good men, things were very different.

The good men

Condemnation of matrimony is amongst the best known of the beliefs espoused by the good men. For them, the Catholic justifications of procreation and sexual continence held little water; they saw no good at all in either of these things. Their position rested upon two interrelated articles of belief: that fleshy matter was the creation of an evil god, and that procreation furthered his aims by creating new corporeal prisons for souls. A misogynistic streak whose theological underpinnings were not always so clearly articulated also placed a taboo on physical contact between consoled Cathar ascetics and members of the opposite sex.

The good men's preaching on marriage was of great interest to the inquisitors, and they routinely asked deponents about it.[89] One of the most detailed responses to this questioning can be found in the deposition of a notary from

87 See Schnell and Shields, 'The Discourse on Marriage in the Middle Ages'. On the importance and influence of preaching in the thirteenth century, see d'Avray, *Medieval Marriage: Symbolism and Society*, chapter 1.

88 Condemnation of sex even within marriage had been a recurring theme in the thought of theologians and canon lawyers, but was less popular in the twelfth and thirteenth centuries. Sex simply for enjoyment was still viewed as sinful, however. On this, see J. A. Brundage, '"Better to Marry Than to Burn?": The Case of the Vanishing Dichotomy', in *Views of Women's Lives in the Western Tradition*, ed. F. R. Keller (New York, 1990), pp. 195–216; reprinted in J. A. Brundage, *Sex, Law and Marriage in the Middle Ages* (Aldershot, 1993), no. III.

89 The questioning is often explicit in the depositions themselves. For instance depositions taken before Geoffroy d'Ablis contain the formula 'asked if he heard the said heretics speaking against the Roman Church or the catholic faith, concerning the sacraments, namely of baptism, of marriage, the sacrifice of the Mass ...': GA, p. 228. Depositions from the 1245–46 enquiry contain many negative responses on this count from which questions can be inferred. The very first deposition in that register contains the following exchange, in which the questions are implicit: 'he said that he believed the heretics to be good men and to have a good faith and to be friends of God, and he heard the heretics saying that God had not made the visible [world] but the said witness did not believe the aforesaid error – of baptism, of the blessed host, of marriage, [and] of the resurrection of the flesh he did not hear the heretics speaking': MS 609, fol. 1v.

Tarascon, Peter of Gaillac.[90] He said that he had heard Peter or Jacques Autier preaching in around 1300 that marriage, as practised by the Roman Church, was a valueless ritual which they had misinterpreted and misconstrued. The preacher used a standard text on marriage, Matthew 16:9, but his interpretation was far from orthodox. Marriage involving a man and a woman could not be the joining of two in one flesh spoken of in the Gospels, he said, because each of the parties quite evidently had their own separate body. The good God *had* instituted matrimony in paradise, but that was the mystical union between an individual's soul and his spirit and had nothing to do with corrupted flesh. True marriage was possible in this world, Autier said, but it was not what the Church called marriage. Instead it was a return to that original union of soul and Holy Spirit, which could only be accomplished through the *consolamentum*. Few testimonies went into as much detail as this, but many people had heard something.

'Marriage is whoring', deponents in the 1240s remembered the good men saying; '[it is] a brothel.'[91] A man could not be saved within marriage, the good men had taught, because there was as much sin with a wife as with any other woman.[92] Domina *Mateuz* remembered it more bluntly – she had heard them saying that a man could not be saved with his wife 'whilst he was doing it with her'.[93] Even after the crusade, the good men were keen to spread the word about marriage. Sicard of Gavaret remembered a debate on marriage between four heretics and four opponents conducted outside the church of Bruyères in 1236.[94] There was nothing in Cathar theology to suggest that marriage was any less harmful to women than to men, although it is difficult entirely to ignore the misogynistic undertone of an argument which focusses on the equality of wife and prostitute and which refers only to the damage marriage did to the salvation of men.

Orthodox writers were wont to claim that the teaching of the good men – along with a lack of ethical regulation for unconsoled members of the community – would lead to widespread sexual licence. Peter of Les Vaux-de-Cernay, who wrote an account of the Albigensian crusade, reported that the heretics believed that no-one could sin below the waist and that they 'said

90 Unusually, Peter – a notary – wrote this deposition himself; the relevant section is GA, p. 336.

91 'matrimonium est meretricium', MS 609, fols. 45v (DT), 66v (DT); 'matrimonium erat lupanar', MS 609, fol. 40r (DT).

92 In the deposition of Ar. Niger, who said that he did not believe it: MS 609, fol. 131r.

93 'habendo rem cum ea', ibid., fol. 130r; translation suggested by Peter Biller.

94 'Dixit etiam quod cum tunc dicti h<eretici> vellent videre Petrum de Montbru et Poncium Vitalis et W. Arnaldi de Vasega, ipse testis de mandato dicti Estolti fecit venire propedictos homines de Vasega addictis hereticis prope ecclesiam de la Brugueira, et ibi disputaverunt de matrimonio, et confabulabantur ad invicem inter se, quo facto dicti heretici recesserunt et tenuerunt viam suam versus Montem Esquivum, … Et sunt X anni vel circa': ibid., fol. 67v (DT).

that it was no greater sin for a man to sleep with his sister than with any other woman'.[95] The former opinion is not found anywhere in the depositions from Languedoc.[96] On the latter, the chronicler may have got the letter of the doctrine right, but he was misinterpreting its spirit. When the good men taught that sex between a woman and her husband was morally equal to that between a prostitute and her customers, they did not mean to praise the latter, but to denigrate the former.[97] In fact, Autier and his contemporaries in the fourteenth century preached that it was a *worse* sin for a man to sleep with his wife, because it was done publicly and without shame.[98]

This was memorable stuff, no doubt, but few who heard such preaching acted on it; most wanted to live conventional lives.[99] This is not to say that they were unaffected, though; as Peter Biller has observed, married men and women who heard their way of life so utterly condemned may well have felt rather uncomfortable with themselves.[100] Others were less easily swayed. One witness – Peter of Luzenac – told the inquisitors in his self-written confession that he had heard one of the good men (though he could not remember whether it was Peter Autier or his brother William) preaching about marriage. 'I do not, however, remember the arguments', he wrote, 'because I wasn't paying much attention, although I contradicted them and they took me for an idiot.'[101]

95 *History of the Albigensian Crusade*, ed. Sibly and Sibly, p. 14.

96 Peter Clergue came close to this sort of opinion, but he was a priest, not a good man, and was probably more concerned with seduction than theology. See Le Roy Ladurie, *Montaillou* (En), especially chapter 9.

97 Sometimes this is ambiguous. For instance, Célestin Douais, discussing 'la doctrine odieuse de l'indifférence des actes' of the Cathars, cites the case of Peter of Mazerolles who confessed 'avoir entendu les hérétiques enseigner que l'homme peut être sauvé "cognoscendo unam mulierem sicut aliam"'. The good man's words might have been a reflection (as Douais suggests) of Cathar 'indifference' towards the mores of lay followers, but they were not necessarily so. A theologically sound Cathar interpretation might also be this: 'any sexually active man has the same chance of salvation whilst he continues to be sexually active – none at all'. This seems to be the sense of the whole item of testimony in context: 'et audiunt eos dicentes quod *ita* potest salvari homo cognoscendo unam mulierem sicut aliam'; emphasis mine. See Célestin Douais, 'Les hérétiques du comté de Toulouse dans la première moitié du XIII siècle d'après l'enquête de 1245', in *Compte rendu du congrès scientifique international des Catholiques tenu à Paris du 1er au 6 avril 1891* (Paris, 1891), p. 13. The deposition in question – not of Peter of Mazerolles but of his wife Ermengaud – is in MS 609, fols. 196v–7r.

98 See GA, pp. 188, 192, 228.

99 Mundy, *Men and Women at Toulouse in the Age of the Cathars*, p. 14.

100 Compare: 'we must conjecture Catharism introducing a dark shadow of sin and co-operation with the devil into the hearts and minds of those many married and Cathar-believing men and women who continued to sleep together and have children': P. Biller, 'Cathars and Material Women', in *Medieval Theology and the Natural Body*, ed. P. Biller and A. J. Minnis (York, 1997), p. 98.

101 GA, p. 374 (fol. 62v).

Self-serving as this story may have been, it nevertheless illustrates an important point – not everyone who heard the good men's teachings agreed with their content. Nor should it be assumed that even ardent supporters accepted every piece of doctrine; on the contrary, deposition after deposition demonstrates that men and women were highly selective in which of the good men's teachings they accepted and which they did not.[102]

What is more, there was no call-to-action from the good men themselves. In Germany – according to the visionary Elizabeth of Schönau – Cathars told people that 'there is no legitimate marriage except between two people who preserve their virginity for the duration of their legal union', but nothing of the sort was advocated in Languedoc.[103] Whilst they loudly derided the institution at every available opportunity, good men in the region did not seek to dissolve or disrupt actual marriages. One deponent in the 1270s told the inquisitors that it was generally suspected that a certain Cale Faure had abstained from marriage because he planned to become a heretic, but this was neither a common practice nor a common suspicion.[104] Occasionally, though, the good men did give direct advice to individuals. Peter Sutor remembered that he had been taught in 1245 by a good-man-relative 'that he should leave his wife and should become a heretic'.[105] In the 1270s, Raymond Hugh told the inquisitors that the good men refused to see one of their supporters because they were 'displeased' that he had married.[106] Pons Coutellier was told by Peter Autier around thirty or forty years later that 'it was a sin to sleep with his wife'.[107] Yet whilst many deponents remembered preaching about marriage, only very occasionally was it applied to real-life situations. It is as if the good men had a clear policy on marriage as a concept, but were uninterested in addressing the reality of existing marriages.

Married life and the Cathar movement

Despite their leaders' abomination of marriage, couples who shared the Cathar faith were often active in the religious life of their community. From

102 On which point, see also Arnold, 'The Preaching of the Cathars', p. 204.

103 *Die Visionen der hl. Elisabeth*, ed. F.W.E. Roth (Brno, 1884), pp. 104–5, quoted in D. Elliott, *Spiritual Marriage: Sexual Abstinence in Medieval Wedlock* (Princeton, 1993), pp. 139–40.

104 'Tamen ipse Cale non habet uxorem, nec unquam habuit quod ipse testis sciat, et hoc, ut creditur, quia ad huc intendit fieri haereticus': D25, fol. 119r–v.

105 MS 609, fol. 70v: 'et tunc … monuit ipsum testem quod dimitteret uxorem suam et fieret hereticus'. The former was, of course, a prerequisite of the latter. The case is also cited by Douais in his 'Les hérétiques du comté de Toulouse dans la première moitié du XIII siècle d'après l'enquête de 1245', p. 13 n. 1.

106 'Sed non vidit eos ibi, quia ipsis hereticis displicebat quia ipse Bernardus duxerat uxorem': D25, fols. 101v–2r.

107 'peccatum erat jacere cum uxore sua': Gui, *Sentences*, I, p. 916.

the earliest inquests, deponents remembered husbands and wives attending sermons and services together.[108] Married couples were also active in the *consolamenta* of their spouses and the arrangements surrounding them, as we shall see in this book's next chapter. Perhaps the most significant intrusion Catharism made into the shared lives of married men and women, though, came in the form of good men seeking shelter and sustenance. To the inquisitors, this was an area of considerable interest.

The Fourth Lateran Council had condemned 'receivers, defenders and supporters' of heresy in the strongest terms, and as such they were subject to focussed inquisitorial questioning.[109] 'The following', wrote Bernard Gui in the *Practica*, 'are suggested questions to be put to believers of the sect of the Manicheans [i.e. the Cathars].' The witness should be asked: has he seen a heretic; where; how often; with whom; when? And then: had he had 'any familiar association with them; when; how and who was responsible for it; also, [has he/she] received any heretical person or persons in his home?'[110] For the deponent who had offered hospitality to heretics, the *Practica* also recommended further questions: '[Ask him/her]', it instructed, 'who he or they were; who brought them there; how long they stayed and who visited them there, and who led them from there and where they went.'[111] This was a profitable area of enquiry for inquisitors because it allowed them to build up a detailed picture of the social networks through which the Cathar community survived.[112] This sort of detailed interrogation is evident in the deposition record long before it was codified by Gui, and it allows us to reconstruct the practical realities of hosting.[113] It reveals a world of negotiation, accommodation and – sometimes – conflict as husband and wife attempted to balance the duties of their faith and the wishes of their partner.

Assistance from the wider community became increasingly important for the good men after the crusade ended in 1229, as increasingly organised persecution drove them into hiding. A swathe of post-war legislation ensured that holders of secular authority were unable to remain neutral in the campaign against heresy, as failure to actively persecute them was itself

108 Abels and Harrison found that in Auriac and Villesiscle between two-thirds and three-quarters of women 'credentes' (as they class them) had had husbands also involved in Catharism: 'The Participation of Women in Languedocian Catharism', pp. 245–6.

109 *Decrees*, ed. Tanner, pp. 233–5.

110 The questions are in Gui, *Practica*, v.I.5, pp. 242–3.

111 Ibid., p. 242.

112 The importance of networks and the expertise of inquisitors in exploiting them has been recently dealt with by Ormerod and Roach, 'The Medieval Inquisition: Scale-Free Networks and the Suppression of Heresy', pp. 645–52.

113 The earliest inquisitorial manual – the *Ordo processus Narbonnensis*, written in 1248 or 1249 – had included similar questioning on 'whether [the witness] gave them [the heretics] lodging or arranged shelter for them ... whether he ate or drank with them or ate bread blessed by them': Wakefield, *Heresy, Crusade and Inquisition*, p. 252.

made a punishable crime.[114] Even ordinary men and women now had to take an oath that they would actively persecute heresy and report it to the ecclesiastical authorities.[115] This atmosphere drove a wedge between the good men and the communities of which they had hitherto been part. Thus, in 1234, the good man Arnold Bos told Isarn Bonhomme that 'we cannot stay in this *castrum*, because no-one here will have us'.[116] In 1242, a gathering of concerned townspeople from Calvirac asked a community of good women to quit their roadside lodgings because of the 'great danger' which their presence brought upon the town.[117] No longer highly visible community leaders, good men and women became increasingly separated from public life. Even as early as 1215, things were becoming difficult. Thus, whilst a woman before the inquisitors remembered that she had seen good men living 'publicly' at Fanjeaux in that year, she was also able around the same time to identify two women to whom she and her husband had given lodging as heretics 'because they left secretly'.[118] Subjects of suspicion, chased by inquisitors, unable either to stay in one place or to travel around independently, the good men became totally reliant on their lay supporters.

Many deponents confessed to having received the good men.[119] The details of these visits were generally negotiated with the prospective hosts by local supporters beforehand. Matters having been settled, the good men (it was almost always men who travelled around in this way) would be brought by a guide to the house of their hosts.[120] Often, in order to avoid suspicion and minimise the chance of discovery, they arrived under the cover of darkness. They would stay for a period of days, weeks or even months, receiving supporters and believers, preaching and visiting others in the area, before leaving once again under the cover of darkness. Using the evidence about these visits gathered by the inquisitors, work has been done to reconstruct

114 See, for example Toulouse 1229 [4–5]: Mansi, XXIII, col. 195, which stated that anyone who permitted heretics in their land 'for any reason' was to forfeit that land forever.

115 Mentioned above, p. 115.

116 D23, fols. 228v–9r.

117 In fact, the women had already been preparing to leave: D23, fols. 68v–9r.

118 'et tunc ipse testis cognovit quod haereticae erant quia occulte recesserant': deposition of Marquesia, wife of the late Isarn of Toulouse: MS 609, fol. 181r.

119 For a discussion of the ways in which the Cathar community sustained its leaders, see Bruschi, *The Wandering Heretics of Languedoc*, pp. 66–74 and pp. 98–9. Whilst she presents a varied picture – from 'hospices' through 'huts' to private residences – Bruschi is primarily concerned with a more institutional level of provision than I have been in this chapter. In general, she sees the process of hosting as a rather more formalised than I do, arguing that the range of hosting dwellings 'all inevitably ended up looking similar to non-Cathar hostels and Catholic places of cult and preaching': p. 98. Whatever form the dwellings took, the good men lodging in them were not self-sufficient, and so the burdens placed on 'hosts' would have been similarly onerous.

120 This sort of evidence evidently informed the questioning set out by Gui in the *Practica* (above, p. 111, n. 110).

the journeys of various good men and women, but far less attention has thus far been dedicated to the hosts.

The widow Blanche of Ferrus told the inquisitors in 1308 that she had often received the good men in her home, 'where they slept, ate and drank'. 'Sometimes', the scribe later recorded on her charge-sheet, 'they stayed for seven days, sometimes three, sometimes four days and nights, and sometimes two.' She saw to their needs whilst they were staying with her, and had prepared for them 'a specific place to sleep in a certain upper-room [*solario*]'. They even had their own 'utensils' at her house.[121] Bruna and her husband Peter sheltered the good man Peter Sans in their house for two months, during which time he ate their food and drank their drink. 'She and her husband provided for their needs,' the inquisitors' scribe recorded, 'and she sometimes washed their clothes.'[122] All this was dangerous, and no doubt expensive, especially as some of the good men had rather refined tastes.[123] Rainier Sacconi – Italian Catholic polemicist and former good man – was of the opinion that the need to compensate for shelter and its associated dangers (the destruction and confiscation of goods) led Cathar ministers to be 'very miserly and tight-fisted', since only the rich could survive in times of persecution.[124] No record of payments made for the provision of shelter survive in the records from Languedoc, however.[125]

The security and secrecy surrounding the visits of the good men became increasingly elaborate in later years. Gaillarde Sicre remembered that one winter's night around 1311 Raymond of Maureville brought a stranger to the house she and her husband shared. The man stayed for two days and nights 'in a secret place, which he entered through a certain opening made in the wall'.[126] William of Rodez and his wife played host to his heretic uncles, Peter and William Autier, in 1301 or thereabouts. Although they could not come in by day – because of the danger – they crept into the town by night. The two men slept side-by-side, his deposition records, 'on a bed which was brought to them by Blanche, wife of the said witness', placed in a lower room of the house, where William kept his grain. He had only had bread and wine to give them, he remembered, and there had not been any fish. In any case,

121 Gui, *Sentences*, I, p. 272, fol. 11r.

122 Ibid., p. 440, fol. 28v. Bernarde Gasc hosted Peter Autier, made his bed and cleaned his shoes and shirts. Bernarde was another witness identified as a widow; the fact that the record describes Peter as having stayed 'in the house of her and her son' implies that her husband was no longer around by the time of his visit: ibid., p. 382, fol. 22r.

123 On which, see Biller, 'Abundance and Scarcity of Food in the Inquisition Records of Languedoc', pp. 263–4.

124 Šanjek, 'Summa de Catharis', p. 47.

125 It would be puzzling for deponents not to have mentioned payments if they had been made, since desire for financial gain could have been presented as a mitigating factor.

126 Gui, *Sentences*, I, p. 606.

William and Blanche had not eaten with them.[127] The notary Peter of Gaillac remembered that he had seen William, Jacques and Peter Autier, along with Prades Tavernier, 'at diverse moments and times ... sometimes for two days, sometimes for five and more' staying in a certain room in his father's house, 'during which time my mother brought them food she had prepared, either with their own supplies or with others'.[128]

If the couple were of similar religious opinions, the good men's nocturnal visits were a shared task, although it has been suggested that the greater part of the burden of hospitality fell upon women.[129] Pons Grand and his wife were obviously in this fortunate position: they hosted, ate with and performed the *melioramentum* to good men together. In 1237 Pons's wife even received two good men in his absence.[130] Other couples were not matched in enthusiasm for the good men. Raymond Roques had welcomed good men into his home, hearing their preaching and performing the *melioramentum* with his then-wife Rixende. It was Raymond's first wife who had begun his association, he told the inquisitors, when she had 'asked him to love the heretics'.[131] Similarly, after they had been introduced to Peter and Jacques Autier, in around 1306, Raymond Peter told his wife Sybille that if these good Christians should come to their house, 'she should receive them well, and hear them, and be careful not to reveal them' because if they should be captured at their house, it would go badly for them. When the men arrived, he went again to talk to his wife and told her that she should 'see them, and hear them speak'. '[If] their words pleased her,' he said, 'she should receive them, but if however they did not please her, she should in no way denounce them or reveal their presence.'[132]

Raymond gave his wife a choice, not an ultimatum. There were other couples who negotiated over matters of faith in this way. 'Asked by his wife', Bernard *Nigri* agreed to receive two good men to stay in his house in the late 1300s. He also 'allowed' her to give them a pair of shoes which had been made in their house.[133] Around the same time, Joanna of Clairac told the inquisitors that her husband Arnold had commended 'a certain man who was a good man, and wanted to come to her house to see her', a request to

127 GA, p. 136.

128 Ibid., pp. 348–50.

129 On this, and for some more examples, see Biller, 'Abundance and Scarcity of Food in the Inquisition Records of Languedoc', where it is suggested (p. 266) that systematic investigation might discover a 'distinct pattern ... [of] girls and women of high estate ... playing a particular role in the feeding of heretics'.

130 MS 609, fol. 26r (DT).

131 'et dixit etiam quor uxor eius prima Alazais rogavit ipsum quod diligeret hereticos': ibid., fol. 215v.

132 JF, II, 405.

133 Gui, *Sentences*, I, p. 780.

which she 'consented'.[134] The two good men who came did not impress her overmuch: although she once made a cake to send to one of them, she put away the blessed bread he sent her, and denied belief in him. In 1309 Bona told the inquisitors that she had often 'urged [*temptavit*] her husband to see and receive heretics in his house and to consent in their deeds'. This persuasion was evidently successful, since Peter Autier and Peter Sans spent 'many days and weeks and months' in their house.[135]

Spouses were not always so easily won over. Bona of Puy's husband Bernard had received good men in their home in the early 1270s, 'which', her deposition records, 'greatly displeased her from the start'.[136] Bona seems to have been won over, though, and told the inquisitors that she had been a firm believer in the good men and their faith.[137] Others were less easily convinced, but swallowed their objections. Bertrande of Lantar told the inquisitors in 1245 that Alaman of Roaix, a man 'condemned for heresy', had called round for her husband one day. He asked her to call for him 'which she did not want to do, but said to her husband "Alamand has asked me to call you for him"'.[138] Otherwise, she said, she had not called her husband. William Faure – who had often had good men in his home, and had lodged them in a barn for a night – told the inquisitors in 1243 that he had often chided his wife 'because she did not want to love the heretics'. Although she had been with them in the house, he later said, he had not thought her to be a believer of theirs.[139]

When persuasion was considered unlikely, deception was sometimes employed. When Na Dyas asked her husband about the 'strangers' who had come to their house, he told her to go to bed and not worry about it. Later, she discovered that they were heretics.[140] It would have been very difficult for husband or wife to keep the night-time visits of good men and women hidden from their partner. This perhaps explains the caution of Petrona Brun who 'could not bear … to bring [a recently returned good man] to the house in which she lived with her husband', but arranged to meet him secretly

134 Ibid., p. 616, fol. 50r.

135 Ibid., p. 378.

136 'quod valde displicuit ipsi testi a principio': D25, fol. 83r–v.

137 Ibid. Her deposition is at fols. 82r–90r.

138 'rogavit ipsam testam quod rogaret maritum suum pro ipso, quod ipsa facere noluit sed dixit viro suo sic quod Alamando rogavit me quod rogarem vos pro ipso. Aliter non rogavit ipsum virum suum pro dicto heretico': MS 609, fol. 212r.

139 D22, fol. 5r: 'saepe increpavit uxorem suam … quia nolebat diligere haereticos'; fol. 9v: 'Item dixit quod vidit Bernardam uxorem eius qui loquitur cum haereticis in domo sua praedicta, sed non credit ipsam fuisse credentem haereticorum'.

140 'et cum quereret a viro suo cuiusmodi homines erant, ipse respondit ei quod non curaret et quod iret iacere. Et tam cito ipsa testis intravit lectum suum. Et post multum temporis audivit dici a viro suo quod heretici fuerant in illa nocte in dicta domo': MS 609, fol. 15r.

in another house she owned.[141] For others, marriage signalled the end of their association with the Cathar faith. After young Raimonde married her husband Bernard of Pujols in 1304, her mother and father instructed her not to talk of the times they had hosted the good man Prades Tavernier. They were cautious, they said, because her new brother-in-law was a cleric, and told her that if she revealed her past contact with heresy, 'afterwards her husband and the others of the household would no longer value her'.[142] These tales of discussion, disagreement and deception reflect a diversity of power relationships within marriages which were governed by personality and circumstance, not normative theories of patriarchal authority.

Religious tensions in some households strained relationships to breaking point. Giving testimony in 1245, Ermessende Viguier told the inquisitors that her husband reproached and 'often beat her' because of her refusal to love the good men.[143] Other men resorted to physical violence against the visitors themselves. Bernarde Farmer told the inquisitors of how two good men had been brought one night to her house at Montgiscard. She let them in, but when her husband returned, he threw them out of the house.[144] Similarly, Peter Pons told the inquisitors matter-of-factly that when he found Guillemette, a relative of his wife, in his house in Baziège, he 'immediately returned her to the chaplain', who in turn sent her back to the bishop of Toulouse.[145]

Sometimes, the threat of violence remained under the surface. After Raymond Borrian and his wife Austorge retired to bed one night in 1234, Raymond's sister and her good-woman companion arrived at their house. 'When she heard the said heretics coming into the house', Austorge's deposition reads, 'she immediately began to weep.' Her husband became very angry, threatening her until she went quiet. Although she did not continue to object, she told the inquisitors, she did not want to talk to the good men 'or even to get out of bed'.[146] Around eighty years later, Gaillarde Sicre was in a similar position. Asked by the inquisitors 'whether she had believed the

141 She appears to have got cold feet about this, however, and did not make the rendezvous: D26, fols. 18v–19r.

142 JF, II, 400.

143 On this case, see the depositions of Martin of Caselis, former chaplain of Auriac (MS 609, fols. 237v–8r), and of Ermessende herself (fols. 239v–40r). Ermessende's case is dealt with in Pegg, *The Corruption of Angels*, pp. 63–4, and in Biller, 'Cathars and Material Women', pp. 61–3.

144 'quando vir suus qui erat foris in platea invenit ibi dicitis hereticis expulit eos de domo': MS 609, fol. 108r (DT).

145 Guillemette is described as a 'consanguinea' of the deponent's wife. The next deponent in the register, William Paire, also claimed to have refused Guillemette, whom he said was his wife's sister, and to have returned her with Peter to the chaplain: ibid., fols. 58v–9r (DT).

146 'quando ipsa testis audivit dictas hereticas intrantes dictum domum incepit statim lacrimari et ideo vir suus fuit multum cominatus ipsam et fecit ipsam tacere sed ipsa testis non voluit loqui dictis hereticabus nec etiam surgere de lecto': ibid., fol. 236v.

heretics were good men, or had a good faith, in which a man could be saved', she said that she had not: in fact, as her deposition records, 'the things which she saw and knew of the aforesaid, she did through fear of her husband'.[147] Another deponent had her sentence commuted on similar grounds: she was spared prison because of her young children 'and because her husband – whom she was afraid of – made her do [these things]'.[148] Fear also plays a part in the deposition of Raymond Saur, who told the inquisitors in 1245 that when two good men had sought shelter with him one night six years previously he had turned them away 'on account of the fear of Raimonde, wife of him the witness, who hated the heretics'.[149]

Unfortunately for Ermessende and other women like her, heresy was not grounds for divorce.[150] Indeed, there were very few legal options for couples whose relationship broke down – the Church considered marriages to be unbreakable as long as both parties lived. This inflexibility can be traced back to the eleventh-century reform movement, whose drive for clerical celibacy had created a class of legislators fundamentally unsympathetic towards the experiences of ordinary married Catholics.[151] Nevertheless, there were two main options for couples seeking separation, which fell under the single term 'divortium' – 'divorce'.[152] The first type of divorce would today be called annulment; parties to this sort of dissolution were permitted to remarry on the grounds that their original 'marriage' had not been valid in the first place. The second type of divorce is more properly thought of as sanctioned estrangement. Remarriage was only allowed in a very small number of such cases, but the process allowed couples for whom married life had become impossible to live apart, exempt from the 'conjugal debt'.[153] Domestic abuse was an accepted cause for this type of separation. Arrangements in Languedoc were not always so formal. One deponent gave testimony in 1245 that her husband

147 Gui, *Sentences*, I, p. 606.

148 Ibid., p. 216, fol. 5r.

149 'propter timorem Rixende uxoris ipsius testis que habebat hodio hereticos': MS 609, fol. 234v. Although Raymond had acquiesced to his wife's fear that night, things had gone his way earlier. He told the inquisitors that he had welcomed the good men into his house 'two or three times'.

150 P. Diehl, P. Landau and J. Mueller, 'Heresy as Grounds for Divorce', in *Proceedings of the Ninth International Congress of Medieval Canon Law, Munich, 13–18 July 1992*, Monumenta iuris canonici 10 (Vatican City, 1997), pp. 975–6.

151 Only a clergy completely divorced from the world of intimate relationships with the opposite sex, the argument goes, would have had the discipline – and lacked the sympathy – necessary to enforce the indissolubility of marriage: d'Avray, *Medieval Marriage: Symbolism and Society*, pp. 88–91.

152 Esmein, *Mariage en droit canonique*, II, 85–9.

153 See Brundage, *Law, Sex, and Christian Society in Medieval Europe*, pp. 199–203 (early decretists), 242–5 (Gratian), 288–9 (Decretists). See also Esmein, *Mariage en droit canonique*, II, 73–9 (Gratian) and chapter 2 (pp. 45–98) as a whole. For a discussion of causation, see d'Avray, *Medieval Marriage: Symbolism and Society*, pp. 74–130.

(whom she had previously claimed to be dead and buried) 'is alive and lives with his first wife at Montgaillard'.[154] It is unclear what sort of reality these few words describe, but whatever the deponent's husband was doing, it was unlikely to have met with Church approval. A particularly humiliating punishment was enforced for bigamists in Albi, where – if they did not pay a fine – they were to be flogged naked through the streets.[155]

Officially sanctioned dissolution was not unheard of, and there were various means for astute men and women to obtain it. Perhaps the easiest method to obtain a 'divorce' was through the discovery – or pretended discovery – that a marriage was invalid. The list of potential impediments to marriage was so lengthy that identifying one was often easy. Canon lawyers lamented this, believing that it devalued the sacrament of marriage by allowing it to be made and broken at will. One commented that the practice of employing false witnesses in divorce proceedings was widespread in France.[156] To reduce the number of divorces, the Fourth Lateran Council had cut the prohibited degrees of relationship in Lateran IV to a more manageable level.[157] The system was still open to exploitation, though, as one deponent found out in 1323, after he was approached by a lawyer friend to testify to the (fictitious) claim that his daughter's marriage was invalidated by an earlier union.[158]

The good men had no complicated regulations: all marriages were equally valueless to them. For some, Catharism thus represented an escape from the demands of home and family. One deponent remembered how as a young woman in 1206 she had 'fled' from her husband to a cloistered Cathar community.[159] Another, Alazais, remembered from around the same time (*c.* 1209) that her mother had left her father to become a good woman, coming back

154 MS 609, fol. 212r, deposition of Rixende 'uxor quondam Ramundi P. dels Sagues': 'Requisita dixit quod vir eius mortuus fuit tholose in pariochia Sancti Stephani. Postea dixit quod eius vivus et manet et manet [sic] cum prima uxore apud montem Gualhardum.'

155 Albi [59]: SS, pp. 30 and 31 n. 1 This punishment was usually elsewhere reserved for adulterers, and was not an unfamiliar sight in Toulouse, apparently. See also Mundy, *Men and Women at Toulouse in the Age of the Cathars*, p. 128 n. 45.

156 John W. Baldwin, *Masters, Princes, and Merchants: The Social Views of Peter the Chanter & His Circle*, 2 vols. (Princeton, 1970), I, 334–5. The canonist Henry of Susa (Hostiensis) gave an example of this practice, also from France, which is discussed in d'Avray, *Medieval Marriage: Symbolism and Society*, pp. 109–10.

157 Canon 50 'On the restriction of prohibitions to matrimony': *Decrees*, ed. Tanner, pp. 257–8.

158 Although the deponent claimed to have refused, the marriage was annulled anyway with the support of eight other 'witnesses' to the earlier marriage. An initial idea to claim impotence on the part of the husband was dismissed, as the girl would have had to undergo (and presumably fail) a physical examination: JF, III, 56–7.

159 'dixit quod ipsa tesitis aufugit a viro suo et venit ad domum Gualharde et sociarum suarum hereticarum': testimony of 'Dulcia quondam uxor Peter Fabri', MS 609, fols. 184v–5r.

secretly to take her young daughter with her.[160] As late as 1246, the servants in one house were gossiping about how their mistress's daughter had 'loved the heretics so much that she had left her husband and wished to become a female heretic'.[161] William Peter Barba had told the inquisitors in the previous year that his wife Raimonde had been a heretic and that 'it was said' that she had been burnt at Montségur – clearly the two were no longer close; perhaps Raimonde was another fugitive from marriage.[162] Another possible late example is that of Pons Viguier, who told the inquisitors in 1246 that 'this year, within the month' his wife had left him to become a heretic – or so he believed – and he had not seen her after.[163]

An orthodox parallel to these events might be dissolution of marriage to become a monk or nun. This was sanctioned by the Church, but only after certain conditions were met; both parties had to consent, and both had to enter the religious life. Only this way could men and women take the veil without undermining the indissolubility of marriage.[164] The good men, whose restraints were not theological but social, seem in contrast to have tolerated, and sometimes actively encouraged, spousal desertion.

Some of their converts seem to have tired of the ascetic life and returned to their families. Guiraude del Riu had left her husband for the heretics, but returned after only six months, and another deponent remembered that her sister had 'left the sect and returned to her husband, and was with [him] for a long time'.[165] Peter Jocglar told the inquisitors that, whilst he had been a good man, he had known Ava – who was to become his wife – for three years, during which time she herself had been a 'vested' good woman.[166]

160 'et inde ipsa forneria mater ipsius testis furtim extraxit ipsam testem'. Alazais, at her mother's urging, subsequently received the consolamentum herself: D24, fols. 204r–5r.

161 'audivit ... quod Orbria filia dicte Austorga uxore Willelmi Sans dilegebat tantum hereticis quod propter monitionem hereticorum dimiserat maritum suum et voluit fieri heretica'. See the depositions of Arnold of Bonabac and his wife, MS 609, fol. 200r–v.

162 'dixit etiam quod Rixenda uxor ipsius testis fuit heretica et dicitur fuisse combusta apud montem securum': MS 609, fol. 24r.

163 'Item dixit quod uxor ipsius testis recessit ab eo hoc anno infra mensem istum et credit quod facta est heretica sed nescit ubi, quia postquam recessit ab ipso teste.' Whilst this could be a case of escape for the purposes of death-bed reception, no mention is made of illness, and the phrasing ('facta est heretica') would be unusual were this the case: ibid., fols. 227v–8r.

164 Earlier rules had allowed unilateral abandonment, but only before either consummation or present consent (depending on the theory of marriage adopted). Twelfth- and thirteenth-century canonists further insisted that a couple could only ever separate prior to consummation, although this requirement was often waived in practice. See Brundage, *Law, Sex and Christian Society*, pp. 375–6 for thirteenth-century canonists' views, and p. 267 for the issue of consent.

165 Guiraude del Riu, D21, fol. 190r; Berbegueira Loubens ('Berbegueira ux<or> den Lobenx'), D24, fol. 136r.

166 'Item dixit quod ava uxor ipsius testis fuit heretica induta et ipse testis vidit eam hereticam per tres annos dum ipse erat hereticus': MS 609, fol. 120r.

Frustratingly, the deposition tells us nothing about the courtship these two must have surreptitiously engaged in before their exit. Such depositions present a dichotomy between marriage and heresy, which suggests that those who gave them had been deeply affected by the good men's teaching on marriage.[167] For some, 'to enter into the sect was to leave the family, to enter the family was to leave the sect'.[168]

In the fourteenth century, there is some evidence that the good men had begun to compromise their ideals about marriage. The good man William Bélibaste encouraged intermarriage amongst those who followed the teachings of his Church. It was better, he said, to marry a poor believer than a rich Catholic, because with the former one would at least have something to talk about.[169] In the same period, the good man William Autier helped a follower pick out a date for his sister's wedding.[170] Arnold Piquier also found that the good men were very interested in his choice of partner.[171] He had first been introduced to them by his first wife Mathilde, he told the inquisitors, who had encouraged him to get to know Peter and Jacques Autier and to offer them hospitality. In Arnold, thanks to Mathilde, the good men found a staunch and reliable ally. When Mathilde died in 1305, however, the comforting certainty of their relationship was threatened, for Arnold married again. 'When the aforesaid heretics knew that he had this second wife … they immediately came to his house', in order to speak with her.

Such outright interest from good men in the marriage choices of their followers appears only amongst the latest depositions from Languedoc. Unlike the *laissez-faire* attitude they had displayed earlier, this new willingness to get involved seems to run counter to their own teaching.[172] It could be seen as an example of the laxity and moral decline of later Catharism, but I do not think this is the case.[173] Rather, there are sound practical reasons for this change, which can help explain why theological discomfort was overridden.

In the highly charged atmosphere of the fourteenth century, 'marrying out' had become increasingly perilous for members of the Cathar commu-

167 This dichotomy is also discussed by Biller, 'Cathars and Material Women', pp. 97–8, which uses similar examples.

168 Douais, 'Les hérétiques du comté de Toulouse dans la première moitie du XIII siècle d'après l'enquête de 1245', p. 13.

169 JF, II, 39: also mentioned in Le Roy Ladurie, *Montaillou* (Fr), p. 263 n. 2.

170 The matter at issue was when the moon would be in a favourable phase: JF, I, 291–2.

171 Arnold's deposition is GA, pp. 164–8, fols. 18r–21r.

172 Jean Duvernoy, on the other hand, sees the interest as 'hardly surprising', since marriage – whilst condemned for the ascetic elite – was considered 'desirable' between believers: JF, I, 293 n. 129.

173 The 'moral decline' argument is principally made in two articles by J.-M. Vidal, 'Les derniers ministres de l'albigéisme en Languedoc: leurs doctrines', *Revue des questions historiques* 79 (1906), 57–107; 'Doctrines et morale des derniers ministers albigeois', *Revue des questions historiques* 86 (1909), 5–48. It is entirely dismissed by Malcolm Lambert in *The Cathars*, pp. 268–71.

nity, risking not just the parties involved, but whole networks and the good men themselves. It may also have become increasingly difficult – Bernard Gui's fourteenth-century inquisitorial manual, for example, contains a form for releasing penitents from the obligation to wear crosses 'in consideration of [their] children', to be used in cases where parental stigma was making it difficult for their children to marry.[174] Members of the (shrinking) Cathar community were thus beginning to find their marriage options limited.

These good men's interest in the marriages of their supporters was thus entirely sensible. In the fourteenth century the men and women who attended their ceremonies were no longer simply potential converts but now also providers of physical protection and aid. It was very important to the good men and the wider Cathar community that those followers who married should continue to be available as hosts and guides. This sort of enlightened self-interest may have something in common with the Cathar peace-making efforts described by Peter Biller. In both cases the good men were taking on essentially orthodox roles – making peace and making (or at least giving advice about) marriage. In both they had self-serving motives of their own.[175] It is important to remember, though, that Cathar ministers' interest in keeping people within their faith community was not only a matter of calculated pragmatism. Abandonment of faith because of marriage might put in jeopardy not just the good men's future safety but also the former believer's chance of salvation. Amongst the good men, it was William Bélibaste who recognised this and stated it most clearly. Believers should marry believers, he said, 'because they could then talk between themselves of their faith and sect without fear, and could also receive and support [*tenere*] the Holy Spirit – that is, the heretic[s] – and hear their preaching, and be received by them at death'.[176]

The relationship between marriage and belief in Cathar Languedoc was a complex one. Despite the well-publicised opinions of their Church, most members of the Cathar community were more likely to marry than not. Marriage was – increasingly – the business of the Catholic Church, however. Even those who were not married with a formal ceremony in church were influenced by orthodox ideas about marriage. The reality of marriage and shared life for our deponents was no doubt very different to that experienced today. Women married younger than men, it seems, and often had less choice in the matter than they might have wanted. We should not assume that this always meant that married life was miserable, though. Some couples were compatible, others not; some marriages were happy, others less so.

174 The formula titled 'Forma alia deponendi seu commutandi cruces alicui intuitu liberorum' can be found in Gui's *Practica*, ii.20, ed. Douais, p. 53.

175 See Biller, 'Cathar Peace-making', pp. 12–13.

176 JF, II, 43.

In a minority community persecuted for its faith, religious differences could have a significant impact on relations between husband and wife. Those who shared an adherence to Catharism were often brought together by the common endeavour of meeting the practical needs of a movement in hiding, but divergent beliefs could cause significant tension. This was sometimes destructive to relationships, but not always. Couples worked to accommodate their differences in various ways. Some wives successfully evangelised their husbands, some husbands their wives, and a lucky few agreed to disagree. Whilst relations in some marriages were dominated by fear, this had as much to do with the characters of the parties involved as it did with their religious faith.

The denigration of marriage was an important and memorable component of Cathar preaching, which must have been uncomfortable for many couples. Taking the message to heart, a number of men and women escaped from their marriages into the welcoming arms of the good men or good women. These, though, were only ever a minority within the movement. For most, the Cathar views on marriage were not a call to practical action. Even the good men themselves do not seem to have been much concerned with the vast majority of marriages amongst their followers. This disinterest was expedient. The good men were increasingly dependent on their supporters for shelter, sustenance, finance and protection. Knowing as they did that so many of those on whom they depended were married, the good men perhaps realised that it was prudent to avoid too much disruption. More direct involvement during the fourteenth century is perhaps also best understood in light of such pragmatic considerations.

This is not the whole story, though, because the outlook of the good men and their supporters was conditioned by more than just doctrine and theology. Cathar communities did not exist in a vacuum – their outlook was also shaped by orthodox theology, liturgy and legislation; Catharism was the current that drew them on, but orthodoxy was the sea in which they swam. Many of the good men had themselves been married before their *consolamenta*, and some kept in contact with their former spouses.

Catharism's relationship with marriage was not a simple one. The story is one of the accommodation of a theoretically versed elite to the realities of their situation and the very different ideals of their followers. This process apparently accelerated over time as the pressures of persecution increased. The most important theme of this chapter, though, has been diversity. Rather than trying to produce a single narrative, it is perhaps better to present as a paradigm the man with whom we began – Peter Autier: father-in-law, husband and good man.

4

Death

William, Peter and Raymond waited in the cemetery of Ax. It was a pitch-dark night in late summer 1311, and it was raining. They had been there for some time. The men had just begun to talk amongst themselves when the guide they had been waiting for arrived, leading a man. 'Well, here he is', she said, '– go! … but don't take the Bath road; go by the Old Town so that no-one will see you.'

Taking her advice, the trio left with their charge. They journeyed on into the night, sleeping when they could go no further beneath the trees of a mountainside wood. The following day they travelled on once more, arriving at Coustassa late in the evening. They were tired from the journey, but their new companion stayed up in the room he had been given by their host and was visited by around six of the locals. The travellers did not have much time to rest that night. After midnight, they rose once more and begun the final leg of their journey to Arques, where they arrived as dawn was breaking. Their two-day journey had covered around sixty miles.[1]

The three men each had different reasons for participating in this strange quest. William Escaunier – who had begun his journey alone – had come to seek out their charge, the good man Prades Tavernier. Prades had been summoned to administer the *consolamentum* to William's mother, Gaillarde, who was nearing death. Gaillarde had been so ill that she was entirely out of her senses, so it had been William's godfather who sent the boys on their way. William should have gone already, he said – it seemed now as if he hardly loved his mother at all. William's brother Raymond became entangled with the mission when he gave the companions a meal at his house in Ax. Raymond did not approve of the good men, and threatened to go to the authorities when he found out they who the travellers were looking for. Although he complained vociferously, he came along in the end to see his dying mother. Peter – a young man sympathetic to the good men – was there almost entirely by chance. He had met William in a drinking house on the road from Arques to Ax, and he had offered himself as a travelling companion.

1 JF, II, 13–14.

The story of this dangerous journey contains many of the themes which will recur throughout this chapter. The urgency of William's quest testifies to the crucial importance of the period surrounding death for those who followed the good men. Yet his tale also presents death and dying in all its complexity. The importance and influence of family is there, but so too is the discord and tension that death could bring to the surface; William sits uncomfortably between the aggressive compulsion of his godfather and the discontented mutterings of his brother. Finally, their difficult journey reveals the very real logistical challenges of deathbed arrangements for Cathar supporters.

Death in Cathar Languedoc is the theme of this chapter, the structure of which follows the stages that the dying and their families would have gone through. We begin at the sickbed, a site of great activity for heterodox and orthodox alike. We then move to the religious rituals and practical arrangements surrounding the dying, exploring family involvement in the last rites, a surprisingly formal process by which men and women were 'released' to the good men by their spouses, and the process of will-making, which had particular complications for supporters of the good men. The importance of timing in administration of the *consolamentum* is then considered, as well as a late development, the 'endura'. Finally, we come to the arrangements for dead bodies in the Cathar community.

Sociability and the sickbed

Medieval death, it has been said, was 'a communal event, not a private one'.[2] Many depositions from Languedoc attest to this, including that of William Serre, a deponent before Jean Galand in 1285.[3] Two years earlier, he told the inquisitor, William had been going about his own business when he encountered a boy whom he knew to belong to the household of his friend Raymond William Mathe. Knowing Raymond to be ill, William enquired after his health. The boy replied 'that he was seriously ill … and that he was having his friends gathered together, and that the said witness should go to his said house'. Following the boy's instruction, William found Raymond on his deathbed, surrounded by a sizeable crowd: his wife, brothers, the butcher, some other mutual acquaintances and 'certain others' whose names William could not remember. Bernard Agasse told a similar story. As a young man in around 1256, he had gone with his family to bring in the harvest at Moustajou.[4] Bernard was not involved in the work himself, perhaps because of a

2 E. Duffy, *The Stripping of the Altars: Traditional Religion in England c.1400–c.1580*, 2nd edn. (New Haven, 2005), p. 322.

3 For what follows, see D26, 273r–4r. Some questions have been raised about the evidence in this register – on these, see pp. 18–19 above.

4 D26, fols. 203r–4v.

recurrent knee complaint that made physical labour difficult, and he stayed in town alone.[5] Seeing men on their way to visit a local man whom he knew to be sick, he had followed them, assuming that their visit indicated that the man was ailing. The assumption was correct; the good men had been called, and Bernard stumbled on a *consolamentum*. He told the inquisitors that he did not know what he was witnessing at the time, meaning that he must have followed the men out of curiosity and sociability, not religious sentiment. Self-serving as this denial was, it is quite plausible that he would have wanted to visit the deathbed of a neighbour. In fact, barring friends and neighbours from the sick-room was strange behaviour and could cause offence in thirteenth-century Languedoc. In 1273, Guillemette of Saint-Flour went to see her friend Raimonde, who had refused to see anyone during her eleven-week illness, to tell her just this. '[Guillemette] came there and said to [Raimonde] that she had done wrong, because she had kept her illness secret in this way, because the same witness [Guillemette], and other neighbours, both men and women, would willingly have visited her.'[6] Raimonde should have known that the deathbed was an important social space for family, friends and others: the central point in a great bustle of activity and competing distractions.

Death was also a time of heightened and urgent religious significance. In the last remaining days and hours of this life, the soul had to be prepared for its passage into the next. The Church stressed the importance of repentance and internal reflection on the world to come. Necessary as these were, though, it was better to have a priest as well, who could administer the last rights of absolution, unction and communion.

The ecclesiastical authorities in Languedoc were anxious that laypeople should receive these sacraments. Synodal statutes issued in the thirteenth century set the lower limit for reception at fourteen: 'the age of discretion'.[7] The statutes issued at Nîmes in 1252 revealed that priests should have been given written instructions for the administration of extreme unction. It was to be administered as often as the illness was severe and the patient requested it, erring on the side of caution.[8] In the same spirit, there was an emphasis on general education. Priests in the diocese of Albi were instructed in 1230 to exhort their parishioners frequently on the necessity of extreme unction.[9] The statutes of Sisteron (to the east of Languedoc, in the Dauphiné) decreed

5 Throughout the series of depositions he gave, Bernard was always careful to note that – unlike others present at *consolamenta* – he had not performed the *melioramentum*. He explained – on two occasions – that this was because he was unable to bend his knees ('non poterat flectere genua'): D26, fols. 205v, 209r.

6 D25, fol. 41r. Dating for Raimonde's death is provided by her daughter: D25, fol. 51r.

7 Bordeaux, 1234 [40]: SS, pp. 64–5; Rodez, 1289, [17]: Mansi, XXIV, col. 1005.

8 Nîmes, 1252 [77–8]: SS, p. 330.

9 Albi, 1230 [48]: ibid., p. 26.

that absolution could be given *in extremis* by a layman ('or even a woman'), whether or not they knew the words. It could be given after death, and was not denied even to those who had committed notorious offences.[10]

Extreme unction, the practice of anointing with oil, had originally been administered with the intent that it would effect a physical cure.[11] With this justification, it had been decreed at the Fourth Lateran Council that doctors should summon a clergyman to the bedside of the dying 'so that as the soul is healed, so more easily might be the body'.[12] This was a little disingenuous, though, as unction was generally thought of in the high Middle Ages as acting on the soul rather than the body.[13] In any case, it is unclear how obediently the Lateran's instruction was followed in Languedoc. For one thing, the practice of administering extreme unction was slow to arrive in the Midi, and was not apparently in usage when Roland of Cremona, who had taught at the university there, wrote his *Summa* in around 1234.[14] It was perhaps for this reason – and no doubt also because they had bigger fish to fry – that provincial councils seem to have ignored it until 1252.[15] Some deponents before early inquisitors reported on medics who were known Cathar or Waldensian sympathisers, and some were even practising good men: none of these would have been in in a hurry to summon clergymen for their patients. In any case, as churchmen were doubtless aware, most people – especially the poor and those in rural areas – were unlikely to be attended by doctors in any illness, fatal or otherwise.

The deposition evidence confirms that the last rites were being administered in thirteenth-century Languedoc. Guillemette of Saint-Flour and her friends had found it notable in 1273 that they 'did not see the body of Christ being brought to [Raimonde, the mother of Fabrissa Vital]' in her final illness.[16] The chaplain of Espinas had come to give communion to Guiraud of Laumière in his last illness, testified Guirauda of Roussiac in 1274.[17] Although he had assented when the host was offered, Guiraud had not in the end received: instead he had 'spat it out, and clenched his teeth', she remembered.

10 Sisteron, 1249 [28–32]: SS, pp. 194–9.

11 On the early development see H. B. Porter, 'The Origin of the Medieval Rite for Anointing the Sick or Dying', *Journal of Theological Studies* n.s. 7 (1956), 211–25.

12 In canon 22, 'That the sick should provide for the soul before the body': *Decrees*, ed. Tanner, pp. 245–6.

13 Porter, 'The Origin of the Medieval Rite'. For a thirteenth-century definition, see the Synodal of Rodez 1289, [17]: Mansi, XXIV, cols. 1004–5.

14 See M.-H. Vicaire, 'Roland de Crémone ou la position de la théologie à l'université de Toulouse', *Cahiers de Fanjeaux* 5 (1970), 150–1. A brief discussion at the Fanjeaux conference on this point is recorded in *Cahiers de Fanjeaux* 6 (1971), 391–2.

15 It appears in the council of Nîmes (etc.) 1252 [59]: SS, p. 59. These statutes were much copied in the region.

16 D25, fol. 41r.

17 D25, fols. 181r–2v.

Whilst Guirauda preferred to believe that this was because he was unable to swallow, the chaplain told people that Guiraud had nearly bitten his finger off; he suspected that the dying man was a heretic who rejected the sacrament. In the early fourteenth century, failure to 'confess and make a will' would stir up similar suspicions of heresy about Arnold Taylor.[18]

Last rites

Catholic last rites were beneficial for salvation, rather than essential to it. For faithful Cathars, however, there was only one way to be saved – through the reception of the *consolamentum*.[19] The ritual was simple. The minister placed a book (containing the New Testament or St John's Gospel) at the believer's head, laid on hands and recited a series of prayers.[20] The consequences were profound, though. A follower received this 'spiritual baptism' from a good man, he was purified of material corruption and his soul was free to ascend to paradise once the bodily 'prison' had perished.[21] The consoled were immediately part of the purified ascetic elite, and were subject to the strict restrictions which governed their lives: daily prayer, fasting, dietary prohibitions and total avoidance of all contact with the opposite sex. If these rules were not followed to the letter, a *consolamentum* would be rendered void, denying its recipient salvation. Yet most people were not cut out for a life of ascetic self-denial, and fewer still were anxious to attempt it.[22] The reception of healthy laypeople was problematic, and most were received only on the point of death. Even with only a few days to live, the position of the newly received remained precarious, and the only way to recover once tainted was to go through the whole process again. A Cathar liturgical handbook from the middle of the thirteenth century implicitly recognised this when it made a distinction between the consolation of sick believers and the reception of

18 JF, II, 196.

19 For a lengthy discussion of this ritual, see Duvernoy, *Religion des Cathares*, pp. 143–70.

20 See *Rituel cathare*, ed. Clédat, pp. xxi–xxvi. On the Cathars' books, see P. Biller, 'The Cathars of Languedoc and Written Materials', in *Heresy and Literacy, 1000–1530*, ed. P. Biller and A. Hudson (Cambridge, 1994), pp. 61–82. Of particular interest here are pp. 70–3.

21 In principle, the rite could be administered by anyone who had themselves received it. In practice, however, it was almost never administered by women. Rainier Sacconi relegated the imposition of hands 'a Catharabus' ('by female Cathars') to times of necessity. See Šanjek, 'Summa de Catharis', pp. 43–4. Some discussion of this and other evidence from Languedoc is in Abels and Harrison, 'The Participation of Women in Languedocian Catharism', pp. 226–7, where it is concluded that 'the activities of female Cathars did not ordinarily include sacerdotal functions'. See also Duvernoy, *Religion des Cathares*, p. 163.

22 As Jean Duvernoy noted, in his *Religion des Cathares*, p. 163, '… il est évident qu'on ne pouvait faire du jour au lendemain d'un laïc consolé un véritable parfait de profession'.

healthy persons beginning lives as good-man and good-woman ascetics.[23] Whilst the two rituals were broadly the same, the consolation of the sick remained provisional. If the consoled believer lived, he should endeavour to receive a second *consolamentum* 'as soon as possible'.[24]

To minimise the risk of transgressing, some people had their final days supervised by the good men themselves. In the first half of the thirteenth century, when good men and women still lived publicly, some had themselves transported to Cathar community houses to die. Guillemette of Canast remembered that, in 1211, two good men had come to her house one night, and at the invitation of her mother had 'carried' her first husband 'to the house which they held publicly at Castelnaudary' where '[he] died in their hands'.[25] In the same year, Odo of Quié 'was hereticated … he had himself carried to the house of the heretics [to be hereticated] … and died a heretic'.[26] Tragedy struck the seven-year-old Raymond Arrufat twice in the years around 1215. His dying mother was carried by two good men from Castelnaudary to Saint-Martin, and his brother 'died in their hands' there, too.[27] Raimonde of Roqueville 'fled in a certain illness … and went to the heretics at Montségur and died there' in 1240.[28] There was apparently a misunderstanding in the case of William Deumer, who had himself carried to a renowned good-man doctor in 1220, but took his cure whilst refusing repeated offers of the *consolamentum*.[29]

Malcolm Lambert has commented that giving oneself over to the good men 'resembled nothing so much as oblation *ad terminum*'.[30] At least one deponent seems to have regarded the two as interchangeable, a Sorèze knight who had 'entered the monastery of Sorèze, and … took on a monk's habit' in his last illness. He told Peter Pictavin that he had entered the monastery to escape the constant nagging of his brothers about the *consolamentum*.[31] William of Maillorgues was perhaps less decisive: he committed himself first to the hands

23 It dedicated separate sections to each; see *Rituel cathare*, ed. Clédat, pp. xxi–xxvi and xi–xxi respectively.

24 Ibid., p. xxvi: 'al pusto[s]t que pusca'. The believer was free to decline, however.

25 MS 609, fol. 29v (DT): 'Dixit etiam quod cum Iohannes de Paracol maritus ipsius testis infirmaretur graviter in domo sua apud Castrumnovum Darri egritudine qua decessit, R. Petit et socius suus hereticus venerunt ibi de nocte et portaverunt dictum infirmum ad domum quam tenebant publice apud Castrumnovum de Arrio, Ermengarda matre ipsa testis invita, et ibi dictus infirmus decessit in manibus hereticorum.'

26 MS 609, fol. 18r: 'Item dixit quod Odo frater suus fuit hereticatus et fecit se deferri ad domum hereticorum … et mortuus fuit hereticus.' The deposition is dated 'as above', where the above deposition, on fol. 17r, is dated to 1256 – presumably the scribe had intended to write 1246, but slipped when noting the date.

27 Ibid., fol. 250r.

28 Ibid., fol. 217r: in the testimony of her husband Raymond.

29 Ibid., fol. 246r. After a month, the good man threw William out.

30 The parallel was noted in Lambert, *The Cathars*, p. 242.

31 D25, fols. 267v–8r.

of the Cathars, and later, the Cistercians.[32] There was an important difference between Catholic and Cathar rites, though. Whilst the Cistercians would have been anxious to ensure that any deathbed entrants were not carelessly abandoning marital obligations, the good men did not always need to be so careful.[33] Thus, when her husband had been carried to the Cathar house at Castelnaudary in 1211, Guillemette of Canast told the inquisitors, she had been asleep in another room, and when the sick Peter *Vipatus* was taken away by a good man to 'a certain hut of his' to receive the *consolamentum* in 1225, he told his wife about it only after he had recovered and returned home.[34]

After the crusade, it became dangerous for the good men to remain in one place, and their public 'houses' quietly disappeared. It had always been more common for deathbed initiates to be visited by the good men, but persecution made this the only option.[35] Hence the emphasis of one instruction in the mid thirteenth century Provençal handbook for good men that 'if the Christians upon whom the service of the Church is conferred [i.e. the good men] should receive a message of an ill believer, *they should go* [to him]'.[36]

Family involvement

Once the good men had gone underground, the role of local Cathar networks – and in particular of close relatives – became vital for sick *consolamentum* candidates. In 1245, Arnold Bruno sought the good men 'at the request, and most great urgency of the said Bruno, his father'.[37] His journey was a difficult one, involving much travelling, an intermediary who needed a great deal of persuasion and a moonlit rendezvous.[38] In 1307, Raymond Issaurat made a round trip of around sixty miles to fetch the good men for his mother's *consolamentum*.[39] Some who were involved in guiding and procuring the good men did it for financial gain – like Peter Bauca of Sorèze, who was said to have

32 This case is cited in Lambert, *The Cathars*, pp. 135, 242, and Duvernoy, *Religion des Cathares*, p. 167. The deposition can be found towards the end of the testimony of William of Canast, MS 609, fol. 8r.

33 On oblation and Canon Law, see Brundage, *Law, Sex and Christian Society*, pp. 375–6.

34 MS 609, fols. 29v (DT), 126r.

35 Cf. Lambert, *The Cathars*, pp. 242–3.

36 *Rituel cathare*, ed. Clédat, p. xii: 'Si crestias als quas le menester de la glesia es comandatz si an message de crezentz malaute, anar i devo'; my emphasis.

37 'Dixit enim ipse testis quod ad preces et maximam instanciam dicti Bruni patris sui nunc defuncti quesivit hereticos ad dictum Brunum patrem suum hereticandum': MS 609, fol. 51r (DT).

38 Ibid., fol. 51r (DT) . When he and his contact met the heretics by night, Arnold told the inquisitors, he did not adore 'because there was then too much light' ('Et quia erat tunc nimis lucens, non adoravit'). I have assumed this to mean moonlight – it could also have been early on in the evening.

39 GA, p. 270.

got an 'iron fist; that is, a great deal of money' from his involvement in one *consolamentum*.[40] Family members acted out of a sense of obligation, though. This was behind the scornful comments of William Escaunier's godfather, who implied that by failing to arrange his mother's reception William was failing her as a son.[41]

William did his duty in the end, but those who had fallen out with their relatives had to make other arrangements. When she came before the inquisitors in 1274, Guillemette of Saint-Flour recalled that her friend Raimonde had said 'she loved [Guillemette] above all' because she could provide shelter for the consoling good men. Raimonde 'did not trust that black peasant Raymond Maurel, her grandson-in-law'.[42] Guiraud Terrier of Sorèze was unable to receive the *consolamentum* before he died in the early 1260s because the only man who could give him 'advice' about the good men was his father, who had not visited him throughout his illness. Guiraud confided to a friend that he was 'in a bad way' with his father.[43] Even when they were not directly involved in securing the good men, family members were often confidants about *consolamenta*. William Calvet remembered discussing the matter with his 'ill and dejected grandson', who told him that 'he thought he was going to die soon and wished by all means to have the heretics if it would be possible'.[44] Similarly, Peter Gaubert was keen to assure himself that his brother would concede to his desire for the *consolamentum*.[45]

Such forward thinking was only sensible, for disgruntled family members could cause serious problems in the increasingly dangerous circumstances under which the good men operated. Pons of Beauteville arrived home from burial preparations for his mother only to clash with his brother over her planned *consolamentum*. Pons disapproved, and chased out the good men who had been brought to receive her.[46] Gerald Colomb of Beauteville told the inquisitors in 1243 that he had had similar reservations about the recep-

40 Peter Bauca should have known about a certain *consolamentum* in 1260. Peter Pictavin told the inquisitors 'quia habuerat inde pugnum ferratum, scilicet magnam peccuniam': D25, 267r.

41 JF, II, 13–14.

42 D25, fol. 41r–v.

43 Ibid., fols. 255r–v.

44 MS 609, fol. 232r: 'dixit quod a xv diebus citra Willelmus calveri nepos ipisus testis in firmus et deiectus dixit ipsi testi quod in brevi credebat mori et omnibus modis vellet habere hereticis si posset'. This wish apparently remained unfulfilled – after waiting all night in a field, the two 'fixers' with whom William's grandson was in contact had been stood up.

45 Ibid., fol. 122r–v.

46 He was later asked by his brother if he would like to be himself consoled and 'replied angrily that he would not' ('quesivit ab ipso teste si volebat se reddere hereticis et ipse testis respondit iratus quod non'): MS 609, fol. 129r. The latter incident is mentioned in Pegg, *The Corruption of Angels*, p. 111.

tion of his uncle, and had threatened to have the good men captured.[47] In 1238, Raymond Fizel 'did not want or allow' good men into the house to console his uncle, whilst Arnold of l'Eglise and his friends 'did not want to tolerate' his brother's reception.[48] The climate was dangerous for good men and their followers in the thirteenth century, and deathbed receptions could not proceed against unless the family allowed them to do so.[49]

Surprisingly, securing spousal consent became a somewhat formalised part of *consolamentum* ritual. When the good man Raymond of Le Vaux came to console the dying Raymond of Toulouse of *Darts* in 1231, the first thing he did was to ask Raymond's wife Tolosana 'whether she wanted to absolve the said invalid, her husband, to God and to the Gospel and to the good men'.[50] Most deponents did not mention a book, instead reporting release 'to God and the good men' or simply 'to the good men'.[51] In 1315, Guillemette Benet formally absolved her husband from 'the bonds of matrimony'.[52] The practice was common in the 1270s and 1280s – of thirty-one *consolamenta* described by Arnold Mazelier to the inquisitor Jean Galand, there were only three at which a spousal release was not mentioned.[53] It was evidently well known to members of the community: Castel Faure had apparently been absolved – at the good men's request – in 1278, 'according to the custom of the heretics when they want to absolve a husband in the presence of his

47 Gerald was outnumbered by equally aggressive believers, though, and chose discretion over valour: D23, fols. 152r–3r.

48 Raymond Fizel: MS 609, fol. 193v; Arnold of l'Eglise: ibid., fol. 204v. Another example: the reception of Aceline Sicre was blocked, according to a witness, because 'other people, whom he [the witness] named, obstructed it': Gui, *Sentences*, I, p. 730. Similarly, the reception of Bernarde Mir had to be postponed through fear that her son-in-law would have the good men captured if they came: GA, pp. 230, 326. It did eventually happen, though: ibid., p. 230.

49 It was, of course, similarly prudent for pious Cathar friends and family members to ensure that the sick person whose *consolamentum* they had arranged actually wanted it. If they did not, the situation could quickly turn ugly. Here are some examples of this. When his mother brought the heretics to his sick brother in 1225, Arnold Chavard told the inquisitors, 'the said invalid did not want [to be hereticated], but instead he spat at them'('dictus infirmus noluit immo conspuit contra ipsos'): MS 609 (DT), fol. 143v. Domina Brulhes of *Fassoneiras* 'really did not want' ('vero noluit') her arranged *consolamentum*: D22, fol. 81v. Barcelona of Villepinte's mother was not received in *c.* 1232 because she 'did not want to consent to their [the heretics'] words' ('noluit verbis eorum consentire'): D23, fol. 123r.

50 D23, fols. 299v–300r.

51 Here are some examples. Alsieu of Massabrac was released 'to the said heretics' by his wife in 1225 or 1229: D22, fols. 114v–15r. The release 'to the good men' by Alazais Aravaut of her 'gravely wounded' husband ('dum iacebat infirmus gravi vulneri') in 1221: MS 609, fol. 93r. The release of William Gontrau 'to God and the good men, that is, the heretics' by his wife in 1240: D23, fols. 330v–1v. The release of Bernard Trilha 'to God and to these heretics' (date unknown): D25, fol. 261r.

52 JF, I, 474: 'a vinculo matrimonii'.

53 His deposition is at D26, fols. 157r–90v.

wife'.[54] Whilst many of the examples given here are of dying men released for the *consolamentum* by their wives, it was also 'their way' – the way of the good men – that women were absolved by their husbands.[55] In only one case, from the early 1230s, did someone refuse to release their partner: Raymond of Toulouse of *Darts*'s wife had answered Raymond of Le Vaux that 'she would not [release her husband], and [had] began to cry out'. Unfortunately, we do not know the outcome of her refusal.[56]

For a movement whose leaders abominated marriage loudly and vociferously, this conscientious attention to spousal consent is strange behaviour indeed. The good men did not explain themselves in any of the testimony recorded by the inquisitors, but I suspect this formal ritual of release was above all a pragmatic response to the needs of lay followers. Recognising the importance of marriage in this way may have gone against the grain for the good men, but it must have made things easier for the dying and their families, smoothing transition that might otherwise have been violent and abrupt. There was also a pragmatic element to it. The good men knew that feuding families disrupted many *consolamenta*, and ignoring a potential initiate's partner could be dangerous. Lombarde Lecger recognised this when she told her friend Sybil that 'if her husband heard about [the *consolamentum* Sybil was advocating] he would strangle her'.[57] The ritual release perhaps developed as a way to avoid these problems. It would not have been sprung on husbands and wives with no warning, but must have been the end-point of much discussion and negotiation. Securing spousal consent was also important when the good men were unable to watch over dying recipients of the *consolamentum*, for husbands and wives were likely to nurse their partner in the last days. It was important that these carers were aware of the new rules by which the consoled had to live, for they would be in large part responsible for upholding them; the words of release served to remind them of this obligation.

54 Ibid., fol. 259r: 'ipsum maritum suum absolvisset, et desamparasset praedictis haereticis secundum quod moris est haereticorum quando volunt uxoratum praesente uxore haereticare'. On Castel, 'one of the most notorious of the Inquisition's suspects', whose case became bound up in the turbulent relationship between the inquisitors and the city of Carcassonne, see Friedlander, *The Hammer of the Inquisitors*, chapter 2, 'The Case of Castel Fabre', pp. 39–65. The evidence concerning this man was thus questioned by contemporaries, and remains contested. Were that evidence to be proven false, however, the inclusion and description of this 'release' would become more interesting, not less so.

55 A few examples from the deposition of Arnold Mazelier: Gilles of Bures released his wife Edelina to the heretics 'secundum modum eorum' *c.* 1283 (D26, fol. 181r–v); the unnamed wife of Raymond Clergue was released by her husband *c.* 1278 (ibid., fols. 175r–6r); the wife of Bernard Isarn was released by her husband *c.* 1277–78 (ibid., fols. 186v–7r).

56 D23, 299v–300r.

57 Gui, *Sentences*, II, p. 888.

Consent was not sought in every case, and the good men continued to receive men and women without their partner present throughout the late thirteenth and early fourteenth centuries. In some cases subterfuge was still encouraged.[58] It may have been the case that when a partner was present, release was requested, but when they were not it was conveniently forgotten – that is to say that it was Cathar custom 'when they want to absolve a husband *in the presence* of his wife', but only then. Formal spousal release is perhaps best thought of as a 'compromise ritual'. Claire Taylor has recently used this term to describe the Cathar practice of blessing bread. Consecrating floury dough was 'meaningless to the heretics', she wrote, 'it neither helped nor harmed' in a spiritual sense, but it was significant for the community, helping to bind it together.[59] Spousal release can also be thought of in this way: a concession by the good men to the needs of their followers.

Wills

As they neared death, men and women turned their minds to the settling of worldly accounts. Making a written will was part of the business of dying in Languedoc, at least for the wealthier elements in society.[60] In the thirteenth century, the Church began to push for wills to be composed in the presence of a clergyman, and legislation on the matter was issued by local synods throughout Languedoc. Failure to summon a priest became a cause of ecclesiastical censure, and sometimes barred the offender from Christian burial.[61] In some jurisdictions, those who notarised such priest-less wills were subject to excommunication.[62] The synodal statutes issued at Béziers in 1246 were frank

58 In an example of the latter, Gaillarde Autier told a friend that if she was worried about her husband's objections, her *consolamentum* could be arranged for a time when he was absent: JF, I, 294.

59 Taylor, *Heresy, Crusade and Inquisition in Medieval Quercy*, pp. 195–6.

60 Some studies on wills in Languedoc are: J. H. Mundy, 'Charity and Social Work in Toulouse', *Traditio* 22 (1966); M.-S. de Nucé de Lamothe, 'Piété et charité publique à Toulouse de la fin du XIIe siécle au milieu du XVe siècle d'après les testaments', *Annales du Midi* 76 (1964), 5–39; M. Bastard-Fournié, 'Mentalités religieuses aux confins du Toulousain et de l'Albigeois à la fin du moyen âge', *Annales du Midi* 85 (1973), 270–1.; K. L. Reyerson, 'Changes in Testamentary Practice at Montpellier on the Eve of the Black Death', *Church History* 47 (1978), 253–69; L. Stouff, 'Les Provençaux et la mort dans les testaments (XIIIe–XVe siécle),' *Cahiers de Fanjeaux* 33 (1998), 199–222; M.-C. Marandet, *Le souci de l'au-delà: la pratique testamentaire dans la région toulousaine (1300–1450)*, 2 vols. (Perpignan, 1998).

61 Such statutes were issued at Narbonne in 1227 [5]: Mansi, XXIII, col. 22; Toulouse in 1229, [16]: Mansi, XXIII, col. 198; Bordeaux, 1234, [82]: SS, p. 60; Béziers, 1246, [44]: Mansi, XXIII, col. 689; Nîmes (etc.), 1252, [111]: SS, p. 358; Albi 1254, [37–8]: Mansi, XXIII, col. 842; Béziers, 1286, [30]: Mansi, XXIV, col. 640.

62 E.g. Béziers 1246 [44]: Mansi, XXIII, col. 689 ; Nîmes (etc), [111–12]: SS, p. 358.

about the purpose of these provisions, which was 'chiefly' to ensure that gifts left to the Church should be rendered faithfully, speedily and without fraud.[63] The effectiveness of these measures is questionable, though. The men and women of Toulouse obtained an exemption from the obligation to summon a priest from Alphonse of Poitiers, their count, in 1255. Thirty-one years later, the town's legal Customs stated that a testament was valid 'in the presence of the chaplain or sub-chaplain, or even in [his] absence' – even, in fact, if a clergyman had not been called at all.[64]

In Languedoc, the Church's interest in testamentary practice was heightened by a perception that Cathars drew particular benefit from the wills of their supporters.[65] The chronicler, cleric and sometime inquisitorial witness William of Puylaurens thought that the heretics received more this way than the Church did in the years before the crusade – they even 'took as legacies their [supporters'] entire beds and their clothes'.[66] This was hyperbole, of course, but William was not entirely off track. As Rainier Sacconi noted, money was very important to the persecuted good men.[67] A thirteenth-century Cathar liturgy written in Provençal twice discussed financial aspects of the *consolamentum*. Before a sick person was received, it instructed, satisfaction had to be given for any debt he had accrued or injury he had done to the (Cathar) church. Those who could settle their debts were still received, as in the case of Bernard Oth, who paid Guilabert of Castres 1,200 Melguiel shillings in restitution for his debts to the 'church of the heretics' when Bernard had thought he was dying in 1230.[68] If the invalid refused to pay, he should be turned away – it was fruitless to pray for a lawbreaker or a dishonest man.[69]

The good men were outlaws with no legal protection, and so unscrupulous relatives of the consoled could refuse payment with no legal consequences. The chronicler of the Albigensian Crusade, Peter of Les Vaux-de-Cernay, made little effort to contain his glee in telling the story of an initiate's son who sought assurance that the *consolamentum* had saved his father's soul, and

63 Béziers 1246, [44]: Mansi, XXIII, col. 689: 'Praesertim ut idem sacerdos, vel locum ejus tenens, valeat de ipso testatore laudabile testimoniam perhibere, ne de ipso aliqua infidelitatis suspicio possint haberi; & maxime ut ea quae in piis causis reliquerit, fidelius & citius sine frauda solvantur.'

64 'presente capellano vel subcapellano vel etiam absente seu etiam non vocato': *Coutumes*, ed. Gilles, p. 130. See ibid., p. 130 n. 3 for the exemption.

65 In fact, this was one of the reasons given by the 1234 council of Arles (in canon 21) for requiring ecclesiastical presence during the formation of wills: Mansi, XXIII, col. 342.

66 *The Chronicle of William of Puylaurens: The Albigensian Crusade and Its Aftermath*, ed. and trans. W. A Sibly and M. D. Sibly (Woodbridge, 2003), p. 9.

67 Šanjek, 'Summa de Catharis', p. 47.

68 'dictus haereticus dixit eidem testi quod ipse testis abstulerat Ecclesiae haereticorum et receperat ab eis multum, et quod restitueret illud eis et tunc ipse testis dedit dictis haereticis pro emenda mille et ducentos solidos melgorienses': D24, fol. 87v.

69 *Rituel cathare*, ed. Clédat, p. xii. Those unable to pay were still admitted, however.

upon gaining it decided that he had no reason to pay the promised legacy.[70] Peter's story was intended to make the heretics look foolish and it may well have been apocryphal, but some of the deponents remembered similar cases in their testimony. Peter Fournier was refused the *consolamentum* in the early 1240s, for example, because he had not yet paid the money his mother and father promised at their deaths, and his subsequent offer to pay in wine and grain was also rejected.[71] Another deponent remembered the good man William Autier grumbling of an unpaid debt in the early fourteenth century.[72] Around this time, Gauzia Clergue was chastised by Guillemette Benet for not having given alms to Prades Tavernier, who – Guillemette told her – had gone very much out of his way to receive her son.[73] Yet most people were punctual and honest about payment. Arnold Mazelier, son of a frequent guide of the good men, gave evidence about thirty-one consolations which had taken place between 1273 and 1284, and all but five of these mention some sort of donation.[74]

The Provençal liturgy stated that such donations were to be put at the disposition of the order as a whole, and it is easy to see why such donations were important, particularly once the good men were excluded from legitimate commerce.[75] In fact, as Andrew Roach has demonstrated, the good men gained most of their income from testamentary bequests.[76] Most sources give no information about the form that Cathar testaments took, and so we are left with questions. Did Cathar followers compose their wills in the presence of the good men? Did they write down their wills at all? One man, Arnold Raymond of Douzens, tried hard to convince the inquisitors that they did.[77]

70 Peter of Les Vaux-de-Cernay, *Historia Albigensis*, i.16: *History of the Albigensian Crusade*, ed. and trans. Sibly and Sibly, pp. 13–14.

71 From the evidence of Bernard Gasc, who saw the exchange when he came in to get his candle lit: MS 609, fol. 159r–v. See also Pegg, *The Corruption of Angels*, p. 103. It apparently occurred in 1242, after his confession to William Arnold at Fanjeaux. That earlier (undated) confession must have been either in 1236–38 or 1241–42. On the dates of the enquiries, see Dossat, *Crises*, pp. 217–20.

72 GA, p. 224.

73 JF, III, 368: 'Guillelma Beneta dixit ipsi loquenti … quod cum dictus bonus homo … tantum laborasset quod venisset de iuxta Taraschonem ad recipiendum et salvandum animam filie eius, quod non faciebat bene quia non dabat aliquid dicto bono homine.'

74 D26, fols. 157r–90v. Some of these depositions involve the good men William Pagès and Bernard Costa, whose existence was questioned by Bernard Délicieux. Friedlander believes that they did in fact exist and has identified a possible earlier sighting: *The Hammer of the Inquisitors*, pp. 62–5. Again, these *consolamenta* do not differ wildly from those described throughout the inquisition record; if they were fabrications, they were carefully researched and plausible ones.

75 On the disposition of testamentary bequests, see *Rituel cathare*, ed. Clédat, pp. xxv–xxvi.

76 On the Cathars' income and expenditure, see Roach, 'The Cathar Economy'.

77 Arnold gave two depositions, this first one is recorded at D26, fol. 142v–6r, and the second at D26, fol. 146r–7v. His story has been covered by various other writers. The most extensive recent treatment is in Friedlander, *The Hammer of the Inquisitors*, pp. 9–12,

In 1286, so he claimed, Arnold found a clay jar in a half-dismantled wall. Arnold was a poor clerk, and he hoped that the jar would contain some money. It did not. Instead, though, he found bundles of documents, amongst which were a number of 'heretical wills'. Unsure of what to do with these testaments, Arnold consulted the local *bailli*, who suggested that the return of the documents might make Arnold new 'friends and benefactors', as well as – ran the not-too-subtle subtext – some money.

The conditions of their storage had not been kind to these documents, but this did not discourage the enterprising Arnold. He copied out the originals, transferred their seals, and put them in a place above his cooking fire where they would absorb its smoke and begin to appear aged. Equipped with these newly legible documents he approached the relatives of their authors. The wills were evidence of heresy, and would have had potentially devastating effects for the testators and their heirs; as predicted, many of them rewarded Arnold for returning the documents.

Arnold was not a reliable witness, and the inquisitor knew it. A second deposition reveals him not as a conscientious returner of goods, but as a confidence trickster and blackmailer.[78] He admitted that his 'discovery' of the cachet of documents was entirely fictitious, and that the 'copies' were in fact entirely his own creation. Yet Arnold continued to claim that he had a genuine Cathar will. His forgeries had, he said, been based on an *exemplum* – the testament his uncle Armanch had made 'in the hands of the heretics'.[79] This second story seems much more plausible, as Arnold would have had little to gain from incriminating his family. In any case, Arnold was not the only deponent to testify about Cathar wills. Bernard Agasse, a scribe when he testified in the 1280s, remembered having been summoned to various sickbeds to notarise wills and had often found the good men already there.[80]

19, 44. For Friedlander, the interest of the episode lies 'in the vivid sense it provides of the climate of fear and suspicion that pervaded the Midi of France at the end of the thirteenth century'. James Given cites him as an example of an individual trying to manipulate the inquisition, in *Inquisition and Medieval Society*, pp. 142–4. The case is also described in in Biller, 'The Cathars of Languedoc and Written Materials', p. 64.

78 D26, fols. 146r–7v.

79 '... ipse testis habuit unum avunculum nomine Armanch militem de Aquisuiuis, qui testamentum suum condiderat in manibus haereticorum, quod testamentum, ut dixit, penes reseruabat': D26, fol. 146v.

80 Here are some examples. Bernard was summoned when Peter of Breil was dying *c.* 1272–74. 'Quadam die de qua dixit se non recordari ivit ad dictum infirmum de mandato magistri Therreni notarii cum quo ipse testis morabatur ad recipiendum testamentum dicti infirmi' – he left 100 sous to the good men: D26 fols. 206r–7r. He was again summoned in 1276 to the bedside of Perrine of Mirepoix, 'quia dictus infirmus volebat condere testamentum' – Perrine left 20 sous to the good men: D26, fols. 207r–8r. Bernard was similarly called to receive the testaments of Edelina of Bures in September *c.* 1283 and her husband Gilles in the same year at the festival of St Michael: D26, fols. 209v–11v. His fellow notary William Sicard was summoned *c.* 1274–76 when Raymond Vital of

Many of those whom Bernard visited left gifts for the good men, although he did not explicitly state whether the Cathar bequests were part of a written will.[81]

In the early thirteenth century, when the Cathar Church was still relatively well organised in Languedoc, the division of payment could be a complex matter and was subject to formal arrangements. Bruno of Renneville thus felt obliged to leave a donation to his local Cathar 'church' even after having recompensed the 'foreign' good men who had been the only ones available to receive him.[82] Elsewhere, something which must have been close to a formal

Cucciaho was dying. 'Filia dicti infirmi veniens ad domum ipsius testis dixit ei quod veniret ad patrem suum infirmum, quia volebat condere testamentum suum.' Raymond was consoled, but there is no mention in the deposition of his will's contents: D26, fols. 222v–3v.

81 Bernard Agasse's testimony is not entirely unproblematic. He and William Serre were allegedly part of a plot to destroy the archives of the Carcassonne inquisition. The depositions concerned are D26, fols. 215v–16v (Bernard Agasse), 250r–4r (Bernard of Lagarrigue), 261v–4v (Arnold Mata, uncle of Bernard of Lagarrigue) and 266r–7r (William Serra). In 1903, Jean-Marie Vidal concluded that the plot was a fabrication, that those who testified to it, including Agasse and Serra, were untrustworthy witnesses, and, of particular interest here, that the 'frappante unanimité' with which they described *consolamenta* was a cause for suspicion: *Un inquisiteur jugé*, pp. 26–31. Lea, on the other hand, thought that 'there must have been some foundation for the story': *A History of the Inquisition of the Middle Ages*, II, 59–60. In 1997, James Given was more equivocal about the plot's existence (*Inquisition and Medieval Society*, pp. 118–19), and in 2000, Alan Friedlander concluded that, in their evidence on the plot, 'the witnesses relate[d] a consistent and plausible train of events' (*The Hammer of the Inquisitors*, p. 17). The most recent examination of the evidence is in Roche, *Une église cathare*. Roche concludes that the plot itself is 'vraisemblablement fondée … [et] est révélatrice du climat de tension qui existe à Carcassonne entre les élites sociales et l'Inquisition' but that evidence about the elite's links with heresy was less likely to have had a basis in reality: ibid, p. 438. See also pp. 418–19 for Roche's survey of the historiography. Roche also specifically questions Agasse's reliability (p. 412), noting that whilst he claimed never to have adored, none of the other witnesses mentioned his exemption from the ritual. Roche does not mention Agasse's 'excuse' (discussed in n. 5 above). Two general points can be made here. First, that whatever the plot's status, the formalism and uniformity of these witness's *consolamenta* descriptions are no greater than those of other witnesses in the Doat collection. Indeed, formulaic regularity is a feature of inquisition records as a whole, and cannot be used to discount their depositions. Second, that if Agasse's testimony was part of an inquisitorial conspiracy to gather false evidence, it would have been in the plotters' interest that what he said was plausible.

82 'Item dixit quod supradictus Pader mandavit ipsum testem et dixit quod legaret IIII solidos hereticis ecclesie de Avinione, quia predicti hereticis non erant de illa ecclesia, sed causa necessitatis venerant ibi. Et ipse testis ad preces dicti Pader legavit illos IIII solidos h., sed postea non persolvit, et hoc fuit hoc anno ante festum Beate Marie Magdalene per XV dies': MS 609, fol. 51r–v (DT); I have expanded some abbreviations in Duvernoy's transcription. The behaviour mirrors regulation around orthodox burial fees, which were due to the home parish even when a body was interred elsewhere. Talk of the 'church of Avignonet', to which the two visiting good men did not belong, seems to contradict the assertion that 'nor, no matter how many times manuscript 609 is read, will a "Cathar

will was remembered from *c.*1237 by Peter Pictavin of Sorèze. Whilst visiting the dying William Raymond with his master, Pictavin had overheard the two men discussing the division of William's estate, which he remembered with surprising detail: of 500 shillings, William had left 100 for 'charity, godchildren and burial', and the remainder to the good men.[83] The responsibility for the arrangement and execution of Cathar-benefiting legacies often fell to relatives of the deceased.[84] It was an enduring practice: recorded in the great inquest of 1245–46, it was still amongst those crimes punished by Bernard Gui.[85] Other deponents remembered more informal arrangements, including payment in cash from a jar buried beneath the lintel of the initiate's house in around 1232.[86] Of course, the good men could never have been legal signatories to a thirteenth- or fourteenth-century will, but in the eyes of those who revered and respected them or their faith their presence doubtless lent a solemn legitimacy to the proceedings for the believers present.

Grief

The deathbed had always been significant for the Cathar community. Once persecution drove the movement underground, though, *consolamenta* were one of the few places ordinary followers came together with their spiritual leaders. As such, they were important centres of community. Aside from the initiate, the good men doing the consoling and his companion(s), *consolamenta* usually gathered together family members, colleagues, close friends and other co-religionists.[87] Often there were upwards of six or seven people crowded into the room, and sometimes many more. The *consolamenta* from

Church" be found' (Pegg, *The Corruption of Angels*, p. 130). NB: the quotation from MS 609 above follows Jean Duvernoy's unpublished transcription, posted online. It must be explicitly noted here that I have been unable to check this passage in the manuscript itself: folio 51 is illegible in the photostat copy which I consulted for this book.

83 D25, fol. 256r.

84 For example, Arnold Isarn promising a sextarius of corn for his son's consolamentum in 1239; testimony of Peter Pages: MS 609, fol. 78r (DT). William Calvet's grandson borrowing money which the latter suspected was for a donation in 1245: MS 609, fol. 232r.

85 Here are some examples. William of Cailhavel giving twenty melgueil sous 'from the legacy of his hereticated father', date unknown: MS 609, fol. 166r. William of Baynac paying to the good men the 'legatum' of his wife: Gui, *Sentences*, I, p. 684. Michael Miron paying the 20 royal sous left by his father: ibid., p. 766.

86 D24, fol. 131v: 'qui infirmus dixit ipsi testi, quod foderet subtus limen dictae domus, et ipse testis fodiit ibi et invenit ibi unam ollam plenam denariis … in qua olla erant sexcenti solidi melgorienses, et amplius'.

87 At the *consolamentum* of Arnold Maistre, two of his lovers were there, Guillemette Compana and Radulfa, both described as 'amasia': testimony of Bernard Tisserand, MS 609, fol. 28v (DT).

Carcassonne recorded in the register of inquisitor Jean Galand in the 1280s and 1290s were particularly well attended.[88] Some believers treated these gatherings as evangelistic opportunities, inviting their friends in the hope that they might be converted.

Sociable as they were, however, *consolamenta* could be distressing occasions for family members. Their grief sometimes manifested itself in the sort of flamboyantly stylised performances that were a feature of Occitan literature at the time.[89] In 1238, for example, Na Azalmurs tore her clothes 'from excessive grief' when arriving at a certain *consolamentum*. Her mother was evidently of the opinion that emotionalism should not get in the way of propriety, however, and roughly forced her to the floor to perform the *melioramentum*.[90] Other overt displays were also subject to censure: in 1215 Mabile of Le Mortier was removed from her husband's reception 'because she was pregnant, and on account of [her] sadness', and Alazais of Tour was 'driven out from her husband's reception' because of 'her cries, from more grief than she could bear' in 1234.[91] Raymond Aiffre did not adore at the *consolamenta* of either his grandson or his brother because of his sadness ('propter dolorem'), and – unlike Na Azalmurs – he was not compelled.[92] Raymond of Mireval and his brothers were 'excused' from the house of their father in 1228 'because of [their] lamentation and grief'.[93] This was a quintessentially Mediterranean performance; the women in these testimonies may have found use for a salve developed by thirteenth-century women from Salerno aimed at soothing sunburn, wind damage, 'excoriations of the face' and 'rivulets and floods made in mourning the dead'.[94]

That both sexes exhibited such emotionalism is perhaps more surprising to twenty-first-century historians than it would have been to contemporaries.

88 Lists of those present at some of these are given in J. Guiraud, *Histoire de l'inquisition au moyen âge*, 2 vols. (Paris, 1935–38), II, 294–302.

89 On literature, see H. Akkari, '"Moult grant duel demener" ou le rituel de la mort', in *Le geste et les gestes au Moyen Age*, ed. Margaret Bertrand and Christian Hory (Aix-en-Provence, 1998), pp. 13–24.

90 MS 609, fol. 192r: 'et cum intrasset domum illius infirmi scidit vestes suas pre nimio dolore … et tunc Alamanda mater ipsius testis dixit ipsi testi quod adoraret dictos hereticos et traxit ipsam testem per vestes et fecit ipsam testem ruere'.

91 Mabile: 'ipsa testis non vidit nec interfuit dicti hereticationi quia fecerunt eam removi quia erat pregnans, propter dolorem quam habebat ipsa testis': MS 609, fol. 162r. Alazais: 'sed ipsa testis non interfuit dicti hereticationi quia pre nimio dolore quam ipsa testis paciebat et propter lamentationem sunt expulsa de domo': MS 609, fol. 141r. Discussion of the former case is in Biller, 'Cathars and Material Women', pp. 99–100, and Pegg, *The Corruption of Angels*, pp. 109–10.

92 D23, fols. 82v, 83v.

93 Ibid., fol. 234r–v: 'propter planctum et dolorem de morte patris ipsius testis erat a domo excussi'.

94 A description of the salve can be found in a contemporary medical handbook from the town. See *Trotula*, ed. and trans. Green, p. 135.

It has, for example, been argued that the representation of grief was 'neither transgressive nor gender-specific' in French literature during the twelfth and early thirteenth centuries.[95] Yet whilst grief at the deathbed-side may not have been limited to women, it was most definitely problematic for some. In fact, dislike of emotional over-exuberance was characteristic of authority during this period.[96] In 1205, the consuls of Toulouse legislated to reduce the size of gatherings around the deceased and ordered that 'any man or any woman' should not, at such occasions, gouge their face, tear their hair and their clothes, or throw themselves to the ground.[97] 'The decency of funerals' was again of concern to the consuls in 1208, and in 1234 a synodal statute from Bordeaux forbade the laity from tearing their skin or hair during funerals, instructing priests to halt the service until calm was restored.[98]

For followers of the good men, grief that drew unwanted attention was not only disruptive but also dangerous.[99] Some grieving relatives tried to restrain themselves. After her brother's reception, Ermessende was observed 'hitting her cheeks with her palms, not daring to cry out until the aforesaid heretics had got a long way away'.[100] Perhaps the most candid testimony to the newly complex politics of grief in Languedoc, however, came from the other side of the orthodox–Cathar divide. Mengard Buscailh told Jacques Fournier that at her mother-in-law Raimonde's graveside in around 1301 she had performed her lamentations, 'but with dry eyes' because she knew that Raimonde had been 'hereticated'.[101]

For the same reason, *consolamenta* were a matter of extreme secrecy after 1209. Since too much privacy around the deathbed also drew suspicion, people had to find creative ways of concealing receptions. In August 1305, some fifty men and women gathered in the sick-room of Gaillarde of Gaillac,

95 L. A. Callahan, 'The Widow's Tears: The Pedagogy of Grief in Medieval France and the Image of the Grieving Widow', in *Constructions of Widowhood and Virginity in the Middle Ages*, ed. C. L. Carlson and A. J. Weisl (Basingstoke, 1999), p. 254.

96 A discussion of the interplay between gender, authority and grief is C. Lansing, *Passion and Order: Restraint of Grief in the Medieval Italian Communes* (Ithaca, 2008).

97 'Et quod aliquis vel aliqua non ingratunet se in facie cum unguibus, nec capillos dilaniet cum manibus, nec scindat vestes, nec in terra se prosternat': R. Limouzin-Lamothe, ed., *La commune de Toulouse et les sources de son histoire (1120–1249): Étude historique et critique suivie de l'édition du cartulaire du consulat* (Toulouse, 1932), p. 360. Those who disobeyed were fined.

98 Mundy, *Liberty and Political Power in Toulouse, 1050–1230*, p. 106; Bordeaux [80]: SS, p. 78.

99 Cf. Pegg, *The Corruption of Angels*, p. 109, where it is suggested that the good men found emotionalism uncomfortable because it was 'a reminder of something inherently human, feminine, and so terrestrial' (i.e. everything that they held in contempt).

100 D25, fols. 253r–4v.

101 JF, I, 490: 'Et cum fuerat mortua, ipsa interfuit sepulture et planxit eam, oculis tamen ciccis, cum ipsa sciret eam esse hereticatam dum viveret'. Cf. Le Roy Ladurie, *Montaillou* (En), p. 224 and *Montaillou* (Fr), p. 334 n. 2.

according to her son Peter's deposition. One of his mother's friends whispered in Peter's ear that he should do all he could to get these people outside 'so that we can do that which you know' – that is, so that William Autier could console her. Thinking quickly, he told the crowd that the excessive heat was tiring out his mother; they left, and the *consolamentum* was administered.[102] When the good men came to console Agnes of Beaupuy, Peter of Mazerolles and his friends gathered 'the men and women and monks of Bria' into the church 'and held them there a long time with talk', so that her reception might proceed undisturbed.[103] In 1230 or 1232, Arnold Roger of Mirepoix was sent from Arnold Ath's sick-room to distract an unwelcome visitor whom it was feared would interrupt his reception.[104] At other *consolamenta*, secrecy was more bluntly enforced. Some people even posted look-outs, as in the case of Arnold Rainault of Saissac, who was 'guarded' by his brother-in-law William in 1225.[105]

Timing

Occasionally, the good men were able to wait by the bedside of newly consoled men and women to give them support and advice. A number of deponents remembered these vigils. In 1215, the good men had stayed for eight days until Arnold of *Bretos*'s consoled mother was convalescing.[106] In 1245, Arnold of Brun remembered, the good men who had received his father stayed on afterwards for three days in the house of a local supporter. They twice visited the sick man before they left the village, and he died immediately after.[107] Yet post-*consolamentum* care was not available to most, and the good men were increasingly reluctant to receive anyone whose death was not imminent. This was pragmatic: an unexpected recovery put the recipient's soul at risk if no-one knowledgeable about the good men's rules for living was to hand. Thus, the good men sought to reassure themselves that their initiates really were dying before administering the *consolamentum*. In August 1301, Peter Autier asked a deathbed candidate to consider 'if he felt, in himself, that he

102 GA, p. 352. Given the number of bodies present, this must have seemed quite plausible.

103 MS 609, fol. 177r. Agnes was apparently the mother of a local monk.

104 D22, fol. 143r–v: 'et alii praedicti rogaverunt ipsum testem quod exiret extra domum, et teneret in verbis Magistrum Arnaldum de Campranha, et non posset habere accessum ad dictum infirmum, dum haeretici consolarent ipsum, et tunc ipse testis exivit extra domum, et cum verbis suis ipse testis tenuit dictum arnaldum de Capranha, quod non intravit ad dictum infirmum ...'.

105 MS 609, fol. 109v (DT), testimony of William of Castilho, knight: 'Dixit etiam quod Poncius Guasc vel Arnaldus frater dicti poncii et P. de Puhsuira faciebant custodiam ...'.

106 D24, fols. 181v–4r.

107 MS 609, fol. 51r (DT).

would not survive the illness', whilst John Maury was encouraged to receive the *consolamentum* only 'after he had already despaired of his life'.[108] Recipients and their families also understood that consolation was better later. The good men were called to Gaillarde Escaunier only when 'it was believed that she would die', and in 1246, one potential recipient even sent them away, saying that he would send word 'if his illness got worse'.[109]

If there was time, the good men preferred to wait with a dying man or woman so that they could receive them at the last possible moment. In 1305 William Autier stayed at Gaillarde of Gaillac's bedside for eight nights in order to console her at the crucial moment.[110] Similarly, in 1312, Pons Sicre was able to arrange for a good man to stay at his house in order to console his wife.[111] Peter Autier told Sybille Peter that the good men had stayed 'in a certain cellar' with Huguette of Larnat, in case they needed to re-console her.[112] This was a common practice by which good men reduced the risk of a newly consoled person breaking their vows.[113] Sometimes, there were other matters to consider. Prades Tavernier said that he would not administer the *consolamentum* to Sybille Peter's husband in 1306 until he was certain to die, 'because if he were able to recover, it would be bad that he had been received, because her husband was, so the said heretic said, a great "pecol", or "foot", of the Church of God, that is, the Church of the heretics'.[114] He was more use to them as a man of the world than as an ascetic in hiding, in other words.

Too much caution in timing the *consolamentum*'s administration could itself cause problems, however. When William Faure fell seriously ill in 1242, the good men were brought to him, with the intention that he should be received. He was so ill, though, that he was unable to speak or recognise people, and

108 JF, II, 484; GA, p. 190.

109 JF, II, 414; D24, fols. 284r–v: 'sed ipse testis noluit se tunc reddere eis, imo dixit ipsis haereticis quod recederent, quia ipse testis mitteret eis nuncium, si eius infirma gravaretur'.

110 GA, pp. 144, 352–3.

111 Apparently, she did not consent to this: Gui, *Sentences*, I, p. 608.

112 JF, II, 426. The good men had been lodged 'in quadam tina'.

113 Here are examples from the thirteenth century. Some good men waited for three days to receive the uncle of the absent Peter of Saint-Michele around 1238. 'Et steterunt ibi praefati haeretici per duas, vel per tres noctes antequam consolarent [at this point the Doat copyist, or someone checking his work, has inserted the letters 'ur' between the current line and that above, apparently correcting 'consolarent' to read 'consolarentur'] ipsum infirmum': D23, fol. 88r–v. Guilabert of Castres and his companion waited for eight days in 1230 at the home of Bernard Oth, who had a severe head-wound, 'ita quod si videretur quod esset necessarium ei reciperet ipsum testem'. They left only when it appeared that he would survive the injury: D24, fol. 86v. Examples from later years: William Autier waited three to four days to console the boy Peter Raymond: GA, p. 342. William Autier waited three or four days to console a child: ibid., p. 342.

114 JF, II, 415–16. Prades was put up by local Cathar supporters whilst he monitored the invalid's condition.

only found out about their visit, he said, after they had left.[115] William probably mentioned his insensibility in order to convince inquisitors that he had not been received. As they knew, consolation – like absolution – required informed consent from the participant. The good men were strict about this, and sometimes refused to receive men and women who could not consent.[116] In the pre-crusade period, they considered *consolamenta* inefficacious if the recipient could not recite the necessary prayers.[117] Such situations were frustrating for all concerned. In the early 1240s one such refusal led Bernard Andreas to angrily dismiss the good men from his brother's bedside.[118]

Some avoided this problem by making a sort of living will with the good men. William *Medici* seems to have made one of these in the mid-1230s. When the good men were brought before him, they were unable to communicate with him, but '[they] then said that the said ill man had formerly made a pact with them that, although he may lose his speech, if the spirit still survived in the body, he should be received'.[119] Jean Duvernoy argues that the good men made two types of pact with their followers. The first was simply a promise to be received by the good men; the second was a more explicit pact for situations where the invalid had lost the power of speech. This last agreement was a late innovation, and appears to have been a practical response by the good men to the pressures of a newly dangerous situation.[120]

115 MS 609, fol. 34v (DT): 'Item dixit quod dum ipse testis infirmaretur gravi infirmitate, B. Alzen adduxit Joule et socium suum hereticum ad domum ipsius testis, et dicti heretici volebant ipsum testem hereticare, sed non poterat loqui nec cognoscebat homines nec vidit ibi dicti heretici, sed postea audivit dici quod dicti heretici stabant in domo sua.'

116 A rare example of the opposite – where consent was assumed rather than explicitly required – is that of Raymond of Saint-Germain who 'made a sign with his hands because he was unable to speak and didn't want to be hereticated', causing the unfortunate good men to be immediately expelled from the house: testimony of Raymond of Roqueville, ibid., fol. 217r.

117 According to the chronicler Peter of Les Vaux-de-Cernay, this question arose after a man died after the laying-on-of-hands portion of the ritual and before reciting the Lord's Prayer. They consulted with a local nobleman, who judged that whilst this man would be saved, others in the same position would not be: *History of the Albigensian Crusade*, ed. Sibly and Sibly, p. 13.

118 D23, fols. 141v–2v.

119 D22, fols. 192v–3r: 'et cum venissent ante dictum infirmum dictus infirmus amiserat loquelam et tunc praedicti haeretici clamando et excuciendo dictum infirmum vocabant ipsum et non potuerunt excutere verbum et tunc praedicti haeretici dixerunt quod dictus infirmus dudum fecerat pactum cum ipsis quod quamvis amisset loquelam tantum modo invenirent spiritum in corpore quod reciperent eum'.

120 Duvernoy, *Religion des Cathares*, p. 159.

The endura

There were other ways of dealing with the problems of timing consolations correctly. One in particular has received a great deal of attention from historians: the exercise in ritual self-starvation known as the 'endura'.[121] Men and women following this extreme path refused all food after their reception in order to hasten death and guarantee their soul's entry to paradise. Since its 'discovery' in Charles Molinier's 1881 article, the practice has been a topic of heated debate.[122] Many – following Molinier – saw the *endura* as an example of the 'vagaries and extravagances' which marked the decline of Catharism in the fourteenth century.[123] Others have questioned its very existence, however. In 1985, R. I. Moore dismissed it as a 'myth' with 'little to support it beyond the remark of Rainier Sacconi', whilst Walter Wakefield considered much of the writing on the subject 'little short of nonsense'.[124] Sacconi, an orthodox polemicist who had converted from Catharism, would certainly have known about the *endura*, but whilst his tirade against the good men discussed suicide and the fatal consequences of extreme asceticism, he did not mention the rite itself.[125] In fact, the most convincing evidence for the rite comes not from orthodox writers, but from the deponents of Languedoc. There is no evidence from before the beginning of the fourteenth century, but the *endura* and its implications were well known amongst members of the Cathar community interviewed by Jacques Fournier and Jean Galand.[126] Peter Maury told

121 Lambert, *The Cathars*, pp. 242–3.

122 See C. Molinier, 'L'Endura, coutume religieuse des derniers sectaires albigeois', *Annales de la Faculté des Lettres de Bordeaux* 3 (1881), 282–99. The discovery is attributed to Molinier in Duvernoy, *Religion des Cathares*, p. 165.

123 Molinier, 'L'Endura', pp. 298–9. The quotation is from Wakefield, *Heresy, Crusade and Inquisition in Southern France 1100–1250*, p. 41. See also Vidal, 'Les derniers ministres de l'albigéisme en Languedoc: leurs doctrines', and idem, 'Doctrines et morale des derniers ministres albigeois'.

124 R. I. Moore, *The Origins of European Dissent* (Oxford, 1985), p. 224; Wakefield, *Heresy, Crusade and Inquisition in Southern France 1100–1250*, p. 40.

125 Sacconi wrote about suicide proper, which, he said, the Cathars 'did not seriously punish'. Shortly after this, he also noted that when sick 'they' (presumably, good men) enjoined their carers not to place any food in their mouths if they (the invalid) did not first recite the Paternoster – since the sick were sometimes unable to do this, he said, 'it is evident that many of them have killed themselves in this way' ('multi ex eis se occiderunt seipsos hoc modo'). Whilst a strict application of the regulations, this is not so much fasting to death as murder. See Šanjek, 'Summa de Catharis,' p. 47. Another Catholic writer, James Capelli, dismissed a 'popular rumour' that the good men 'kill [sick believers] by strangulation, so that they may be martyrs or confessors'. This bears neither upon the *endura* nor upon Sacconi's comments: it merely reveals that misinformation was circulating about a (different) supposed Cathar practice. See W. L. Wakefield and A. P. Evans, eds., *Heresies of the High Middle Ages* (New York, 1969), pp. 303–4.

126 Molinier and Duvernoy both saw the *endura* as a late innovation: Duvernoy, *Religion des Cathares*, p. 167; Molinier, 'L'Endura', p. 294. This view was challenged in 1948 by

Fournier in 1325 that he had heard from a friend that Gaillarde Escaunier had been placed in the *endura*.[127] Also testifying before Fournier, Sybille Peter remembered hearing about 'a certain woman of Alairac' who had been '*en la endura* for a long time'.[128] The term *endura* was probably used by the deponents themselves; unlike other technical terms ('hereticated', for example), which were imposed during the translation process by inquisitorial scribes, it appears 'embedded' in the Provençal.[129]

Self-starvation following deathbed reception was a recognised practice even amongst those who did not use the term. Joanna of Lantar, for instance, told the inquisitors in 1310 that she could be certain of her husband's heretication because 'from then on [i.e. after the good men arrived] he did not eat, but drank only sugared water which she gave to him, and [because] when she was giving it, he said "Our Father"'.[130] Whether the good men thought the *endura*'s value to be spiritual or solely pragmatic, the wider community had begun to see it as closely defined rite.[131] For some, it was a bone of contention. John Maury angrily told William Bélibaste that it was not he who should decide when to end his life, but God.[132] Sybille Peter told the inquisitors that whilst she believed the heretics to be good on many counts, 'she thought and believed that they were not good men, but bad, because they were very greedy and jealous *and because they led people to die in the endura*'.[133] On the other hand, apparently admiring stories began to circulate of particularly lengthy instances of *endura*. Guillemette Faure managed fifteen days in the *endura*; an

Yves Dossat, who identified a case from Pavia in 1275 where 'un évadé des prisons de l'Inquisition se soumet au jeûne rituel': 'L'évolution des rituels cathares', *Revue de Synthèse* n.s. 22–3 (1948), 30. This supposed case was cited as D25, fol. 300. It appears that Dossat was mistaken, though. The case which seems most likely to have been that to which he was referring (located not at his reference, but at fol. 307v) was that of Peter Maurel ('qui fugit de carcere inquisitorum'), who had placed himself in the 'abstinence' of the heretics ('ad abstinentiam haereticorum') and appears as part of a list of people living ('morantur') at Genoa. At fault appears to be a misreading of 'morantur' (they reside) as 'moritur' (he dies) and a misinterpretation of 'abstinence', which probably referred simply to the normal ascetic observance of all good men. My thanks to Peter Biller for help with this material.

127 JF, III, 143. This piece of testimony comes in a section where Peter was listing men and women from the vale of Arches whom he knew to be believers. The *endura* was presumably mentioned because it was a sure sign of commitment.

128 Ibid., II, 413.

129 A. Murray, *Suicide in the Middle Ages* (Oxford, 1998), I, 189.

130 Gui, *Sentences*, I, p. 822. The good man was Peter Autier; see the *culpa* of Joanna of Lantar. Sugared water was not a usual proscription, as others have noted; see Lambert, *The Cathars*, p. 242 n. 47.

131 Lambert argues that the term 'endura' ('fasting' or 'hungering' in Occitan) took on a 'precise and technical' meaning amongst them: not simply fasting, but the specific act of rejecting all food after reception into the Cathar sect: *The Cathars*, pp. 241–2.

132 JF, II, 484.

133 Ibid., II, 424; my emphasis.

unidentified woman from Coustessa apparently lasted twelve weeks![134] It is not too much of a leap to imagine that prolonged submission to the *endura*'s rigours began to draw a sort of horrified admiration from some quarters. Yet the *endura* was never an automatic consequence of consolation, and the good men still preferred to wait if they could. It has in fact been suggested that the *endura* was a 'practical answer' to the pressures of persecution and 'the normal consequence of the *consolamentum*' in a fourteenth-century context, rather than a rite in and of itself.[135]

Burial

After death, bodies had to be laid to rest. Men and women in thirteenth-century Languedoc took funeral arrangements very seriously. In a deposition from 1276, Rodrigo Fernandes, a priest, remembered an angry exchange with Pons of Mons on this topic. Pons had been 'moved and disturbed' and had told the Rodrigo that he would be 'against the Church for his whole life', because 'the priests and clerics of the church of La Garde wanted to bury [his niece] without candles'.[136] Candles were also important for Gaubert of Bénas, who clashed with the local chaplain because his wife was saving good wax for their funeral and giving inferior stuff to the Church.[137] Another rare detail on thirteenth-century death practice can be found in the deposition of Peter Pictavin, who remembered that one morning he had 'heard the bells rung' for a man who had died the previous day.[138] Funerary practice was generally of little interest to the inquisitors, though, and so these fragments are all that remains in the deposition evidence.

134 Guillemette: ibid., II, 235 (on the 'heroism' of this, see Le Roy Ladurie, *Montaillou* (Fr), p. 325 n. 3); the woman from Coustessa: GA, p. 226. Here are other examples. Montolive Francis, six weeks: Gui, *Sentences*, I, p. 292. 'A certain man of Coustessa', 'a long time': GA, p. 196. William Sabatier, seven weeks: ibid., pp. 282, 306, 316. Some of these, along with other cases, can also be found in G. Rottenwöhrer, *Der Katharismus*, 4 vols. (Bad Honnef, 1982–193), II/2, 586–604. I had initially supposed the more lengthy of these to have been implausible exaggerations. There are, however, some well-documented cases of extraordinary endurance from more recent times which suggest that long survival without food is not intrinsically implausible. One example is that of Terence MacSwiney, the Sinn Féin Mayor of Cork, who was on hunger strike for seventy-four days in 1920.

135 See Lambert, *The Cathars*, pp. 241 ('practical answer'), 244; JF, I, 235–6 n. 93 ('normal consequence'); M. Barber, *The Cathars: Dualist Heretics in Languedoc in the High Middle Ages* (Harlow, 2000), p. 103; in 2nd edn (Harlow, 2013), pp. 114–15.

136 D25, fol. 228r.

137 D25, fol. 24v. On the translation of this difficult passage, see *Inquisitors and Heretics in Thirteenth-Century Languedoc*, ed. Biller, Bruschi and Sneddon, p. 231 n. 8.

138 D25, fol. 255r.

Burial, by contrast, was of great interest to the inquisitors, and the depositions are full of material about it. In Languedoc, the broad story of Christian burial is one of a move from segregation to integration, as interment gradually moved from specially designated sites outside city or town walls to graveyards at the heart of communities. This move was driven by the growth of the parish, and of cities, towns and villages themselves.[139] By the thirteenth century, most people were buried in cemeteries in the grounds of their parish church. These were made up of a confusion of semi-permanent interments; family graves were often shared, and the burial of a new family member necessitated the tomb's re-opening and their corpse's placement on top of its current contents. Burial within the church itself was a way to avoid this messiness, but was only an option for those of substantial means. Burial fees were an important source of income, and hence an area of fierce competition in some areas.[140] Synodal statutes sought to regulate this by protecting parish incomes and forbidding priests from touting for burial business with flattery, gifts or deception.[141]

A number of groups were denied Christian burial. By the thirteenth century these included duellists, usurers, those who had failed to attend annual confession or pay tithes and – of course – heretics. [142] Before the crusade, according to William of Puylaurens, the heretics ran 'cemeteries in which they openly buried those whom they had hereticated'.[143] William was not a scandal-monger – deposition testimony reveals that these 'heretic cemeteries' really did exist.[144] In 1245, Stephen John testified that the good men had had 'their own cemetery' in Montesquieu and named ten or eleven recipients of the *consolamentum* who had been buried there in the early thirteenth century.[145] In the 1240s and 1250s a small number of other deponents

139 See J.-C. Hélas, 'Cimetières médiévaux et rites funéraires en Languedoc: l'apport de l'archéologie', *Cahiers de Fanjeaux* 33 (1998), especially pp. 286–92. See also the early chapters of P. Ariés, *The Hour of Our Death*, trans. H. Weaver (London, 1981).

140 See Reyerson, 'Changes in Testamentary Practice at Montpellier on the Eve of the Black Death', pp. 255–6, for one local example.

141 Nîmes (etc.), 1252 [124, 121, 121–9]: SS, pp. 364–72.

142 On duellists and userers, see Lateran III, canons 21 and 25; *Decrees*, ed. Tanner, pp. 221, 223; Albi 1230 [40]: SS, p. 22; Bordeaux 1234 [128–30]: ibid., p. 102 – the wives of usurers were allowed deathbed sacraments if they promised to try to convince their husbands to repent. On those who failed to pay tithes or confess, see Lateran IV, canon 21, *Decrees*, ed. Tanner, p. 245; Albi 1230 [40]: SS, p. 22; Bordeaux 1234 [128–30]: ibid., p. 102. On heretics, see Lateran III, canon 27 and Lateran IV, canon 3; *Decrees*, ed. Tanner, pp. 224, 233–5.

143 *The Chronicle of William of Puylaurens*, ed. Sibly and Sibly, p. 9. See also the story (ibid., pp. 13–14) of the relative of the bishop of Albi who rejected burial at Gaillac Candeil or Albi, and instead wanted to go to the good men.

144 For an introduction to these, see W. L. Wakefield, 'Burial of Heretics in the Middle Ages', *Heresis* 5 (1985), 29–32.

145 MS 609, fol. 99r (DT).

also mentioned these apparently well-known and well-used burial grounds. Using their testimony, further three cemeteries can be located at Lordat, Puylaurens and Saint-Paul-Cap-de-Joux.[146]

These special cemeteries did not survive the crusade and had entirely disappeared by the time the inquisitors began their work. Many continued to be buried in orthodox burial places. In 1308, Blanche of Rodes's dying brother Bernard made his desire for the *consolamentum* very clear, but he nevertheless wanted an ecclesiastical burial.[147] Heretic and orthodox remains also shared space in the cemetery of fourteenth-century Montaillou.[148] It should not be supposed that orthodox burial for Cathar followers was exclusively a late development, and some deponents from the earlier period remembered the bodies of the consoled receiving conventional burial.[149] Only a small number of 'Cathar' cemeteries seem to have existed, and we must assume that supporters were routinely buried in orthodox cemeteries before the crusade. Had this not been the case, there would have been no need for the intensely unpopular inquisitorial practice of disinterring the bodies of those posthumously convicted of heresy.[150]

Persecution brought a new need for secrecy, and ad hoc private burials in woods, fields or gardens were sometimes necessary. Two (separate) incidents that have drawn some attention were remembered by Bernard Gralh in 1244: the body of one good man had been dropped into the river Tarn, he told the inquisitors, another tossed into an old pit.[151] On another occasion, a body was apparently buried in the local gravel pit.[152] Other good men were buried

146 Lordat: D24, fol. 277v; Puylaurens: D24, fol. 127v; Saint-Paul-Cap-de-Joux: D23, fols. 75v–6v. A possible fifth cemetery was located at Saint-Martin. Its existence was first proposed by Griffe, *Le Languedoc cathare de 1190 à 1210*, p. 125. Evidence rests upon testimony that two members of the Arrufat family were carried to that town 'in obitu', and subsequently died 'in the hands of' the good men: MS 609, fol. 250r, cited also in Wakefield, 'Burial of Heretics in the Middle Ages', pp. 30, 32 n. 11. As an actual cemetery at Saint-Martin is not specifically mentioned by any deponent, its existence is questionable.

147 GA, p. 224. Blanche told the inquisitors in 1309 that she saw her brother's corpse 'in ecclesia quem volebant sepelire'.

148 JF, III, 182.

149 Examples in Wakefield, 'Burial of Heretics in the Middle Ages', p. 32 nn. 17–18.

150 A fact also noted by Yves Dossat in his 'Les Cathares d'après les documents de l'inquisition', *Cahiers de Fanjeaux* 3 (1968), 71–104.

151 D22, fols. 47v–8r, 49v. See Wakefield, 'Burial of Heretics in the Middle Ages', p. 30. On the latter of these, Wakefield states that the body was 'placed', though the Latin ('proiecierunt') implies less respect. The incident took place at Fontauser, according to the deponent, not, as he states, Villemur. These cases are also noted in Biller, 'Cathar Peace-making', p. 2.

152 'in quodam graverio': D22, fol. 189r–v. Wakefield says 'men placed him in a gravel pit'; the deponent, however, uses 'sepelierunt', 'they buried'. Wakefield, 'Burial of Heretics in the Middle Ages', p. 30. (The reference in this article has also been mis-printed as 'Doat XXIV': ibid., p. 32 n. 22.)

in gardens and woods, as sometimes were their followers.[153] Beyond their location, we know very little about these burials.[154] It has been suggested that this variety of practice finds its roots in a conflict between the conventional desires of ordinary followers and the contempt for materiality of the Cathar elite.[155] It is true that the bodies of good men were sometimes treated carelessly, but these 'disposals' have more to do with fear of discovery than Cathar theology. This secrecy was very much justified, as Raymond Baussan found out when the Lombard cellar in which he had buried the good man Pons Boer was searched – in vain – at an inquisitor's command.[156] For the most part, there is no reason to suspect that the remains of good men and their followers were treated without care, even when they were kept hidden.

For those who believed what the good men taught, death was a time of unparalleled significance. The *consolamentum* was the most important ceremony in which they would ever take part: it promised to rescue their soul from eternal imprisonment in a corrupt and corrupting world. Only at death did most have the chance of participating in this salvific ritual. Yet the last hours of those who wanted to be consoled were also a time of tension and danger. In the very early part of the thirteenth century some fortunate members of the Cathar community may have been able to carry out their last wishes with minimal trouble, but after 1209 things were never again so easy.

During most of the period surveyed in this chapter, *consolamenta* were exceptionally difficult to organise. The good men could not travel easily or stay in one place for very long, and so it became more important than ever that reception and death should follow in quick succession. To this end, they sought a kind of living will from their followers and – in some cases – encouraged initiates into a regime of extreme fasting that would shorten their lives. Timing was only one of the problems faced by dying believers, though. Utter reliance on friends and family was another. In a climate of persecution, the good men had to be contacted and collected with absolute secrecy. Local support networks – often made up of family members – bore the responsibility for this. For those who disapproved of their relatives' allegiances, on

153 See Wakefield, 'Burial of Heretics in the Middle Ages', p. 32 nn. 21–7, 32–4.

154 Cf. Wakefield, 'Burial of Heretics in the Middle Ages', p. 30 and nn. 25–6, where Wakefield comments that a good man was buried 'with little ceremony'. The deposition, however, records only the burial's occurrence, not its form: 'et tunc Raymundus Aolric predictus decessit, et fuit sepultus in aperio, sicut … retulerunt ipsi testi et hostenderunt sibi locum': Douais, ed., *Documents*, II, 289.

155 By Peter Biller in his 'Cathar Peace-making', pp. 21–2. Biller proposes an 'analytic triad' of pure Catharism, tradition and Catholicism. Bernard Hamilton interprets the evidence for conventional funerals presented in Wakefield, 'Burial of Heretics in the Middle Ages', as straightforwardly demonstrating family pressure. Hamilton's comments are in 'The Cathars and Christian Perfection', p. 22 n. 82.

156 D25, fols. 145r, 304r–5v; D26, fol. 16v.

the other hand, external danger afforded new opportunities to disrupt or derail proceedings.

A few of the most ardent believers viewed death as a blessed release, but most friends and relatives still found the occasion one for sadness.[157] Like their orthodox counterparts, the good men sometimes reacted censoriously to overt displays of emotionalism, which could be not only distracting but also dangerous. Yet at this time of heightened emotion, they also displayed unexpected respect towards the matrimonial vows of some followers, requiring men and women to 'release' their dying spouse before he or she could be consoled. The development of this 'compromise ritual' demonstrates once again that Cathar practice was influenced by the needs and expectations of ordinary followers.[158] Similar pragmatism may have been behind the creation of 'Cathar' cemeteries in the twelfth century; these seem inimical to the good men's views on corporeality, but nevertheless served a social function.

The deathbed in Languedoc was the busy site of many competing influences, where orthodoxy and Catharism, family and piety, finance and spirituality all vied for limited attention and where – for Cathar followers – expectations of sociability clashed with an urgent need for secrecy. Whatever high-minded sentiments might have been espoused by theologians, Cathar and orthodox, the story of dying in thirteenth- and early fourteenth-century Languedoc is that of the attempt, successful or otherwise, to balance these disparate elements.

157 Two rare exceptions are: JF, I, 462 (see Le Roy Ladurie, *Montaillou* (En), p. 224, and *Montaillou* (Fr), p. 333) and JF, I, 193. This last case is discussed by J. H. Arnold, 'Inquisition, Texts and Discourse', in *Texts and the Repression of Medieval Heresy*, ed. C. Bruschi and P. Biller (York, 2003), pp. 72–7.

158 The phrase 'compromise ritual' is from Taylor, *Heresy, Crusade and Inquisition in Medieval Quercy*, pp. 195–6.

Conclusion

On the feast day of St Denis 1273, Durand of Rouffiac testified at Toulouse before the inquisitor Ranulph of Plassac and a panel of three witnesses. A scribe recorded his testimony. The inquisitor had a pre-prepared list of questions for Durand, based upon a catalogue of jovial anti-clericalisms that had been sent to him and his colleagues earlier.[1] It did not take Plassac long to get Durand to confess – he admitted scorning the Eucharist, questioning the existence of the soul and advocating usury. Here, it seems, was someone who enjoyed saying the unsayable. There was little substance to his utterances, though. Durand was no evangelist, and when we read his claim that he had not really meant what he said, there seems little reason for scepticism.

The inquisitor was not quite so trusting. The following day, Plassac asked Durand again about a report that he had questioned divine power – something he had previously denied. This time, a different story came out:

> Item: he added on the above item concerning the divine power that when his son, named Peter of Rouffiac, whom the same witness loved very much, had gone overseas with merchants, four years ago, to Alexandria, and the same witness had prayed and begged God day and night to bring him back alive and well, he at last learned that he had died at Acre. And, devastated by this, he said that it did a man as much good if he prayed to God as if he did not.[2]

This extract is striking not just because of its emotional frankness, but also because of the unexpected way in which Durand presents his religious life. His belief is presented as intertwined with something entirely secular: concern for an absent son. By all accounts – and certainly by the account sent to his inquisitor – Durand was not an overly pious man. He prayed, it seems, because he was a father; this was what concerned parents were supposed to do. When his son died, the effect on Durand was not just emotional but religious too: he renounced prayer. This was not the first time Durand had related a chronology of belief. He had been reported as saying that 'when he was young he crossed himself frequently, and nothing good happened to him, but when he had grown up he left off crossing himself, and many good

1 An account of 'everything he knew' about Durand's statements was given by William Orset of Espinas to Raymond of Livron, 'who sent it in writing to the inquisitor': D25, fol. 178r.

2 Ibid., fol. 23v.

things happened to him'.[3] Here again, Durand's testimony dangles tantalising questions about the relationship between the ephemeral realm of belief and the hard-and-fast realities of 'real life'.

It was this singular deposition that first prompted my interest in two of this book's primary themes: the interplay between faith and other facets of life, and the ways in which it could change over time. A closer acquaintance with the sources soon revealed that such self-conscious accounts of life-cycle change in religious practice were rare. Deponents did not give coherent and continuous narratives of their lives, but instead recounted a series of disjointed snapshots dictated by inquisitorial questioning and the limits of memory. As I read, another way of approaching the question began to suggest itself. Rather than study the changing patterns of belief over individual lives, I would instead use the life-cycle model as an organising principle for the diverse evidence contained within the deposition record. This approach has proven to be a very productive one, which has revealed a number of overarching themes. Before reprising these, a brief recap of the material that has been covered will be of benefit.

We began with children, whose experiences can be divided into two stages. Before the crusade, girls and (especially) boys mixed with good men freely in their local communities. After persecution drove Cathar ministers into hiding, however, children were much less likely to encounter them outside the family home and without adult supervision. The encounters that they subsequently had were imbued with a glamour that had as much to do with the good men's status as fugitives and outlaws as it did with their status as holy ascetics. In both periods, some good men cultivated relationships with children, whilst others remained more aloof – a divergence which is probably best explained by the diversity of individual characters and attitudes.

The Catholic Church took an interest in children at a more institutional level. It had long placed a heavy emphasis on the baptism of children, which message was successful to the extent that the rite enjoyed widespread take-up and genuine public approval. Ecclesiastical legislators were also beginning in the thirteenth century to promote the doctrinal instruction and church attendance of minors. These attempts were in their early stages, though, and followers of the good men had no such encouragement. The extent to which children took part in Cathar ritual was largely a matter for their parents and guardians. Attitudes on this matter varied widely. Some adults actively encouraged – and even required – the participation of minors in their care, whilst others were more censorious. To whatever extent children participated in religious life, however, the consensus opinion amongst deponents and inquisitors alike seems to have been that those below 'the age of discretion' – pre-teens – were capable of obedient adherence, but not real understanding.

3 D25, fols. 22v–3r.

This problematises the idea of 'family transmission' of Catharism as a belief system. For contemporaries, at least, there was a clear distinction between the adherence that children learnt, and real faith.

On the face of it, the presumed absence of childhood belief makes the reception of young children to live as good men and good women – with pairs of Cathar guardians or in small communities – appear a rather confusing anomaly. It was not so much that life as Cathar ascetics was beyond children – though the day-to-day reality of their experience remains largely hidden – but the fact of reception itself. Given the emphasis the good men placed upon the need for informed consent, and their derision of infant baptism for lacking exactly this, it was a strange practice indeed. It is also unclear what the adult relatives who were often the principal agents behind the reception of young children saw as its purpose, or how they viewed the fact that many left the sect after a relatively brief period. By the fourteenth century, men and women no longer needed to ponder such questions: the reception of children seems to have ceased around the middle of the thirteenth century, no doubt because persecution made it unworkable. Later good men – particularly those around Peter Autier – were thus able to take a much more hard-line stance against the reception of children. In fact, the theological justification behind this fascinatingly contradictory practice had always been unclear. One suspects that the good men who consoled children in the twelfth and thirteenth centuries had not yet worked out how the practice fitted coherently within contemporary understandings of childhood and their own focus on consent.

Compared to the rich evidence on children, material about youths was much scarcer. As a life stage, youth was distinctively marked out within social and legal frameworks, yet neither the Catholic Church nor the good men placed much emphasis on it. An impressionistic picture can be constructed, though. Moving beyond the family home afforded the young greater opportunities to mix with the good men. When the latter still lived and traded publicly, in the early thirteenth century, some young people were employed as apprentices in their workshops. Contemporary Catholic writers' suspicions that these places were in fact thinly disguised seminaries seem to have been mistaken: the boys who worked there really were learning a trade. Nevertheless, they were perhaps inevitably exposed to some Cathar theology from their masters. Even those apprentices whose masters were not consoled members of the Cathar Church's formal hierarchy still sometimes found themselves socialised into the faith community through their work. During this period, young people formed associations which would last for many years, and which – for some – blurred the boundary between business and religion. Youths were more active participants in Cathar ritual and community life than younger children, although older adults viewed them with condescension. Youthfulness was considered by inquisitors a reason for leniency, however, which apparently stemmed from an appreciation of their still-limited independence from adult influence and supervision.

Women were often identified by their matrimonial status, which perhaps explains why evidence about female youth is so sparse within the deposition record. Surveys of the available demographic evidence from thirteenth-century Languedoc have suggested that men married somewhat later than did women, although the former were probably always more likely to appear as independent actors within the depositions. The Cathars were of course famous for their preaching against marriage at whatever age it was contracted, a stance which was in stark contrast to a largely positive image promoted by (some) Catholic theologians and pastors. Despite their ministers' abomination of marriage, however, most men and women in the Cathar community did marry. In fact, there is some evidence to suggest that an increasing number may have done so with the involvement of the Catholic Church. Many factors affected marriage choice, amongst which religious faith was of increasing significance for members of the persecuted Cathar community.

The character of married people's relationships varied widely, as did the impact of religious affiliations upon them. Some people – women as well as men – were able to convince their spouses of the good men's worthiness through argument and persuasion. Many married 'shelterers' worked together as hosts. Others had relationships that were characterised more by the threat of violence than by amicability. It is unclear whether or not such conditions were as common as has sometimes been supposed, however, and they were certainly seen as undesirable by contemporaries. The good men did welcome some (mostly female) converts who had 'fled' their spouses to become Cathar ascetics, but it was not the norm. As many deponents, in fact, reported having abandoned asceticism to marry. For the most part, though, the good men did not attempt to intervene in actual marriages. This may have been more to do with a pragmatic assessment of the important support role played by married couples than with a *laissez-faire* attitude towards the unconsoled. Indeed, as the number of their followers shrank, some good men began to take active interest in the marriage choices of their followers. This was an innovation, although they had for a long time been making concessions to its binding power during the administration of the *consolamentum*.

That last ritual, administered on the deathbed, was the central event in the spiritual life of any Cathar follower. It was also an important community event, which enhanced the already social nature of death in medieval Languedoc. The exact timing of the *consolamentum* was always a matter of great importance, which only became more crucial once persecution set in. Once again, the role of ordinary community members was vital. Friends and relatives of the deceased played important parts in procuring the good men, facilitating *consolamenta*, and in watching over dying initiates once they had been received. They were also often responsible for the execution of financial business that took place at the bedside. Those who did not agree with the choices of their relatives, on the other hand, could cause great disruption, whose effects can only have been increased by persecution.

Death was a time of sadness for many, whatever their religious beliefs. It is true that the good men found their followers' sometimes extravagant displays of grief uncomfortable. It is unclear, however, whether this was for theological reasons or as a result of a more mundane fear of discovery, and it should in any case be noted that this censorious attitude mirrored that of secular and Catholic authorities. Another area in which Cathar and orthodox provisions apparently paralleled each other – at least before the beginning of the Albigensian Crusade – was the provision of burial places. This is a little strange, given the good men's very vocal condemnation of all things corporeal. The disjunction between doctrine and practice was not explicitly explained by any deponent, but it must have had something to do with the enduring power of social norms for both good men and their followers.

Many interesting themes have emerged across these different stages of life, all of which would benefit from further investigation. In closing, however, I wish to highlight what are – I think –the three most important.

First, the boundary between Cathar and orthodox practice has in many cases been shown to be more porous than previously imagined. Many people, in fact, drew on elements from both traditions. This should not be surprising: the good men had little to offer people at some crucial moments in their lives. There was no Cathar alternative to infant baptism, marriage blessings or – during most of the period we have studied – burial. What is more, both the good men and their lay supporters were drawn from a society whose institutional framework and broader character owed a heavy debt to the Catholic faith and its ecclesiastical hierarchy. In some ways, then, the categories we employ in the discussion of 'heresy and orthodoxy' are unnecessarily rigid. To think of these two as mutually exclusive opposites is, in the words of John Mundy, 'an argument from law rather than the description of a religious state of mind'.[4]

A second theme is the crucially important role played by 'ordinary' (i.e. unordained) people in maintaining Catharism as a vibrant and active faith. Laypeople provided practical services as hosts and guides; they introduced children to the faith and policed their behaviour; they provided financial support in the form of legacies, and many of them were active proselytisers amongst friends, relatives and loved ones. The good men were more conscious of this than those who study them have sometimes appreciated, and as their faith had very little to say about community relations, their responses to real-world problems raised by followers were often less formally constrained than those of their orthodox equivalents. In fact, two rather unexpected Cathar practices – requiring formal dissolution of marriage ties during the *consolamentum* and providing cemeteries for the dead – can be seen as concessions to secular expectations.

4 J. H. Mundy, *Liberty and Political Power in Toulouse, 1050–1230* (New York, 1954), pp. 76–7.

Finally, and perhaps most importantly, we have seen that people's experience of Catharism was characterised by variety. The life-cycle model adopted here has allowed us to see the ways in which expectations and practices varied over the course of peoples' lives. From the circumscribed activities of children, through the expanded interactions for youths, to co-operation or tension during marriage and through to the final climactic moment of death, a person's stage of life impacted very greatly upon their experience of religious faith. At any given stage of the life cycle, though, a great number of external forces and individual motivations also worked to guide and direct people's actions. Some people (especially children) performed the *melioramentum* because they were ordered to; others bent their knees in response to subtler social pressures. Some welcomed the good men into their homes because a spouse whose opinion they respected had asked them to, whilst others did so through fear or ignorance. Many who did not themselves believe were encouraged to arrange their parents' *consolamenta* because it was considered to be a family duty. All these things and more lay behind deponents' engagement with the good men and their faith.

This richly complex reality is one which the language of much Cathar historiography obscures with a dualistic divide between good men and 'believers'. Even the 'categories of transgression' employed by the inquisitorial courts were more nuanced than this. Legislators divided those who had come into contact with the good men into distinct groups – from heretics and believers through to hiders (those who knew about heresy but did not report it), concealers (those who maliciously hid the truth), receivers, defenders and supporters.[5] Historians could do worse than to adopt similar groupings. Their origins and associations may be somewhat distasteful, but working with such categories would allow for the separation of action from the singular motivation of 'belief', which so often marks the endpoint of enquiry. A more sensitive picture of lived experience would thus be allowed to emerge.

I do not argue that we should eradicate belief from our discourse. This would be entirely counter-productive, not to mention anachronistic. In fact, many people who first engaged with the good men because of obedience, guilt or obligation also believed, or came to believe, that they were noble examples of holiness who held the keys to salvation. Yet this belief alone cannot 'explain' those men and women. As the depositions they gave have repeatedly demonstrated, the 'Cathar' portion of people's lives was not a discrete set of experiences to be extracted from the broader whole, but instead part of a messily human continuum in which sacred and profane, religious and secular were often entirely interwoven.

5 These are taken from the 1242 council of Tarragona, in Mansi, XXIII, cols. 5538. On that council, see H. Maisonneuve, *Études sur les origines de l'inquisition*, 2nd edn (Paris, 1960), pp. 287–92. A list of the eleven categories (in English) is given in Arnold, *Inquisition and Power*, pp. 42–3.

Glossary

Adoring
See *Melioramentum*.

Albigensian Crusade
A series of military campaigns from 1209–1229, triggered by the murder of papal legate Peter of Castelnau 1208 and ending with the Peace of Paris in 1229. The crusade was principally made up of northern barons, led by Simon de Montfort until his death in 1218. It saw the loss of many southern lands to the invaders. The county of Toulouse was – eventually – absorbed into the lands of the French Crown, as a result of a marriage alliance in the peace treaty.

Castrum
Fortified town, typical of Languedoc and the Lauragais region at the turn of the thirteenth century.

Consolamentum
Rite roughly analogous to baptism, by which men and women entered into the ranks of the good men and good women. Anyone who had received the *consolamentum* was guaranteed salvation, but any minor infraction of the rules of life that it bound them to invalidated this. Most ordinary followers thus received the *consolamentum* as adults, and only when they knew they were on the verge of death. The ritual was referred to as 'heretication' by inquisitors.

Deponent
Man or woman giving evidence before the inquisitors. Depositions were normally taken in front of two inquisitors, a scribe, and a panel of clerical witnesses. They were given in the vernacular, but were translated into Latin by the scribe and later abbreviated and written up into reference works. It is these documents that survive today.

Endura
A practice that developed amongst recipients of the *consolamentum* in late-thirteenth and early-fourteenth-century Languedoc. The consoled who were on the verge of death at reception placed themselves 'en la endura', refusing all food and water and effectively starving themselves to death. This reduced the chance of an accidental breach of the new rules governing their lives, and so maximised their chance of salvation.

Good man, Good woman

Men and women who had received the *consolamentum* and undertaken a life of ascetic purity. Only good men could administer the *consolamentum* and thus salvation was entirely under their control. Prohibitions on the good men and good women included a near-vegan diet (all animal products were taboo, save fish), regular prayers (including before meals), and an absolute taboo on physical contact with the opposite sex. Whilst they also received the *consolamentum*, and were subject to the same rigid rules of life, female members of the sect seem to have had a diminished role, particularly in public. (Note that 'good man' was not used to designate death-bed recipients of the *consolamentum* who played no continuing role in the life of the sect.)

Heretic

In the depositions from Languedoc, 'heretic' used without qualification is not a generic term but refers exclusively to good men (Latin 'hereticus') or good women (Latin 'heretica'). This is most obvious to the reader in the standard inquisitors' question 'did you ever see a heretic or a Waldensian'.

Inquisition

Both an institution and a legal procedure, the medieval inquisition used the legal procedure of *inquisitio* which allowed them to try cases *ex officio*, without first requiring an accusation from within a community. In Languedoc, inquisitors were first appointed in 1233. They usually worked in pairs, were generally drawn from the Dominican order, and after 1242 were based in urban centres, notably Toulouse and Carcassonne. Whilst there was no formal institutional structure, inquisitors were united across geographic and temporal divides by their mission, by buildings and custom, and by an exceptionally well-developed documentary archive.

Melioramentum

Ritual series of genuflexions and petitions to 'pray to God for me', usually performed when followers met or left the good men, and between the good men themselves. This rite was referred to as 'adoring' by inquisitors.

Waldensian

A preaching movement begun by Valdes (Waldo) of Lyons in the latter half of the twelfth century. Waldensians embraced poverty and preaching, but despite being active against the good men in Languedoc, themselves fell afoul of the Church because they refused to respect its monopoly on preaching. They were pursued as heretics by inquisitors.

Bibliography

Unpublished primary works

Paris, Bibliothèque nationale de France
Collection Doat, 21–6

Toulouse, Bibliothèque municipale
MS 609

Published primary works

Cartulaire de Notre-Dame de Prouille: précédé d'une étude sur l'albigéisme languedocien aux XIIe & XIIIe siècles, ed. J. Guiraud (Paris, 1907).

The Chronicle of William of Puylaurens: The Albigensian Crusade and Its Aftermath, ed. and trans. W. A. Sibly and M. D. Sibly (Woodbridge, 2003).

Les coutumes de Toulouse (1286) et leur premier commentaire (1296), ed. H. Gilles (Toulouse, 1969).

Decrees of the Ecumenical Councils, ed. and trans. N. Tanner, 2 vols. (London, 1990).

Douais, C., ed., *Documents pour servir à l'histoire de l'inquisition dans le Languedoc*, 2 vols. (Paris, 1900).

Durand, William, *Rationale divinorum officiorum I–IV*, ed. A. D'avril and T. M. Thibodeau, Corpus Christianorum, Continuatio Medievalis 140 (Turnhout, 1995).

Duvernoy, J., ed., *L'inquisition en Quercy: le registre des pénitences de Pierre Cellan, 1241–1242*, (Castelnaud la Chapelle, 2001).

——, ed., *Le registre d'inquisition de Jacques Fournier, évêque de Pamiers (1318–1325)*, Bibliothèque Méridionale, series 2, 41, 3 vols. (Toulouse, 1965).

——, *Le registre d'inquisition de Jacques Fournier, évêque de Pamiers (1318–1325): corrections* (Toulouse, 1972).

——, ed. and trans., *Le registre d'inquisition de Jacques Fournier (évêque de Pamiers) 1318–1325*, 3 vols. (Paris, 1978).

Gui, Bernard, *De fundatione et prioribus conventuum provinciarum Tolosanae et Provinciae Ordinis Praedicatorum*, ed. P. A. Amargier, *Monumenta ordinis fratrum praedicatorum historica* 24 (Rome, 1961).

——, *Le livre des sentences de Bernard Gui: 1308–1323*, ed. A. Pales-Gobilliard, 2 vols. (Paris, 2002).

——, *Practica inquisitionis heretice pravitatis*, ed. C. Douais (Paris, 1886).

L'Inquisiteur Geoffroy d'Ablis et les Cathares du comté de Foix (1308–1309), ed. and trans. A. Pales-Gobilliard (Paris, 1984).

The Inquisition at Albi 1299–1300, ed. G. W. Davis (New York, 1974).

Inquisitors and Heretics in Thirteenth-century Languedoc: An Edition and Translation of Toulouse Inquisition Depositions, 1273–1282, ed. P. Biller, C. Bruschi, and S. Sneddon (Leiden, 2011).

Limouzin-Lamothe, R., ed., *La commune de Toulouse et les sources de son histoire (1120–1249) étude historique et critique suivie de l'édition du cartulaire du consulat* (Toulouse, 1932).

Livre des deux principes, ed. C. Thouzellier, Sources Chrétiennes 198 (Paris, 1973).

Mansi, G. D., ed., *Sacrorum conciliorum nova et amplissima collection*, 53 vols. (1757–98).

Le manuscrit 609 de la bibliothèque municipale de Toulouse: Lauragais 1245–1246, 1253 (PDF format, 3 parts), ed. J. Duvernoy. http://jean.duvernoy.free.fr/text/listetexte.htm (accessed 1 November 2006).

Le Nouveau Testament: traduit au XIIIe siècle en langue provençale suivi d'un rituel cathare, ed. L. Clédat (Geneva, 1968).

Patrologiae: cursus completus series Latina, ed. J.-P. Migne, 221 vols. (Paris, 1844–64).

Peter of les Vaux-de-Cernay: The History of the Albigensian Crusade, ed. and trans. W. A. Sibly and M. D. Sibly (Woodbridge, 1998).

Petri Vallium Sarnaii monachi hystoria albigensis, ed. P. Guébin and E. Lyon, 3 vols. (Paris, 1926–39).

Saisimentum Comitatus Tholosani, ed. Y. Dossat (Paris, 1966).

Šanjek, F., 'Raynerius Sacconi O.P. Summa de Catharis', *Archivum Fratrum Praedicatorum* 44 (1974), 31–60.

Les statuts synodaux français du XIIIe siècle, précédés de l'historique du synode diocésain depuis ses origines, ed. O. Pontal, 2 vols. (Paris, 1971).

The Trotula: A Medieval Compendium of Women's Medicine, ed. and trans. M. H. Green, (Philadelphia, 2001).

Wakefield, W. L., and Evans, A. P., ed. and trans., *Heresies of the High Middle Ages* (New York, 1969).

Secondary works

Abels, R., and Harrison, E., 'The Participation of Women in Languedocian Catharism', *Mediaeval Studies* 41 (1979), 215–51.

Akkari, H., '"Moult grant duel demener" ou le rituel de la mort', in *Le geste et les gestes au Moyen Age*, ed. M. Bertrand and C. Hory (Aix-en-Provence, 1998), pp. 13–24.

Albaret, L., *Les inquisiteurs: portraits de défenseurs de la foi en languedoc, XIIIe–XIVe siècles* (Toulouse, 2001).

Ames, C. C., 'Does Inquisition Belong to Religious History?', *American Historical Review* 110 (2005), 11–37.

——, *Righteous Persecution: Inquisition, Dominicans, and Christianity in the Middle Ages* (Philadelphia, 2009).

Amundsen, D. W., and Diers, C. J., 'The Age of Menarche in Medieval Europe', *Human Biology; an International Record of Research* 45 (1973), 363–9.

Andrews, F., 'A Safe-Haven for Children? The Early Humiliati and Provision for Children', in *Youth in the Middle Ages*, ed. P. J. P. Goldberg and F. Riddy (York, 2004), pp. 73–84.

Ariès, P., *Centuries of Childhood*, trans. R. Baldick (London, 1962).
——, *L'enfant et la vie familiale sous l'ancien régime* (Paris, 1960).
——, *The Hour of Our Death*, trans. H. Weaver (London, 1981).
Armargier, P., 'Éléments pour un portrait de Bernard Gui', *Cahiers de Fanjeaux* 16 (1981), pp. 19–37.
Arnold, J. H., *Belief and Unbelief in Medieval Europe* (London, 2005).
——, 'The Historian as Inquisitor: The Ethics of Interrogating Subaltern Voices', *Rethinking History* 2 (1998), 379–86.
——, *Inquisition and Power: Catharism and the Confessing Subject in Medieval Languedoc* (Philadelphia, 2001)
——, 'Inquisition, Texts and Discourse', in *Texts and the Repression of Medieval Heresy*, ed. C. Bruschi and P. Biller (York, 2003).
——, 'The Preaching of the Cathars', in *Medieval Monastic Preaching*, ed. C. Muessig (Leiden, 1998), pp. 183–205.
——, 'Review: Malcolm Barber, The Cathars', IHR Reviews in History (2001) http://www.history.ac.uk/reviews/paper/ArnoldJohn.html.
Baldwin, J. W., *Masters, Princes, and Merchants: The Social Views of Peter the Chanter & His Circle*, 2 vols. (Princeton, 1970).
Barber, M., *The Cathars: Dualist Heretics in Languedoc in the High Middle Ages* (Harlow, 2000; 2nd edn, 2013).
Bastard-Fournié, M., 'Mentalités religieuses aux confins du Toulousain et de l'Albigeois à la fin du moyen âge', *Annales du Midi* 85 (1973), 266–87.
Biller, P., 'Abundance and Scarcity of Food in the Inquisition Records of Languedoc', in *Cross, Crescent and Conversion: Studies on Medieval Spain and Christendom in Memory of Richard Fletcher*, ed. S. Barton and P. Linehan (Leiden, 2008), pp. 263–76.
——, 'Bernard Gui, Sex and Luciferanism', *Praedicatores inquisitores I: The Dominicans and the Mediaeval Inquisition. Acts of the 1st International Seminar on the Dominicans and the Inquisition*, Dissertationes Historicae 29 (Rome, 2004), 455–70.
——, 'Cathar Peace-making', in *Christianity and Community in the West: Essays for John Bossy*, ed. S. Ditchfield (Aldershot, 2001), pp. 1–23.
——, 'Cathars and Material Women', in *Medieval Theology and the Natural Body*, ed. P. Biller and A. J. Minnis (York, 1997), pp. 61–107.
——, 'The Cathars of Languedoc and Written Materials', in *Heresy and Literacy, 1000–1530*, ed. P. Biller and A. Hudson (Cambridge, 1994), pp. 61–82.
——, 'The Common Woman in the Western church in the Thirteenth and Early Fourteenth Centuries', *Studies in Church History* 27 (1990), 127–57.
——, *The Measure of Multitude: Population in Medieval Thought* (Oxford, 2000).
——, 'Popular Religion in the Central and Later Middle Ages', in *Companion to Historiography*, ed. M. Bentley (London, 1997), pp. 221–46.
——, 'Review of *The Corruption of Angels*, by M. Pegg', *Speculum* 78 (2003), 1366–70.
——, 'Umberto Eco et les interrogations de Bernard Gui', in *Inquisition et pouvoir*, ed. G. Audisio (Aix-en-Provence, 2004), pp. 257–68.
Bossy, J., *Christianity in the West, 1400–1700* (Oxford, 1985).
Boyle, L. E. 'Montaillou Revisited: Mentalité and Methodology', in *Pathways to Medieval Peasants*, ed. J. A. Raftis (Toronto, 1981), pp. 120–40.
Brooke, C., *The Medieval Idea of Marriage* (Oxford, 1989).

Brown, E. A. R., 'Authority, the Family, and the Dead in Late Medieval France', *French Historical Studies* 16 (1990), 803–32.

Brundage, J. A., '"Better to Marry Than to Burn?": The Case of the Vanishing Dichotomy', in *Views of Women's Lives in the Western Tradition*, ed. F. R. Keller (New York, 1990), pp. 195–216.

——, 'Domestic Violence, Medieval and Modern', in *Violence in Medieval Society*, ed. Richard W. Kaeuper (Woodbridge, 2000), pp. 183–97.

——, *Law, Sex, and Christian Society in Medieval Europe* (Chicago, 1987).

——, *Sex, Law and Marriage in the Middle Ages* (Aldershot, 1993).

Bruschi, C., '"Magna diligentia est habenda per inquisitorem": Precautions Before Reading Doat 21–26', in *Texts and the Repression of Medieval Heresy*, ed. C. Bruschi and P. Biller (York, 2003), pp. 81–110.

——, *The Wandering Heretics of Languedoc* (Cambridge, 2009).

Burrow, J. A., *The Ages of Man: A Study in Medieval Writing and Thought* (Oxford, 1986).

Callahan, L. A., 'The Widow's Tears: The Pedagogy of Grief in Medieval France and the Image of the Grieving Widow', in *Constructions of Widowhood and Virginity in the Middle Ages*, ed. C. L. Carlson and A. J. Weisl (Basingstoke, 1999), pp. 245–63.

Carbonell, C.-O., 'Vulgarisation et récupération: le Catharisme à travers les mass-médias', *Cahiers de Fanjeaux* 14 (1979), 361–80.

Cramer, P., *Baptism and Change in the Early Middle Ages, c. 200–c. 1150* (Cambridge, 1993).

d'Avray, D. L., *Medieval Marriage: Symbolism and Society* (Oxford, 2005).

de la Presle-Evesque, A., 'Le manuscrit BNF latin 12856. Analyse, texte, traduction' (unpublished Ph.D. thesis, École Pratique des Hautes Études, Section des Sciences Religieuses, 1995).

Demaitre, L., 'The Idea of Childhood and Child Care in Medical Writings of the Middle Ages', *Journal of Psychohistory* 4 (1977), 467–90.

Diehl, P., Landau, P. and Mueller, J., 'Heresy as Grounds for Divorce', in *Proceedings of the Ninth International Congress of Medieval Canon Law, Munich, 13–18 July 1992*, Monumenta iuris canonici 10 (Vatican, 1997), pp. 975–6.

Dossat, Y., 'Les Cathares d'après les documents de l'inquisition', *Cahiers de Fanjeaux* 3 (1968), 71–104.

——, *Les crises de l'inquisition Toulousaine au XIIIe siècle (1233–1273)* (Bordeaux, 1959).

——, 'L'évolution des rituels cathares', *Revue de Synthèse* n.s. 22–3 (1948), 27–30.

——, 'Une figure d'inquisiteur: Bernard de Caux', *Cahiers de Fanjeaux* 6 (1971), 253–72.

——, 'Les vaudois méridionaux d'après les documents de l'inquisition', *Cahiers de Fanjeaux* 1 (1967), pp. 207–26.

Douais, C., 'Les hérétiques du comté de Toulouse dans la première moitié du XIII siècle d'aprés l'enquête de 1245', in *Compte rendu du congrès scientifique international des Catholiques* (Paris, 1891), pp. 148–62.

Dove, M., *The Perfect Age of Man's Life* (Cambridge, 1986).

Duffy, E., *The Stripping of the Altars: Traditional Religion in England c.1400–c.1580*, 2nd edn. (New Haven, 2005).

Dusan, B., 'De Manso Sanctarum Puellarum', *Revue Archéologique du Midi de la*

France: recueil de notes, mémoires, documents relatifs aux monuments de l'histoire et des beaux-arts dans les pays de langue d'Oc 2 (1868), Appendix (separately paginated), 1–12.

Duvernoy, J., *Le Catharisme: la religion des Cathares* (Toulouse, 1976).

Elliott, D., *Spiritual Marriage: Sexual Abstinence in Medieval Wedlock* (Princeton, 1993).

Esmein, A., *Le mariage en droit canonique*, 2 vols. (Paris, 1891).

Fass, P. S., 'The World is at Our Door: Why Historians of Children and Childhood Should Open Up', *Journal of the History of Childhood and Youth* 1 (2008), 11–31.

Feuchter, J., *Ketzer, Konsuln und Büsser: Die städtischen Eliten von Montauban vor dem Inquisitor Petrus Cellani (1236/1241)*, Spätmittelalter, Humanismus, Reformation 40 (Tübingen, 2007).

——, 'Le pouvoir de l'inquisition à travers ses peines: Le cas de Montauban (1241)', in *Inquisition et Pouvoir*, ed. Gabriel Audisio (Aix-en-Provence, 2004), pp. 236–55.

Fisher, J. D. C., *Christian Initiation: Baptism in the Medieval West* (London, 1965).

Forrest, I., *The Detection of Heresy in Late Medieval England* (Oxford, 2005).

Friedlander, A., *The Hammer of the Inquisitors: Brother Bernard Délicieux and the Struggle against the Inquisition in Fourteenth-Century France* (Leiden, 2000).

Given, J., *Inquisition and Medieval Society: Power, Discipline, and Resistance in Languedoc* (Ithaca, 1997).

——, 'A Medieval Inquisitor at Work: Bernard Gui, 3 March 1308 to 19 June 1323', in *Portraits of Medieval and Renaissance Living: Essays in Memory of David Herlihy*, ed. S. K. Cohn and S. Epstein (Ann Arbor, 1996), pp. 207–32.

Goldberg, P. J. P., 'Masters and Men in Later Medieval England', in *Masculinity in Medieval Europe*, ed. Dawn Hadley (New York, 1998), pp. 56–70.

——, 'Orphans and Servants: The Socialisation of Young People Living away from Home in the English Later Middle Ages', in *Adoption et fosterage*, ed. M. Corbier (Paris, 1999), pp. 231–46.

——, 'What was a servant?', in *Concepts and Patterns of Service in the Later Middle Ages*, ed. A. Curry and E. Matthew (Woodbridge, 2000), pp. 1–20.

——, *Women, Work and Life Cycle in a Medieval Economy* (Oxford, 1992).

Goldberg, P. J. P., and Riddy, F., eds., *Youth in the Middle Ages* (York, 2004).

Graham-Leigh, E., *The Southern French Nobility and the Albigensian Crusade* (Woodbridge, 2005).

Griffe, É., *Le Languedoc cathare de 1190 à 1210* (Paris, 1971).

Grundmann, H., *Religious Movements in the Middle Ages*, trans. S. Rowan (Notre Dame and London, 1995).

Guiraud, J., *Histoire de l'inquisition au moyen age*, 2 vols. (Paris, 1935–38).

——, *Questions d'histoire et d'archéologie chrétienne* (Paris, 1906).

Haas, L. and J. Rosenthal, 'Historiographical Reflections and the Revolt of the Medievalists', in *Essays on Medieval Childhood: Responses to Recent Debates*, ed. J. Rosenthal (Donington, 2007).

Hajnal, J., 'European Marriage Patterns in Perspective', in *Population in History: Essays in Historical Demography*, ed. D. V. Glass and D. E. Eversley (London, 1965), pp. 100–43.

Hamilton, B., 'The Cathars and Christian Perfection', in *The Medieval Church: Universities, Heresy, and the Religious Life: Essays in Honour of Gordon Leff*, ed.

P. Biller and B. Dobson, Studies in Church History Subsidia 11 (Woodbridge, 1999), pp. 5–23.
——, 'The Legacy of Charles Schmidt to the Study of Christian Dualism', *Journal of Medieval History* 24 (1998), 191–214.
——, 'Review of *The Corruption of Angels*, by M. Pegg', *American Historical Review* 107 (2002), 925–6.
Hanawalt, B., 'Historical Descriptions and Prescriptions for Adolescence', *Journal of Family History* 17 (1992), 341–51.
Herlihy, D., 'Review: Montaillou: Cathars and Catholics in a French Village, 1294–1324', *Social History* 4 (1979), 517–20.
Herlihy, D., and Klapisch-Zuber, C., *Toscans et leurs familles: une étude du catasto florentin de 1427* (Paris, 1978).
——, *Tuscans and their Families: A Study of the Florentine Catasto of 1427*, Yale series in economic history (New Haven, 1985).
Hélas, J.-C., 'Cimetières médiévaux et rites funéraires en Languedoc: l'apport de l'archéologie', *Cahiers de Fanjeaux* 33 (1998), 283–318.
James, E., 'Childhood and Youth in the Early Middle Ages', in *Youth in the Middle Ages*, ed. P. J. P. Goldberg and F. Riddy (York, 2004), pp. 11–23.
Johnson, C., 'Marriage Agreements from Twelfth-Century Southern France', in *To Have and to Hold: Marrying and its Documentation*, ed. P. L. Reynolds and J. Witte Jr (Cambridge, 2007), pp. 215–59.
Jordan, W. C., 'Adolescence and Conversion in the Middle Ages: a Research Agenda', in *Jews and Christians in Twelfth-century Europe*, ed. M. A. Signer and J. H. Van Engen, Notre Dame Conferences in Medieval Studies 10 (Notre Dame, 2001).
Justice, S., 'Inquisition, Speech and Writing: A Case from Late Medieval Norwich', in *Criticism and Dissent in the Middle Ages*, ed. Rita Copeland (Cambridge, 1996), pp. 289–322.
Kelly, H. A., 'Inquisition and the Prosecution of Heresy: Misconceptions and Abuses', *Church History* 58 (1989), 439–51.
Kieckhefer, R., 'The Office of the Inquisition and Medieval Heresy: The Transition from Personal to Institutional Juristiction', *Journal of Ecclesiastical History* 46 (1995), 47–53.
Koch, G., *Frauenfrage und Ketzertum im Mittelalter* (Berlin, 1962).
Lambert, M., *The Cathars* (Oxford, 1998).
Lansing, C., *Passion and Order: Restraint of Grief in the Medieval Italian Communes* (Ithaca, 2008).
——, *Power and Purity: Cathar Heresy in Medieval Italy* (New York, 1997).
Laribière, G., 'Le mariage à Toulouse au XIVe–XVe siécles', *Annales du Midi* 79 (1967), 335–61.
Le Roy Ladurie, E., *Montaillou: The Promised Land of Error*, trans. B. Bray (London, 1978).
——, *Montaillou, village occitan de 1294 à 1324* (Paris, 1975).
Lea, H. C., *A History of Auricular Confession and Indulgences in the Latin Church*, 3 vols. (Philadelphia, 1896).
——, *A History of the Inquisition of the Middle Ages*, 3 vols. (New York, 1887–88).
Maisonneuve, H., *Études sur les origines de l'inquisition*, 2nd edn. (Paris, 1960).

Marandet, M.-C., *Le souci de l'au-delà: la pratique testamentaire dans la région toulousaine (1300–1450)*, 2 vols. (Perpignan, 1998).
McCaffrey, E., 'Imagining the Cathars in Late-Twentieth-Century Languedoc', *Comtemporary European History* 11 (2002), 409–27.
Metz, R., 'L'Enfant dans le droit canonique medieval: orientations de recherche', *Recueils de la Société Jean Bodin pour l'histoire comparative des institutions* 36 (1976), 9–97.
Molin, J.-B., and Mutembe, P., *Le rituel du mariage en France du XIIe au XVIe siècle*, Theologie historique 26 (Paris, 1974).
Molinier, C., 'L'Endura, coutume religieuse des derniers sectaires albigeois', *Annales de la Faculté des Lettres de Bordeaux* 3 (1881), 282–99.
——, *L'Inquisition dans le Midi de la France au XIIIe et au XIVe siècle* (Toulouse, 1880).
Moore, R. I., *The Origins of European Dissent* (Oxford, 1985).
——, *The War on Heresy* (Cambridge, MA, 2012).
Mundy, J. H., 'Charity and Social Work in Toulouse', *Traditio* 22 (1966).
——, *Liberty and Political Power in Toulouse, 1050–1230* (New York, 1954).
——, 'Le mariage et les femmes à Toulouse au temps des Cathares', *Annales ESC* 42 (1987), 117–34.
——, *Men and Women at Toulouse in the Age of the Cathars* (Toronto, 1990).
——, *Society and Government at Toulouse in the Age of the Cathars* (Toronto, 1997).
——, *Studies in the Ecclesiastical and Social History of Toulouse in the Age of the Cathars* (Aldershot, 2006).
Murray, A., *Suicide in the Middle Ages* (Oxford, 1998).
Nickson, M. A. E., 'Locke and the Inquisition of Toulouse', *British Museum Quarterly* 36 (1971), 83–92.
Noonan, J. T., 'Marriage in the Middle Ages 1: Power to Choose', *Viator* 4 (1973), 419–32.
Nucé de Lamothe, M.-S., 'Piété et charité publique à Toulouse de la fin du XIIe siécle au milieu du XVe siécle d'après les testaments', *Annales du Midi* 76 (1964), 5–39.
Omont, H., 'La Collection Doat à la Bibliothèque Nationale: Documents sur les recherches de Doat', *Bibliothéque de l'École des Chartes* 77 (1916), 286–336.
Orme, N., 'Children and the Church in Medieval England', *Journal of Ecclesiastical History* 45 (1994), 563–87.
——, *Medieval Children* (New Haven, 2001).
Ormerod, P., and Roach, A., 'The Medieval Inquisition: Scale-Free Networks and the Suppression of Heresy', *Physica A: Statistical Mechanics and its Applications* 339 (August 2004), 645–52.
Paterson, L. M., 'L'enfant dans la littérature occitane avant 1230', *Cahiers de civilisation médiévale, Xe–XII siécles* 32 (1989), 233–45.
——, 'The Occitan Squire in the Twelfth and Thirteenth Centuries', in *The Ideals and Practice of Medieval Knighthood I*, ed. C. Harper-Bill and R. Harvey (Woodbridge, 1986), pp. 133–49.
——, *The World of the Troubadours: Medieval Occitan Society, c. 1100–c. 1300* (Cambridge, 1993).
Paul, J., 'Famille et hérésie', *Cahiers de Fanjeaux* 43 (2008), 349–72.
Pegg, M. G., *A Most Holy War: The Albigensian Crusade and the Battle for Christendom* (Oxford, 2008).

——, 'Albigenses in the Antipodes: An Australian and the Cathars', *Journal of Religious History* 35 (2011), 577–600.

——, *The Corruption of Angels: The Great Inquisition of 1245–1246* (Princeton, 2001).

——, 'Heresy, Good Men, and Nomenclature', in *Heresy and the Persecuting Society in the Middle Ages: Essays on the Work of R. I. Moore*, ed. Michael Frassetto, Studies in the History of Christian Traditions 129 (Leiden, 2006), pp. 227–39.

——, 'On Cathars, Albigenses, and Good Men of Languedoc', *Journal of Medieval History* 27 (2001), 181–95.

Pontal, O., *Les statuts synodaux*, Typologie des sources du Moyen Age occidental 11 (Turnhout, 1975).

Porter, H. B., 'The Origin of the Medieval Rite for Anointing the Sick or Dying', *Journal of Theological Studies* n.s. 7 (1956), 211–25.

Resnick, I. M., 'Marriage in Medieval Culture: Consent Theory and the Case of Joseph and Mary', *Church History* 69 (2000), 350–71.

Reyerson, K. L., 'The Adolescent Apprentice/Worker in Medieval Montpellier', *Journal of Family History* 17 (1992), 353–70.

——, 'Changes in Testamentary Practice at Montpellier on the Eve of the Black Death', *Church History* 47 (1978), 253–69.

Roach, A., 'The Cathar Economy', *Reading Medieval Studies* 12 (1986), 51–71.

——, 'Penance and the Making of the Inquisition in Languedoc', *Journal of Ecclesiastical History* 52 (2001), 409–33.

Roche, J., *Une église cathare: l'évêché du Carcassès* (Cahors, 2005).

Rottenwöhrer, G., *Der Katharismus*, 4 vols. (Bad Honnef, 1982–93).

Rouse, R. H., and Rouse, M. A., '*Statim Invenire*: Schools, Preachers, and New Attitudes to the Page', in *Renaissance and Renewal in the Twelfth Century*, ed. R. L. Benson, G. Constable and C. D. Lanham (Oxford, 1982), pp. 201–25.

Russell, J. B., 'Review: Montaillou: The Promised Land of Error', *Catholic Historical Review* 66 (1980), 678–80.

Sackville, L. J., *Heresy and Heretics in the Thirteenth Century: The Textual Representations*, Heresy and Inquisition in the Middle Ages 1 (York, 2011)

Schnell, R. and Shields A., 'The Discourse on Marriage in the Middle Ages', *Speculum* 73 (1998), 771–86.

Schultz, James A. 'Medieval Adolescence: The Claims of History and the Silence of German Narrative', *Speculum* 66 (1991), 519–39.

——, *The Knowledge of Childhood in the German Middle Ages, 1100–1350* (Philadelphia, 1995).

——, 'No Girls, No Boys, No Families: On the Construction of Childhood in Texts of the German Middle Ages', *Journal of English and Germanic Philology* 94 (1995), 59–81.

Sears, E., *The Ages of Man: Medieval Interpretations of the Life Cycle* (Princeton, 1986).

Shahar, S., *Childhood in the Middle Ages* (New York, 1990).

——, *Growing Old in the Middle Ages: 'Winter Clothes Us in Shadow and Pain'* (London, 1997).

Smith, R. M., 'Hypothéses sur la nuptialité en Angleterre aux XIIIe–XIVe siécles', *Annales: ESC* 38 (1983), 107–36.

——, 'The People of Tuscany and Their Families in the Fifteenth Century: Medieval or Mediterranean?', *Journal of Family History* 6 (1981), 107–26.

——, 'Some Reflections on the Evidence for the Origins of the "European Marriage

Pattern" in England', in *The Sociology of the Family: New Directions for Britain*, ed. C. Harris, Sociological Review Monograph 28 (Keele, 1979), pp. 74–112.

Stouff, L., 'Les Provençaux et la mort dans les testaments (XIIIe–XVe siécle)', *Cahiers de Fanjeaux* 33 (1998), 199–222.

Swanson, J., 'Childhood and Childrearing in ad status Sermons by Later Thirteenth Century Friars', *Journal of Medieval History* 16 (1990), 309–31.

Tanner, N., and Watson, S., 'Least of the Laity: The Minimum Requirements for a Medieval Christian', *Journal of Medieval History* 32 (2006), 395–423.

Taylor, C., 'Evidence for Dualism in Inquisitorial Registers of the 1240s: A Contribution to a Debate', *History* 98 (2013), 319–45.

——, *Heresy, Crusade and Inquisition in Medieval Quercy*, Heresy and Inquisition in the Middle Ages 2 (York, 2011).

——, *Heresy in Medieval France: Dualism in Aquitaine and the Agenais, 1000–1249* (Woodbridge, 2005).

Vicaire, M.-H., 'L'action de saint Dominique sur la vie régulière des femmes en Languedoc', *Cahiers de Fanjeaux* 23 (1988), 217–40.

——, 'Roland de Crémone ou la position de la théologie à l'université de Toulouse', *Cahiers de Fanjeaux* 5 (1970), 145–78.

——, *Saint Dominic and His Times* (New York, 1964).

Vidal, J. M., 'Les derniers ministres de l'albigéisme en Languedoc: leurs doctrines', *Revue des questions historiques* 79 (1906), 57–107.

——, 'Doctrines et morale des derniers ministres albigeois', *Revue des questions historiques* 86 (1909), 5–48.

——, *Un inquisiteur jugé par ses 'victims': Jean Galand et les Carcassonnais (1285–1286)* (Paris, 1903).

——, *Le tribunal d'inquisition de Pamiers* (Toulouse, 1906).

——, 'Le tribunal d'inquisition de Pamiers: Notice sur le registre de l'évêque Jacques Fournier', *Annales de Saint-Louis-des Français* 8 (1903–04), 377–435; continued in 9 (1904–05), 5–87, and 10 (1905–06), 5–52.

Wakefield, W. L. 'Burial of Heretics in the Middle Ages', *Heresis* 5 (1985), 29–32.

——, 'The Family of Niort in the Albigensian Crusade and Before the Inqusition', *Names* 18 (1970), 97–117, 286–303.

——, 'Friar Ferrier, Inquisitor', *Heresis* 7 (1986), 33–41.

——, *Heresy, Crusade and Inquisition in Southern France 1100–1250* (London, 1974).

——, 'Heretics and Inquisitors: The Case of Auriac and Cambiac', *Journal of Medieval History* 12 (1986), 225–37.

——, 'Heretics and Inquisitors: The Case of Le Mas-Saint-Puelles', *Catholic Historical Review* 69 (1983), 209–26.

Wei, I. P., *Intellectual Culture in Medieval Paris: Theologians and the University, c. 1100–1330* (Cambridge, 2012).

Wilson, A., 'The Infancy of the History of Childhood: An Appraisal of Philippe Ariès', *History and Theory* 19 (1980), 132–53.

Zingerle, I. V., *Das deutsche Kinderspiel im Mittelalter* (Innsbruck, 1873).

Index

Adoring 45–6
children performing 27, 46–8
compulsion 47, 139
Age of Discretion 27, 41–2, 64–8, 46 n. 103, 125
Albigensian Crusade 34, 68
Apprenticeship 60–1, 78–83
Apparelamentum 43–4
Ariès, Philippe 28–9, 72
Arnold Isarn (deponent) 47, 86–88, 138 n. 84
Avignonet 63, 79, 137 n. 82

Baptism 65, 39–41, 90
preaching of good men against 40–1
Belief
childhood and 38, 27, 29–30, 64–8
family conflict and 71, 76,130–1
Bernard Agasse (deponent) 83, 124, 136, 137 n. 81
Bernard of Caux (inquisitor) 11–14
Bernard Gui (inquisitor) 20–2 (*see also* *Practica* and Youth, leniency towards)
Blackmail 135–6
Book of the two principles 66

Cemeteries 146–9
Catharism
historiography of xi, 1–7, 10
in popular culture 1
Children
attending church 42
as deponents 30–1
Confirmation (sacrament of) 90
Consolamentum
children and 29, 48–64, 69–70
conflict and 130–1
consent of spouse 130–1
consent of recipient 143
difficulty of arranging 149–50
death and 27, 127–9
form of 127–8
pact to receive 143
timing of 141–3
as social occasion 138–9, 140–1
Corpses, treatment of 148–9
Crosses, punishment of wearing 16, 55, 88–9, 121

Deathbed, sociability of 124, 140–1
Divorce 117–19
Doat Collection 14–19
Doat, Jean de 14, 18 n. 83
Domestic abuse 94–5, 117–18
Dominic Guzman (St Dominic) 51, 55, 58, 61 n. 170
Dowry 63, 80, 99
Dualism 4–5

Ermessende Viguier 9 n. 36, 116, 117
Endura 9–10, 144–6

Faith, loss of 151
Ferrier (inquisitor) 17, 27 n. 2
Forgery 135–6
Funerals 146

Good Men
and food 33–4, 35, 50
as fugitives 35, 112–14
giving and receiving gifts 27, 33
as peacemakers 121
preaching 32
public life 32
houses of 52–3, 55
Grief 138–141, 151
Guides for good men
importance of 129–31
youths as 71, 75–6, 80, 123–4
Guillemette of Saint-Flour (deponent) 9 n. 36, 100, 125–6, 130

Heretication *see Consolamentum*
Hosts of good men 111–17

Inquisition
effect on good men 34
opposition to 19, 20, 62–3, 137 n. 81

institution of xi–xii
questioning by 13, 23, 24, 40, 44, 65, 107 n. 89, 111, 112 n. 120, 151
registers of 10–26
historians and 24–6

Jacques Fournier (inquisitor) 22–4
Jacques Autier (good man) 90–1, 108, 114, 120
Jean Galand (inquisitor) 11 n. 48, 18–19
Jean of Saint Pierre (inquisitor) *see* Bernard of Caux (inquisitor)
Joanna del Pas (good woman) 48–52, 61, 63–4
John Maury (deponent) 41, 73, 142, 145

Last rites (Catholic) 125–7
Life cycle in medieval thought 8–9
Love 106

Marriage
abandonment of 118–20, 128–9
advice on from good men 120–1
age at 92, 97–8
Canon Law and 96, 98, 99, 100–102, 105–6, 117–19
ceremony of 103–5
conflict in 115–17
preaching against by good men 107–110
second 98, 117
Melioramentum see adoring
Montaillou (book) 2–3, 20, 25

Oblation *ad terminum* (Catholic) 128–9

Perfect xi, 15 n. 70
Peter Autier (good man) 40, 65, 69, 90, 94–5, 108–10, 113–15, 120, 122, 141–2
Peter Sella (inquisitor) 16–17, 87 n. 88
Peter of Gaillac (deponent) 20 n. 97, 91, 108, 114, 141
Peter of Les-Vaux-de-Cernay 52, 108, 134–5, 143 n. 117
Peter of Luzenac (deponent) 20 n. 97, 65 n. 183, 109
Peter Pictavin (deponent) 46, 78–9, 89, 128, 130 n. 40, 138, 146
Pregnancy 9–10
Prouille 51, 62
Parenthood 9–10, 94–5, 151
Puberty 74
Practica, inquisitorial manual of Bernard Gui 31, 67, 87, 89, 111, 121

Rainier Sacconi 43, 61 n. 172, 113, 127 n. 21, 134, 144

Sex 95–6, 108–9, 105, 107 n. 88
Squires 76–7

Toulouse MS 609 11–14
Cathar Church in 4, 137 n. 82

Viaticum 126–7

Waldensianism 17, 21 n. 100, 67 n. 199, 73 n. 73, 75, 126
Weaving 81–2
Wills
notorisation of 136–7
priest required for 133–4
plot to forge 135–6
William Autier (good man) 40, 45 n. 91, 96, 113–14, 120–1, 135, 141–2, 145
William Bélibaste (good man) 40, 45 n. 91, 96, 120–1, 145
William Escaunier (deponent) 41, 75, 123, 130

Youth
family life of 75–6
leniency of inquisitors towards 86–9
in medieval thought 72–5
in Occitan society 74

YORK MEDIEVAL PRESS: PUBLICATIONS

God's Words, Women's Voices: The Discernment of Spirits in the Writing of Late-Medieval Women Visionaries, Rosalyn Voaden (1999)

Pilgrimage Explored, ed. J. Stopford (1999)

Piety, Fraternity and Power: Religious Gilds in Late Medieval Yorkshire 1389–1547, David J. F. Crouch (2000)

Courts and Regions in Medieval Europe, ed. Sarah Rees Jones, Richard Marks and A. J. Minnis (2000)

Treasure in the Medieval West, ed. Elizabeth M. Tyler (2000)

Nunneries, Learning and Spirituality in Late Medieval English Society: The Dominican Priory of Dartford, Paul Lee (2000)

Prophecy and Public Affairs in Later Medieval England, Lesley A. Coote (2000)

The Problem of Labour in Fourteenth-Century England, ed. James Bothwell, P. J. P. Goldberg and W. M. Ormrod (2000)

New Directions in later Medieval Manuscript Studies: Essays from the 1998 Harvard Conference, ed. Derek Pearsall (2000)

Cistercians, Heresy and Crusadse in Occitania, 1145–1229: Preaching in the Lord's Vineyard, Beverly Mayne Kienzle (2001)

Guilds and the Parish Community in Late Medieval East Anglia, c. 1470–1550, Ken Farnhill (2001)

The Age of Edward III, ed. J. S. Bothwell (2001)

Time in the Medieval World, ed. Chris Humphrey and W. M. Ormrod (2001)

The Cross Goes North: Processes of Conversion in Northern Europe, AD 300–1300, ed. Martin Carver (2002)

Henry IV: The Establishment of the Regime, 1399–1406, ed. Gwilym Dodd and Douglas Biggs (2003)

Youth in the Middle Ages, ed. P. J. P. Goldberg and Felicity Riddy (2004)

The Idea of the Castle in Medieval England, Abigail Wheatley (2004)

Rites of Passage: Cultures of Transition in the Fourteenth Century, ed. Nicola F. McDonald and W. M. Ormrod (2004)

Creating the Monastic Past in Medieval Flanders, Karine Ugé (2005)

St William of York, Christopher Norton (2006)

Medieval Obscenities, ed. Nicola F. McDonald (2006)

The Reign of Edward II: New Perspectives, ed. Gwilym Dodd and Anthony Musson (2006)

Old English Poetics: The Aesthetics of the Familiar in Anglo-Saxon England, Elizabeth M. Tyler (2006)

The Late Medieval Interlude: The Drama of Youth and Aristocratic Masculinity, Fiona S. Dunlop (2007)

The Late Medieval English College and its Context, ed. Clive Burgess and Martin Heale (2008)

The Reign of Henry IV: Rebellion and Survival, 1403–1413, ed. Gwilym Dodd and Douglas Biggs (2008)

Medieval Petitions: Grace and Grievance, ed. W. Mark Ormrod, Gwilym Dodd and Anthony Musson (2009)

St Edmund, King and Martyr: Changing Images of a Medieval Saint, ed. Anthony Bale (2009)

Language and Culture in Medieval Britain: The French of England c.1100–c.1500, ed. Jocelyn Wogan-Browne et al. (2009)

The Royal Pardon: Access to Mercy in Fourteenth-Century England, Helen Lacey (2009)

Texts and Traditions of Medieval Pastoral Care: Essays in Honour of Bella Millett, ed. Cate Gunn and Catherine Innes-Parker (2009)

The Anglo-Norman Language and its Contexts, ed. Richard Ingham (2010)

Parliament and Political Pamphleteering in Fourteenth-Century England, Clementine Oliver (2010)

The Saints' Lives of Jocelin of Furness: Hagiography, Patronage and Ecclesiastical Politics, Helen Birkett (2010)

The York Mystery Plays: Performance in the City, ed. Margaret Rogerson (2011)

Wills and Will-making in Anglo-Saxon England, Linda Tollerton (2011)

The Songs and Travels of a Tudor Minstrel: Richard Sheale of Tamworth, Andrew Taylor (2012)

Sin in Medieval and Early Modern Culture: The Tradition of the Seven Deadly Sins, ed. Richard G. Newhauser and Susan J. Ridyard (2012)

Socialising the Child in Late Medieval England, c. 1400–1600, Merridee L. Bailey (2012)

Barking Abbey and Medieval Literary Culture: Authorship and Authority in a Female Community, ed. Jennifer N. Brown and Donna Alfano Bussell (2012)

Christians and Jews in Angevin England: The York Massacre of 1190, Narratives and Contexts, ed. Sarah Rees Jones and Sethina Watson (2013)

Reimagining History in Anglo-Norman Prose Chronicles, John Spence (2013)

Henry V: New Interpretations, ed. Gwilym Dodd (2013)

Rethinking Chaucer's Legend of Good Women, Carolyn P. Collette (2014)

York Studies in Medieval Theology

I *Medieval Theology and the Natural Body*, ed. Peter Biller and A. J. Minnis (1997)

II *Handling Sin: Confession in the Middle Ages*, ed. Peter Biller and A. J. Minnis (1998)

III *Religion and Medicine in the Middle Ages*, ed. Peter Biller and Joseph Ziegler (2001)

IV *Texts and the Repression of Medieval Heresy*, ed. Caterina Bruschi and Peter Biller (2002)

York Manuscripts Conference

Manuscripts and Readers in Fifteenth-Century England: The Literary Implications of Manuscript Study, ed. Derek Pearsall (1983) [Proceedings of the 1981 York Manuscripts Conference]

Manuscripts and Texts: Editorial Problems in Later Middle English Literature, ed. Derek Pearsall (1987) [Proceedings of the 1985 York Manuscripts Conference]

Latin and Vernacular: Studies in Late-Medieval Texts and Manuscripts, ed. A. J. Minnis (1989) [Proceedings of the 1987 York Manuscripts Conference]

Regionalism in Late-Medieval Manuscripts and Texts: Essays celebrating the publication of 'A Linguistic Atlas of Late Mediaeval English', ed. Felicity Riddy (1991) [Proceedings of the 1989 York Manuscripts Conference]

Late-Medieval Religious Texts and their Transmission: Essays in Honour of A. I. Doyle, ed. A. J. Minnis (1994) [Proceedings of the 1991 York Manuscripts Conference]

Prestige, Authority and Power in Late Medieval Manuscripts and Texts, ed. Felicity Riddy (2000) [Proceedings of the 1994 York Manuscripts Conference]

Middle English Poetry: Texts and Traditions. Essays in Honour of Derek Pearsall, ed. A. J. Minnis (2001) [Proceedings of the 1996 York Manuscripts Conference]

Manuscript Culture in the British Isles

I *Design and Distribution of Late Medieval Manuscripts in England*, ed. Margaret Connolly and Linne R. Mooney (2008)

II *Women and Writing, c.1340–c.1650: The Domestication of Print Culture*, ed. Anne Lawrence-Mathers and Phillipa Hardman (2010)

III *The Wollaton Medieval Manuscripts: Texts, Owners and Readers*, ed. Ralph Hanna and Thorlac Turville-Petre (2010)

IV *Scribes and the City: London Guildhall Clerks and the Dissemination of Middle English Literature, 1375–1425*, Linne R. Mooney and Estelle Stubbs (2013)

Heresy and Inquisition in the Middle Ages

Heresy and Heretics in the Thirteenth Century: The Textual Representations, L. J. Sackville (2011)

Heresy, Crusade and Inquisition in Medieval Quercy, Claire Taylor (2011)